Law Lit

Also by Thane Rosenbaum

NONFICTION
The Myth of Moral Justice

FICTION
The Golems of Gotham
Second Hand Smoke
Elijah Visible: Stories

Law Lit

From Atticus Finch to
The Practice:
A Collection of Great
Writing About the Law

Edited by
Thane Rosenbaum

THE NEW PRESS

NEW YORK
LONDON

Requests for permission to reproduce selections from this book should be mailed to:
Permissions Department, The New Press, 38 Greene Street, New York, NY 10013.

Published in the United States by The New Press, New York, 2007
Distributed by W. W. Norton & Company, Inc., New York

LIBRARY OF CONGRESS CATALOGING-IN-PUBLICATION DATA
Law lit : from Atticus Finch to The practice / edited by Thane Rosenbaum.
p. cm.
ISBN 978-1-59558-194-5 (hc.)
1. Law—Literary collections.   2. Justice, Administration of—Literary collections.
I. Rosenbaum, Thane.
PN6071.L33L39 2007
808.8'03554—dc22
2007017330

The New Press was established in 1990 as a not-for-profit alternative to the large, commercial publishing houses currently dominating the book publishing industry. The New Press operates in the public interest rather than for private gain, and is committed to publishing, in innovative ways, works of educational, cultural, and community value that are often deemed insufficiently profitable.

www.thenewpress.com

Composition by NK Graphics
This book was set in AGaramond

Printed in the United States of America

2 4 6 8 10 9 7 5 3 1

For Razi

CONTENTS

EDITOR'S NOTE

The reading pleasure of *Law Lit* is far more than a revolving carousel of dramatic trial scenes. For those readers who love their lawyers gliding around courtrooms like gazelles, dazzling juries with their wickedly wise ways and Hollywood-handsome smiles, unraveling witnesses and extracting confessions like truth surgeons, galvanizing judges into pounding their gavels, *Law Lit* is your book. But you don't necessarily need *Law Lit* if that's all you want from an anthology that bills itself as "great writing about the law." Anyone watching reruns of *Perry Mason* or *Law & Order* well knows the familiar depictions of riveting lawyers, contemplative judges, earnest jurors, and spellbound spectators.

Law Lit is all that and more. After teaching a course on law and literature for nearly fifteen years to more than twelve hundred law students, and writing a book and various essays on cultural and literary representations of the legal system, I can assure you that *Law Lit* has assembled the classics of the genre, among them Dickens's *Bleak House*, Kafka's *The Trial*, Camus's *The Stranger*, Dostoevsky's *The Brothers Karamazov*, Shakespeare's *The Merchant of Venice*, and Herman Melville's *Billy Budd, Sailor*.

Yet, *Law Lit* is not just for lawyers and law students. I would not have edited an inside baseball book for barristers—certainly not in our culture, where the obsession with baseball is no greater than it is for law, and where the legal system can seriously lay claim to being America's true national pastime. Everyone enamored of the way the legal system makes for stunning entertainment and dramatic spectacle will appreciate the selections that have been gathered in this volume. Nevertheless, *Law Lit* has an even higher purpose, creating a symphony of voices that express the many shadings of law and longings for justice that animate the soul of humankind.

It is for this reason that *Law Lit* includes the song lyrics of Bob Dylan and Johnny Cash, because once a criminal trial is over, human life somehow still endures—even in prison. And there are excerpts from screenplays and TV scripts, from David Mamet's *The Verdict* to David E. Kelley's *The Practice*, where religious faith and emotional honesty are introduced into a legal system that is too often satisfied with numbingly cold results. From Alexandre Dumas we learn about the moral impulse for revenge. By Margaret Atwood, Dr. Martin Luther King Jr., and E.L. Doctorow we are reminded that sometimes, in response to the law's failure, the law is undeserving of our respect and obedience.

The great moral lessons that derive from the law, as seen through the imagination of the artist, are not limited to courtrooms. The courtroom and its showpiece, the trial, may be the epicenter of the law's aspiration for social peace and the main marquee on the town square, but the law lurks everywhere, and so does the literature that has been inspired by it.

Thane Rosenbaum

INTRODUCTION

Throughout history and nearly all over the world, there has been no greater and more paradoxical love-hate relationship than the one between laymen and lawyers. Lawyer jokes are as old as Adam and Eve's special pleading in the Garden of Eden. And the lawyer's lair is regarded as even more dreaded than the dentist's chair.

Yet, when we find ourselves in irresolvable trouble; when we have been bitterly betrayed; when promises made to us have been casually broken; when our contracts have been breached, our bodies damaged, our property defaced, our wealth stolen, our reputations maligned; when our friends, neighbors, and the strangers among us remain self-righteously defiant and refuse to apologize and make amends, where do we go—where must we go?

Instead of seeking revenge, before taking matters into our own hands, we retain lawyers who bring us before the law—the refuge of last resort. More than anything else, we need counsel. The law, after all, is not consumer friendly. All the signposts are written in legalese, unpronounceable fine print, pig latin for lawyers. There are too many forms to fill out and motions to make. In the end, we are ignorant and far too fragile to represent ourselves.

It is in a courtroom where rage and moral outrage are deemed out of order, where enemies sit at opposing tables dressed in their Sunday finery and on their best behavior. Civil societies insist that we forgo the ruinous violence of self-help in favor of law and order. So we are welcomed into the pacifying cocoon of courtrooms, at taxpayers' expense, where cooler heads are thought to prevail and where final judgments can be handed down by wise judges and impartial peers.

It is here, in the courtroom, where one form of violence is substituted for another. Lawyers are deployed as mercenaries, sharks, and attack dogs, Terminators with time sheets. The legal system offers a bloodless way of moving the fight from the streets to wood-paneled, marble-walled arenas where the pounding of a gavel is presumed to soften the blow. And once inside the courtroom, everyone is aroused by the spectacle of warring combatants dressed in coats of Armani, arguing subtle points, disputing facts, badgering witnesses, distorting truths, doing whatever it takes to win. Ironically, dating back as far as ancient Greece, the courtroom as Coliseum, with lawyers as gladiators, is the civilized way of transforming human conflict into tragic opera. Anyone who was obsessed with the O.J. Simpson trial has seen the modern version of this ancient gauntlet.

And obsession is the best way to describe it. While many have a poor opinion of lawyers and the legal profession, these same people can't seem to get enough of the law when it comes to their consumption of culture. Whether it appears in the form of paperback legal thrillers, TV courtroom dramas, Court TV, *Judge Alex*, feature films from *12 Angry Men* to *A Few Good Men*, or classic works of literature, many of which are excerpted in this volume, the public can't resist the natural drama and emotional conflict that arises from a trial.

Judgment proclaimed at the public square is intoxicating. We all become helpless and mesmerized witnesses, with a jury present and the community watching and a stenographer tapping away, recording the moment for posterity. The difference between guilt and innocence, between liability and blamelessness, dramatically withheld until the final verdict, with tensions mounting and anticipation swelling, makes the courthouse—overly heated with emotion or just from the temperature—like nowhere else on the planet. This is what justice looks like—justice as art and entertainment—observed from a distance and distilled through our imaginations.

But while justice is purportedly blind, we are not. We know that the law often does not feel moral or just. The legal system makes mistakes. The resolution and remedy we seek never come. Final judgments lack the necessary emotional finality. Those whom we call upon in a crisis to advocate on our behalf we ultimately come to resent. The parties return home unrelieved of their misery, and the community loses faith in the law as an institution.

This is where the artist enters, the intersection between the longing for law and the consequences of law. From Sophocles to Shakespeare, from Dickens and Dostoevsky to Kafka and Camus, the artist sees what the legal system itself does not—or will not. Some of the finest writers in the world—poets, novelists, playwrights, screenwriters, songwriters, and essayists—have focused their insights and imaginations on the law and the nature of judgment, justice, punishment, and revenge. The range of literary offerings assembled in *Law Lit* spans from five hundred years before Christ to several years after 9/11. The allure of the law is immune to time frames and geographical borders. When it comes to the legal system as plot device, as set piece, as central character, there are no limits on its capacity to enthrall and entertain. The law frustrates and intoxicates every culture and every age. It also, ironically, takes no prisoners. What a surprising number of *Law Lit* narratives have in common is that they are, for the most part, emblems of the bitter disappointment that arises from the law's failure.

The literature that has been inspired by the law is not a genre of happy, redemptive endings. The relationship between the legal system and the artistic imagination is a case study in miscarriage and misfortune, of justice denied. The machinery of justice is represented as unmercifully slow and unmerciful. Imprisonment occurs even before the guilty are actually incarcerated. Hard time is first served in the courthouse. And the innocent are imprisoned, too, without anyone throwing away the key. The artist's rendering of the law is as brutally honest as the legal system can be brutally heartless. And yet implicit in these portrayals of law as labyrinth, as soulless enterprise, as grinding, bureaucratic machine, is also the desire for reform, for a legal system that is as adept at delivering personal salvation as it is at dispensing misery.

Paradoxically, this genre of literature that is universally fixated on the theme of law as menace has the potential, in some transcendent way, to humanize the legal system, as well. Lawyers make for good fictional characters, as any Atticus Finch fan well knows. We long for the moral attorney who takes on lost causes without regard to personal consequence. There is high drama in lives laid bare before the bench, the soul-crushing dimensions of the law resisted; the soul, improbably, remains.

Law Lit reveals the human experience that is antiseptically left out of legal opinions. Judges and novelists, lawyers and poets, see different things when they witness a trial. The novelist is interested in the idiosyncrasy of his characters, what set of psychological factors make them act in ways that the court, invariably, misunderstands. The lawyer, by contrast, wishes to objectify and impersonalize conduct, evaluating it according to the standard of what a "reasonable man" would do in the same situation. The artist is more interested in what the irrational man has to say, and whether he, too, is permitted a day in court.

The parties enter the courtroom riding a crest of backstory that informs their grievances better than any cause of action. And when it crashes, which it must, the judge and assembled attorneys typically miss the force of its impact, the weight of its own authority. They are too focused on the externalized frontstory, the one that plays itself out only in front of the jury and tells little about who the parties are as people and what manner of heartache preceded their troubles and flirtations with the law.

Does truth matter to the legal system? When the law fails, is it complicit in compounding the original injury? Is revenge as moral an impulse as any obedience to the rule of law? Is the legal system capable of reform, or have all attorneys lost their inner Atticus Finch?

These are but a few of the questions that *Law Lit* lyrically, amusingly, and achingly asks of the law. And, in doing so, *Law Lit* promises to prove, beyond any reasonable doubt, that no sphere of the human experience is as alluring and lurid, lamentable and lust provoking, as the law.

Thane Rosenbaum

PART I

The Law Elevated

When the law achieves what's right; when law and morality are in complete harmony; when lawyers are righteous, impassioned, and wise; when judges are honest and fair; when the good cause unites with the good fight; when good men refuse the easy anonymity of indifference; then there is every reason to defend the law, and honor it with our trust, and, most of all, take comfort in it.

Harper Lee

from TO KILL A MOCKINGBIRD

The following excerpt is taken from southern writer Harper Lee's first and only novel, To Kill a Mockingbird, *which was later made into a feature film starring Gregory Peck as attorney Atticus Finch. Of all fictional lawyers, Finch perhaps best embodies the longing for the heroic lawyer, the moral attorney, the advocate of uncompromising righteousness. In this impassioned summation to an all-white jury in defense of Tom Robinson, a black man in 1930s Alabama falsely accused of raping a white woman, Finch appeals to the jurors' sense of balance and fairness and asks them to look beyond their southern prejudices and do what the law demands and what decency deserves, despite the politics of the Jim Crow South.*

"Gentlemen," he was saying, "I shall be brief, but I would like to use my remaining time with you to remind you that this case is not a difficult one, it requires no minute sifting of complicated facts, but it does require you to be sure beyond all reasonable doubt as to the guilt of the defendant. To begin with, this case should never have come to trial. This case is as simple as black and white.

"The state has not produced one iota of medical evidence to the effect that the crime Tom Robinson is charged with ever took place. It has relied instead upon the testimony of two witnesses whose evidence has not only been called into serious question on cross-examination, but has been flatly contradicted by the defendant. The defendant is not guilty, but somebody in this courtroom is.

"I have nothing but pity in my heart for the chief witness for the state, but my pity does not extend so far as to her putting a man's life at stake, which she has done in an effort to get rid of her own guilt.

"I say guilt, gentlemen, because it was guilt that motivated her. She has committed no crime; she has merely broken a rigid and time-honored code of our society, a code so severe that whoever breaks it is hounded from our midst as

unfit to live with. She is the victim of cruel poverty and ignorance, but I cannot pity her: she is white. She knew full well the enormity of her offense, but
because her desires were stronger than the code she was breaking, she persisted
in breaking it. She persisted, and her subsequent reaction is something that all
of us have known at one time or another. She did something every child has
done—she tried to put the evidence of her offense away from her. But in this
case she was no child hiding stolen contraband: she struck out at her victim—
of necessity she must put him away from her—he must be removed from her
presence, from this world. She must destroy the evidence of her offense.

"What was the evidence of her offense? Tom Robinson, a human being. She
must put Tom Robinson away from her. Tom Robinson was her daily reminder of what she did. What did she do? She tempted a Negro.

"She was white, and she tempted a Negro. She did something that in our
society is unspeakable: she kissed a black man. Not an old Uncle, but a strong
young Negro man. No code mattered to her before she broke it, but it came
crashing down on her afterwards.

"Her father saw it, and the defendant has testified as to his remarks. What
did her father do? We don't know, but there is circumstantial evidence to indicate that Mayella Ewell was beaten savagely by someone who led almost exclusively with his left. We do know in part what Mr. Ewell did: he did what
any God-fearing, persevering, respectable white man would do under the
circumstances—he swore out a warrant, no doubt signing it with his left hand,
and Tom Robinson now sits before you, having taken the oath with the only
good hand he possesses—his right hand.

"And so a quiet, respectable, humble Negro who had the unmitigated
temerity to 'feel sorry' for a white woman has had to put his word against two
white people's. I need not remind you of their appearance and conduct on the
stand—you saw them for yourselves. The witnesses for the state, with the exception of the sheriff of Maycomb County, have presented themselves to you
gentlemen, to this court, in the cynical confidence that their testimony would
not be doubted, confident that you gentlemen would go along with them on
the assumption—the evil assumption—that *all* Negroes lie, that *all* Negroes
are basically immoral beings, that *all* Negro men are not to be trusted around
our women, an assumption one associates with minds of their caliber.

"Which, gentlemen, we know is in itself a lie as black as Tom Robinson's
skin, a lie I do not have to point out to you. You know the truth, and the truth

is this: some Negroes lie, some Negroes are immoral, some Negro men are not to be trusted around women—black or white. But this is a truth that applies to the human race and to no particular race of men. There is not a person in this courtroom who has never told a lie, who has never done an immoral thing, and there is no man living who has never looked upon a woman without desire."

Atticus paused and took out his handkerchief. Then he took off his glasses and wiped them, and we saw another "first": we had never seen him sweat—he was one of those men whose faces never perspired, but now it was shining tan.

"One more thing, gentlemen, before I quit. Thomas Jefferson once said that all men are created equal, a phrase that the Yankees and the distaff side of the Executive branch in Washington are fond of hurling at us. There is a tendency in this year of grace, 1935, for certain people to use this phrase out of context, to satisfy all conditions. The most ridiculous example I can think of is that the people who run public education promote the stupid and idle along with the industrious—because all men are created equal, educators will gravely tell you, the children left behind suffer terrible feelings of inferiority. We know all men are not created equal in the sense some people would have us believe—some people are smarter than others, some people have more opportunity because they're born with it, some men make more money than others, some ladies make better cakes than others—some people are born gifted beyond the normal scope of most men.

"But there is one way in this country in which all men are created equal— there is one human institution that makes a pauper the equal of a Rockefeller, the stupid man the equal of an Einstein, and the ignorant man the equal of any college president. That institution, gentlemen, is a court. It can be the Supreme Court of the United States or the humblest J.P. court in the land, or this honorable court which you serve. Our courts have their faults, as does any human institution, but in this country our courts are the great levelers, and in our courts all men are created equal.

"I'm no idealist to believe firmly in the integrity of our courts and in the jury system—that is no ideal to me, it is a living, working reality. Gentlemen, a court is no better than each man of you sitting before me on this jury. A court is only as sound as its jury, and a jury is only as sound as the men who make it up. I am confident that you gentlemen will review without passion the evidence you have heard, come to a decision, and restore this defendant to his family. In the name of God, do your duty."

Scott Turow

from PRESUMED INNOCENT

The exonerated know and appreciate their liberty in ways that the rest of us either take for granted or can't even comprehend. In Scott Turow's bestselling 1987 novel, Presumed Innocent, *which influenced a cultural revolution of the legal thriller, Rusty Savich, a prosecutor, is found not guilty of having murdered his former lover and colleague. In this excerpt, he revels in the relief of his newfound freedom and reflects on the extreme emotional toll that the trial took on his life.*

Only the poets can truly write of liberty, that sweet, exhilarant thing. In my life, I have not known an ecstasy as dulcet or complete as the occasional instants of shivering delight when I again realize this peril is behind me. Over. Done. Whatever the collateral consequences, whatever the smirking, the unvoiced accusations, the contumely or scorn with which others might treat me, to my face or, more certainly, behind my back—whatever they say, the terror is over; the sleepless early-morning hours I spent trying to catapult myself ahead in time, envisioning a life of mindless toil during the day, and nights working like half the other inmates on my endless train of *habeas corpus* petitions and, finally, the wary fearful hours of half-sleep on some prison bunk, awaiting whatever perverse terror the night would bring—that horror is past me. And with a sense of earned relief. Every sin of my life seems truly expiated. My society has judged; no punishment is due. Every sticky cliché is right: an enormous weight has been lifted; I feel as if I could fly, like a million bucks, ten feet tall. I feel free.

And then, of course, the shadow moves, and I think what I have been through, with enormous anger and bitterness and a swooping descent into depression. As a prosecutor I lost cases, more, naturally, than I would have liked, and had my chance to observe the acquitted defendant in the instant of victory. Most wept; the guiltier they were, the harder they cried. I always thought it was relief, and guilt. But it is, I tell you, this disbelief that this ordeal, this—think of the word—trial has been endured for no apparent point but your disgrace, and your uncompensable damage.

The return to life is slow: an island on which a soft wind moves. The first two days the phone does not stop. How people who did not speak to me for the last four months can imagine that I could accept their glib congratulations astounds me. But they call. And I am calculating enough to know they may be needed again; I accept their good wishes with some aplomb. But I spend most of my time alone. I am overwhelmed by the desire to be out in the waning summer and the stirring fall. One day I hold Nat out of school and we go fishing from a canoe. The day passes and we say almost nothing; but I am content to be with my boy and I feel he knows it. Other days I walk in the forest for hours. Very slowly, I begin to see things and therefore notice what I did not see before. My life for four months has been an oblivion, a hopeless storm of feeling so wild that there was nothing outside it. Every face that presented itself to my imagination did so with cyclonic impact in my interior reaches, which now, gradually, are growing still, and which, I finally realize, will in time again require movement.

Mark Twain

from THE TRAGEDY OF

PUDD'NHEAD WILSON

American novelist Mark Twain's pre–Civil War novel The Tragedy of Pudd'n-
head Wilson, *published in 1894, is a detective story dealing with slavery and
racial identity. In this excerpt from the trial scene, fingerprint identification is used
to determine the truth of who committed the murder of Judge Driscoll. It was perhaps the first time in fiction that such a technique for establishing proof was presented. Twain's comedic sensibility and use of southern African American dialect
make for a dramatic and clever tactical trial.*

"I beg the indulgence of the court while I make a few remarks in explanation
of some evidence which I am about to introduce, and which I shall presently
ask to be allowed to verify under oath on the witness stand. Every human being carries with him from his cradle to his grave certain physical marks which
do not change their character, and by which he can always be identified—and
that without shade of doubt or question. These marks are his signature, his
physiological autograph, so to speak, and this autograph can not be counter-
feited, nor can he disguise it or hide it away, nor can it become illegible by the
wear and mutations of time. This signature is not his face—age can change
that beyond recognition; it is not his hair, for that can fall out; it is not his
height, for duplicates of that exist; it is not his form, for duplicates of that exist also, whereas this signature is each man's very own—there is no duplicate
of it among the swarming populations of the globe! [The audience were interested once more.]

"This autograph consists of the delicate lines or corrugations with which
Nature marks the insides of the hands and the soles of the feet. If you will look
at the balls of your fingers—you that have very sharp eyesight—you will observe that these dainty curving lines lie close together, like those that indicate
the borders of oceans in maps, and that they form various clearly defined pat-

terns, such as arches, circles, long curves, whorls, etc., and that these patters differ on the different fingers. [Every man in the room had his hand up to the light now, and his head canted to one side, and was minutely scrutinizing the balls of his fingers; there were whispered ejaculations of "Why, it's so—I never noticed that before!"] The patterns on the right hand are not the same as those on the left. [Ejaculations of "Why, that's so, too!"] Taken finger for finger, your patterns differ from your neighbor's. [Comparisons were made all over the house—even the judge and jury were absorbed in this curious work.] The patterns of a twin's right hand are not the same as those on his left. One twin's patterns are never the same as his fellow twin's patterns—the jury will find that the patterns upon the finger balls of the twins' hands follow this rule. [An examination of the twins' hands was begun at once.] You have often heard of twins who were so exactly alike that when dressed alike their own parents could not tell them apart. Yet there was never a twin born into this world that did not carry from birth to death a sure identifier in this mysterious and marvelous natal autograph. That once known to you, his fellow twin could never personate him and deceive you."

Wilson stopped and stood silent. Inattention dies a quick and sure death when a speaker does that. The stillness gives warning that something is coming. All palms and finger balls went down now, all slouching forms straightened, all heads came up, all eyes were fastened upon Wilson's face. He waited yet one, two, three moments, to let his pause complete and perfect its spell upon the house; then, when through the profound hush he could hear the ticking of the clock on the wall, he put out his hand and took the Indian knife by the blade and held it aloft where all could see the sinister spots upon its ivory handle; then he said, in a level and passionless voice:

"Upon this haft stands the assassin's natal autograph, written in the blood of that helpless and unoffending old man who loved you and whom you all loved. There is but one man in the whole earth whose hand can duplicate that crimson sign"—he paused and raised his eyes to the pendulum swinging back and forth—"and please God we will produce that man in this room before the clock strikes noon!"

Stunned, distraught, unconscious of its own movement, the house half rose, as if expecting to see the murderer appear at the door, and a breeze of muttered ejaculations swept the place. "Order in the court!—sit down!" This from the sheriff. He was obeyed, and quiet reigned again. Wilson stole a glance at Tom, and said to himself, "He is flying signals of distress now; even people who despise him are pitying him; they think this is a hard ordeal for a young fellow who has lost his benefactor by so cruel a stroke—and they are right." He resumed his speech:

"For more than twenty years I have amused my compulsory leisure with collecting these curious physical signatures in this town. At my house I have hundreds upon hundreds of them. Each and every one is labeled with name and date; not labeled the next day or even the next hour, but in the very minute that the impression was taken. When I go upon the witness stand I will repeat under oath the things which I am now saying. I have the finger-prints of the court, the sheriff, and every member of the jury. There is hardly a person in this room, white or black, whose natal signature I cannot produce, and not one of them can so disguise himself that I cannot pick him out from a multitude of his fellow creatures and unerringly identify him by his hands. And if he and I should live to be a hundred I could still do it. [The interest of the audience was steadily deepening now.]

"I have studied some of these signatures so much that I know them as well as the bank cashier knows the autograph of his oldest customer. While I turn my back now, I beg that several persons will be so good as to pass their fingers through their hair, and then press them upon one of the panes of the window near the jury, and that among them the accused may set THEIR finger marks. Also, I beg that these experimenters, or others, will set their fingers upon another pane, and add again the marks of the accused, but not placing them in the same order or relation to the other signatures as before—for, by one chance in a million, a person might happen upon the right marks by pure guesswork, ONCE, therefore I wish to be tested twice."

He turned his back, and the two panes were quickly covered with delicately lined oval spots, but visible only to such persons as could get a dark background for them—the foliage of a tree, outside, for instance.

Then upon call, Wilson went to the window, made his examination, and said:

"This is Count Luigi's right hand; this one, three signatures below, is his left. Here is Count Angelo's right; down here is his left. How for the other pane: here and here are Count Luigi's, here and here are his brother's." He faced about. "Am I right?"

A deafening explosion of applause was the answer. The bench said:

"This certainly approaches the miraculous!"

Wilson turned to the window again and remarked, pointing with his finger:

"This is the signature of Mr. Justice Robinson. [Applause.] This, of Constable Blake. [Applause.] This of John Mason, juryman. [Applause.] This, of the sheriff. [Applause.] I cannot name the others, but I have them all at home, named and dated, and could identify them all by my fingerprint records."

He moved to his place through a storm of applause—which the sheriff stopped, and also made the people sit down, for they were all standing and struggling to see, of course. Court, jury, sheriff, and everybody had been too absorbed in observing Wilson's performance to attend to the audience earlier.

"Now then," said Wilson, "I have here the natal autographs of the two children—thrown up to ten times the natural size by the pantograph, so that anyone who can see at all can tell the markings apart at a glance. We will call the children A and B. Here are A's finger marks, taken at the age of five months. Here they are again taken at seven months. [Tom started.] They are alike, you see. Here are B's at five months, and also at seven months. They, too, exactly copy each other, but the patterns are quite different from A's, you observe. I shall refer to these again presently, but we will turn them face down now.

"Here, thrown up ten sizes, are the natal autographs of the two persons who are here before you accused of murdering Judge Driscoll. I made these pantograph copies last night, and will so swear when I go upon the witness stand. I ask the jury to compare them with the finger marks of the accused upon the windowpanes, and tell the court if they are the same."

He passed a powerful magnifying glass to the foreman.

One juryman after another took the cardboard and the glass and made the comparison. Then the foreman said to the judge:

"Your honor, we are all agreed that they are identical."

Wilson said to the foreman:

"Please turn that cardboard face down, and take this one, and compare it searchingly, by the magnifier, with the fatal signature upon the knife handle, and report your finding to the court."

Again the jury made minute examinations, and again reported:

"We find them to be exactly identical, your honor."

Wilson turned toward the counsel for the prosecution, and there was a clearly recognizable note of warning in his voice when he said:

"May it please the court, the state has claimed, strenuously and persistently, that the bloodstained fingerprints upon that knife handle were left there by the assassin of Judge Driscoll. You have heard us grant that claim, and welcome it." He turned to the jury: "Compare the fingerprints of the accused with the fingerprints left by the assassin—and report."

The comparison began. As it proceeded, all movement and all sound ceased, and the deep silence of an absorbed and waiting suspense settled upon the house; and when at last the words came, "THEY DO NOT EVEN RESEMBLE," a thundercrash of applause followed and the house sprang to its feet, but was quickly repressed by official force and brought to order again. Tom was altering his position every few minutes now, but none of his changes brought repose nor any small trifle of comfort. When the house's attention was become fixed once more, Wilson said gravely, indicating the twins with a gesture:

"These men are innocent—I have no further concern with them. [Another outbreak of applause began, but was promptly checked.] We will now proceed to find the guilty. [Tom's eyes were starting from their sockets—yes, it was a cruel day for the bereaved youth, everybody thought.] We will return to the infant autographs of A and B. I will ask the jury to take these large pantograph facsimiles of A's marked five months and seven months. Do they tally?"

The foreman responded: "Perfectly."

"Now examine this pantograph, taken at eight months, and also marked A. Does it tally with the other two?"

The surprised response was:

"NO—THEY DIFFER WIDELY!"

"You are quite right. Now take these two pantographs of B's autograph, marked five months and seven months. Do they tally with each other?"

"Yes—perfectly."

"Take this third pantograph marked B, eight months. Does it tally with B's other two?"

"BY NO MEANS!"

"Do you know how to account for those strange discrepancies? I will tell you. For a purpose unknown to us, but probably a selfish one, somebody changed those children in the cradle."

This produced a vast sensation, naturally; Roxana was astonished at this admirable guess, but not disturbed by it. To guess the exchange was one thing, to guess who did it quite another. Pudd'nhead Wilson could do wonderful things, no doubt, but he couldn't do impossible ones. Safe? She was perfectly safe. She smiled privately.

"Between the ages of seven months and eight months those children were changed in the cradle"—he made one of this effect-collecting pauses, and added—"and the person who did it is in this house!"

Roxy's pulses stood still! The house was thrilled as with an electric shock, and the people half rose as if to seek a glimpse of the person who had made that exchange. Tom was growing limp; the life seemed oozing out of him. Wilson resumed:

"A was put into B's cradle in the nursery; B was transferred to the kitchen and became a Negro and a slave [Sensation—confusion of angry ejaculations]—but within a quarter of an hour he will stand before you white and free! [Burst of applause, checked by the officers.] From seven months onward until now, A has still been a usurper, and in my finger record he bears B's name. Here is his pantograph at the age of twelve. Compare it with the assassin's signature upon the knife handle. Do they tally?"

The foreman answered:

"TO THE MINUTEST DETAIL!"

Wilson said, solemnly:

"The murderer of your friend and mine—York Driscoll of the generous hand and the kindly spirit—sits in among you. Valet de Chambre, Negro and slave—falsely called Thomas a Becket Driscoll—make upon the window the fingerprints that will hang you!"

Tom turned his ashen face imploring toward the speaker, made some impotent movements with his white lips, then slid limp and lifeless to the floor.

Wilson broke the awed silence with the words:

"There is no need. He has confessed."

Roxy flung herself upon her knees, covered her face with her hands, and out through her sobs the words struggled:

"De Lord have mercy on me, po' misasble sinner dat I is!"

The clock struck twelve.

The court rose; the new prisoner, handcuffed, was removed.

Richard Wright

from NATIVE SON

In Richard Wright's classic novel of racial injustice in 1930s Chicago, Native Son *(1940), is an unvarnished portrait of the poverty and hopelessness of Bigger Thomas, a black man who is on trial for murdering a young white woman. In this excerpt, defense attorney Boris Max pleads for his client's freedom by passionately arguing the history of race in America—the desperate and forbidding circumstances of African American men and the nature of prejudice and hatred to which they are routinely subjected—as a way to mitigate and comprehend the crime that his client committed.*

"Everybody rise, please. . . ."

Everybody stood up. Bigger felt Max's hand touching his arm and he rose and stood with Max. A man, draped in long black robes and with a dead-white face, came through a rear door and sat behind a high pulpit-like railing. That's the judge, Bigger thought, easing back into his seat.

"Hear ye, hear ye. . . ." Bigger heard the hollow voice booming again. He caught snatches of phrases: ". . . this Honorable Branch of the Cook County Criminal Court. . . . now in session. . . . pursuant to adjournment. . . . the Honorable Chief Justice Alvin C. Hanley, presiding. . . ."

Bigger saw the judge look toward Buckley and then toward him and Max. Buckley rose and went to the foot of the railing; Max also rose and went forward. They talked a moment to the judge in low voices and then each went back to his seat. A man sitting just below the judge rose and began reading a long paper in a voice so thick and low that Bigger could only hear some of the words.

". . . indictment number 666-983. . . . the People of the State of Illinois vs. Bigger Thomas. . . . The Grand Jurors chosen, selected and sworn in and for the said County of Cook, present that Bigger Thomas did rape and inflict sexual injury upon the body. . . . strangulation by hand. . . . smother to death and dispose of body by burning same in furnace. . . . did with knife and hatchet sever head from body. . . . said acts committed upon one Mary Dalton, and contrary to the form of the statute in such case made and provided, against the peace and dignity of the People of the State of Illinois. . . ."

The man pronounced Bigger's name over and over again and Bigger felt that he was caught up in a vast but delicate machine whose wheels would whir no matter what was pitted against them. Over and over the man said that he had killed Mary and Bessie; that he had beheaded Mary; that he had battered Bessie with a brick; that he had raped both Mary and Bessie; that he had shoved Mary in the furnace; that he had thrown Bessie down the air-shaft and left her to freeze to death; and that he had stayed on in the Dalton home when Mary's body was burning and had sent a kidnap note. When the man finished, a gasp of astonishment came from the court room and Bigger saw faces turning and looking in his direction. The judge rapped for order and asked,

"Is the defendant ready to enter a plea to this indictment?"

Max rose.

"Yes, Your Honor. The defendant, Bigger Thomas, pleads guilty."

Immediately Bigger heard a loud commotion. He turned his head and saw several men pushing through the crowd toward the door. He knew that they were newspapermen. The judge rapped again for order. Max tried to continue speaking, but the judge stopped him.

"Just a minute, Mr. Max. We must have order!"

The room grew quiet.

"Your Honor," Max said, "after long and honest deliberation, I have determined to make a motion in this court to withdraw our plea of not guilty and enter a plea of guilty.

"The laws of this state allow the offering of evidence in mitigation of punishment, and I shall request, at such a time as the Court deems best, that I be given the opportunity to offer evidence as to the mental and emotional attitude of this boy, to show the degree of responsibility he had in these crimes. Also, I want to offer evidence as to the youth of this boy. Further, I want to prevail upon this Court to consider this boy's plea of guilty as evidence mitigating his punishment. . . ."

"Your Honor!" Buckley shouted.

"Allow me to finish," Max said.

Buckley came to the front of the room, his face red.

"You cannot plead that boy both guilty and insane," Buckley said. "If you claim Bigger Thomas is insane, the State will demand a jury trial. . . ."

"Your Honor," Max said, "I do not claim that this boy is legally insane. I shall endeavor to show, through the discussion of evidence, the mental and emotional attitude of this boy and the degree of responsibility he had in these crimes."

"That's a defense of insanity!" Buckley shouted.

"I'm making no such defense," Max said.

"A man is either sane or insane," Buckley said.

"There are degrees of insanity," Max said. "The laws of this state permit the hearing of evidence to ascertain the degree of responsibility. And, also, the law permits the offering of evidence toward the mitigation of punishment."

"The State will submit witnesses and evidence to establish the legal sanity of the defendant," Buckley said.

There was a long argument which Bigger did not understand. The judge called both lawyers forward to the railing and they talked for over an hour. Finally, they went back to their seats and the judge looked toward Bigger and said,

"Bigger Thomas, will you rise?"

* * *

Max rose, ran his hand through his white hair and went to the front of the room. He turned and half-faced the judge and Buckley, looking out over Bigger's head to the crowd. He cleared his throat. "Your Honor, never in my life have I risen in court to make a plea with a firmer conviction in my heart. I know that what I have to say here today touches the destiny of an entire nation. My plea is for more than one man and one people: Perhaps it is in a manner fortunate that the defendant has committed one of the darkest crimes in our memory; for if we can encompass the life of this man and find out what has happened to him, if we can understand how subtly and yet strongly his life and fate are linked to ours—if we can do this, perhaps we shall find the key to our future, that rare vantage point upon which every man and woman in this nation can stand and view how inextricably our hopes and fears of today create the exultation and doom of tomorrow.

"Your Honor, I have no desire to be disrespectful to this Court, but I must be honest. A man's life is at stake. And not only is this man a criminal, but he is a black criminal. And as such, he comes into this court under a handicap, notwithstanding our pretensions that all are equal before the law.

"This man is *different*, even though his crime differs from similar crimes only in degree. The complex forces of society have isolated here for us a symbol, a test symbol. The prejudices of men have stained this symbol, like a germ stained for examination under the microscope. The unremitting hate of men has given us a psychological distance that will enable us to see this tiny social symbol in relation to our whole sick social organism.

"I say, Your Honor, that the mere act of understanding Bigger Thomas will be a thawing out of icebound impulses, a dragging of the sprawling forms of dread out of the night of fear into the light of reason, an unveiling of the unconscious ritual of death in which we, like sleep-walkers, have participated so dreamlike and thoughtlessly.

"But I make no excessive claims, Your Honor. I do not deal in magic. I do not say that if we understand this man's life we shall solve all our problems, or that when we have all the facts at our disposal we shall automatically know how to act. Life is not that simple. But I do say that, if, after I have finished, you feel that death is necessary, then you are making an open choice. What I want to do is inject into the consciousness of this Court, through the discussion of evidence, the two possible courses of action open to us and the inevitable consequences flowing from each. And then, if we say death, let us mean it; and if we say life, let us mean that too; but whatever we say, let us know upon what ground we are putting our feet, what the consequences are for us and those whom we judge.

"Your Honor, I would have you believe that I am not insensible to the deep burden of responsibility I am throwing upon your shoulders by the manner in which I have insisted upon conducting the defense of this boy's life, and in my resolve to place before you the entire degree of his guilt for judgment. But, under the circumstances, what else could I have done? Night after night, I have lain without sleep, trying to think of a way to picture to you and to the world the causes and reasons why this Negro boy sits here a self-confessed murderer. But every time I thought I had discovered a vital piece of evidence bearing upon his fate, I could hear in my mind's ear the low, angry muttering of that mob which the state troops are holding at bay beyond that window.

"How can I, I asked myself, make my voice heard with effect above the hungry yelping of hounds on the hunt? How can I, I asked myself, make the picture of what has happened to this boy show plain and powerful upon a screen of sober reason, when a thousand newspaper and magazine artists have already drawn it in lurid ink upon a million sheets of public print? Dare I, deeply mindful of this boy's background and race, put his fate in the hands of a jury (not of his peers, but of an alien and hostile race!) whose minds are already conditioned by the press of the nation; a press which has already reached a decision as to his guilt, and in countless editorials suggested the measure of his punishment?

"No! I could not! It would be better if we had no courts of law, than that justice should be administered under such conditions! An outright lynching would be more honest than a 'mock trial'! Rather that courts be abolished and each man buy arms and proceed to protect himself or make war for what he thinks is rightfully his own, than that a man should be tried by men who have already made up their minds that he is guilty. I could not have placed at the disposal of a jury the evidence, so general and yet so confoundingly specific, so impalpable and yet so disastrous in its terrible consequences—consequences which have affected my client and account for his being here today before the bar of judgment with his life at stake—I could not have done that and have been honest with myself or with this boy.

"So today I come to face this Court, rejecting a trial by jury, willingly entering a plea of guilty, asking in the light of the laws of this state that this boy's life be spared for reasons which I believe affect the foundations of our civilization.

"The most habitual thing for this Court to do is to take the line of least resistance and follow the suggestion of the State's Attorney and say, 'Death!' And that would be the end of this case. But that would not be the end of this crime! That is why this Court must do otherwise.

"There are times, Your Honor, when reality bears features of such an impellingly moral complexion that it is impossible to follow the hewn path of expediency. There are times when life's ends are so raveled that reason and sense cry out that we stop and gather them together again before we can proceed.

"What atmosphere surrounds this trial? Are the citizens soberly intent upon seeing that the law is executed? That retribution is dealt out in measure with the offense? That the guilty and only the guilty is caught and punished?

"No! Every conceivable prejudice has been dragged into this case. The authorities of the city and state deliberately inflamed the public mind to the point where they could not keep the peace without martial law. Responsible to nothing but their own corrupt conscience, the newspapers and the prosecution launched the ridiculous claim that the Communist Party was in some way linked to these two murders. Only here in court yesterday morning did the State's Attorney cease implying that Bigger Thomas was guilty of other crimes, crimes which he could not prove. And, because I, a Jew, dared defend this Negro boy, for days my mail has been flooded with threats against my life. The manner in which Bigger Thomas was captured, the hundreds of innocent Negro homes invaded, the scores of Negroes assaulted upon the streets, the dozens who were thrown out of their jobs, the barrage of lies poured out from every source against a defenseless people—all of this was something unheard of in democratic lands.

"The hunt for Bigger Thomas served as an excuse to terrorize the entire Negro population, to arrest hundreds of Communists, to raid labor union headquarters and workers' organizations. Indeed, the tone of the press, the silence of the church, the attitude of the prosecution and the stimulated temper of the people are of such a nature as to indicate that *more* than revenge is being sought upon a man who has committed a crime."

* * *

"We must deal here with the raw stuff of life, emotions and impulses and attitudes as yet unconditioned by the strivings of science and civilization. We must deal here with a first wrong, which, when committed by us, was understandable and inevitable; and then we must deal with the long trailing black sense of guilt stemming from that wrong, a sense of guilt which self-interest and fear would not let us atone. And we must deal here with the hot blasts of hate engendered in others by that first wrong, and then the monstrous and horrible crimes flowing from that hate, a hate which has seeped down into the hearts and molded the deepest and most delicate sensibilities of multitudes.

"We must deal here with a dislocation of life involving millions of people, a dislocation so vast as to stagger the imagination; so fraught with tragic consequences as to make us rather not want to look at it or think of it; so old that we would rather try to view it as an order of nature and strive with uneasy conscience and false moral fervor to keep it so."

Benjamin N. Cardozo

from THE NATURE OF
THE JUDICIAL PROCESS

Benjamin Cardozo was a U.S. Supreme Court Justice, but fashioned his most lively and evocative writings when he served as a judge, and then chief judge, on the New York Court of Appeals, from 1917 to 1932, where his opinions oftentimes rose to the level of art. Judge Cardozo's rulings were also notable because they sometimes mocked the rigid, soulless application of law in favor of decisions that made emotional and moral sense. In this excerpt from a series of 1921 lectures delivered at Yale Law School that were eventually published as a book about the nature of the judicial process, Judge Cardozo explains, among other things, how judges should come to their decisions.

In these days, there is a good deal of discussion whether the rule of adherence to precedent ought to be abandoned altogether. I would not go so far myself. I think adherence to precedent should be the rule and not the exception. I have already had occasion to dwell upon some of the considerations that sustain it. To these I may add that the labor of judges would be increased almost to the breaking point if every past decision could be reopened in every case, and one could not lay one's own course of bricks on the secure foundation of the courses laid by others who had gone before him. Perhaps the constitution of my own court has tended to accentuate this belief. We have had ten judges, of whom only seven sit at a time. It happens again and again, where the question is a close one, that a case which one week is decided one way might be decided another way the next if it were then heard for the first time. The situation would, however, be intolerable if the weekly changes in the composition of the court were accompanied by changes in its rulings. In such circumstances there is nothing to do except to stand by the errors of our brethren of the week before, whether we relish them or not. But I am ready to concede that the rule of adherence to precedent, though it ought not to be abandoned, ought to be in some degree relaxed. I think that when a rule, after it has been duly tested by experience, has been found to be inconsistent with the sense of justice or in the social welfare, there should be less hesitation in frank avowal and full abandonment. We have had to do this sometimes in the field of constitutional law. Perhaps we should do so oftener in fields of private law where considerations of social utility are not so aggressive and insistent. There should be greater readiness to abandon an untenable position when the rule to be discarded may not reasonably be supposed to have determined the conduct of the litigants, and particularly when in its origin it was the product of institutions or conditions which have gained a new significance or development with the progress of the years. . . .

* * *

Our survey of judicial methods teaches us, I think, the lesson that the whole subject-matter of jurisprudence is more plastic, more malleable, the moulds less definitively cast, the bounds of right and wrong less preordained and constant, than most of us, without the aid of some such analysis, have been accustomed to believe. We like to picture to ourselves the field of the law as accurately mapped and plotted. We draw our little lines, and they are hardly down before we blur them. As in time and space, so here. Divisions are working hypotheses, adopted for convenience. We are tending more and more toward an appreciation of the truth that, after all, there are few rules; there are chiefly standards and degrees. It is a question of degree whether I have been negligent. It is a question of degree whether in the use of my own land, I have created a nuisance which may be abated by my neighbor. It is a question of degree whether the law which takes my property and limits my conduct, impairs my liberty unduly. So also the duty of a judge becomes itself a question of degree, and he is a useful judge or a poor one as he estimates the measure accurately or loosely. He must balance all his ingredients, his philosophy, his logic, his analogies, his history, his customs, his sense of right, and all the rest, and adding a little here and taking out a little there, must determine, as wisely as he can, which weight shall tip the scales. If this seems a weak and inconclusive summary, I am not sure that the fault is mine. I know he is a wise pharmacist who from a recipe so general can compound a fitting remedy. But the like criticism may be made of most attempts to formulate the principles which regulate the practice of an art. W. Jethro Brown reminds us in a recent paper on "Law and Evolution" that "Sir Joshua Reynolds' book on painting, offers little or no guidance to those who wish to become famous painters. Books on literary styles are notoriously lacking, speaking as a rule, in practical utility." After the wearisome process of analysis has been finished, there must be for every judge a new synthesis which he will have to make for himself. The most that he can hope for is that with long thought and study, with years of practice at the bar or on the bench, and with the aid of that inward grace which comes now and again to the elect of any calling, the analysis may help a little to make the synthesis a true one.

* * *

I have spoken of the forces of which judges avowedly avail to shape the form and content of their judgments. Even these forces are seldom fully in consciousness. They lie so near the surface, however, that their existence and influence are not likely to be disclaimed. But the subject is not exhausted with the recognition of their power. Deep below consciousness are other forces, the likes and the dislikes, the predilections and prejudices, the complex of instincts and emotions habits and convictions, which make the man, whether he be litigant or judge. I wish I might have found the time and opportunity to pursue this subject farther. I shall be able, as it is, to do little more than remind you of its existence. There has been a certain lack of candor in much of the discussion of the theme, or rather perhaps in the refusal to discuss it, as if judges must lose respect and confidence by the reminder that they are subject to human limitations. I do not doubt the grandeur of the conception which lifts them into the realm of pure reason, above and beyond the sweep of perturbing and deflecting forces. None the less, if there is anything of reality in my analysis of the judicial process, they do not stand aloof on these chill and distant heights; and we shall not help the cause of truth by acting and speaking as if they do. The great tides and currents which engulf the rest of men, do not turn aside in their course, and pass the judges by. We like to figure to ourselves the processes of justice as coldly objective and impersonal. The law, conceived of as a real existence, dwelling apart and alone, speaks, through the voices of priests and ministers, the words which they have no choice except to utter. That is an ideal of objective truth toward which every system of jurisprudence tends. It is an ideal of which great publicists and judges have spoken as of something possible to attain. "The judges of the nation," says Montesquieu, "are only the mouths that pronounce the words of the law, inanimate beings, who can moderate neither its force nor its rigor."

* * *

I remember that this statement when made, aroused a storm of criticism. It betrayed ignorance, they said, of the nature of the judicial process. The business of the judge, they told us, was to discover objective truth. His own little individuality, his tiny stock of scattered and uncoordinated philosophies, these, with all his weaknesses and unconscious prejudices, were to be laid aside and forgotten. What did men care for his reading of the eternal verities? It was not worth recording. What the world was seeking, was the eternal verities themselves. Far am I from denying that this is, indeed, the goal toward which all of us must strive. Something of Pascal's spirit of self-search and self-reproach must come at moments to the man who finds himself summoned to the duty of shaping the progress of the law. The very breadth and scope of the opportunity to give expression to his finer self, seem to point the accusing finger of disparagement and scorn. What am I that in these great movements onward, this rush and sweep of forces, my petty personality should deflect them by a hairbreadth? Why should the pure light of truth be broken up and impregnated and colored with any element of my being? Such doubts and hesitations besiege one now and again. The truth is, however, that all these inward questionings are born of the hope and desire to transcend the limitations which hedge our human nature. . . .

I have no quarrel, therefore, with the doctrine that judges ought to be in sympathy with the spirit of their times. Alas! Assent to such a generality does not carry us far upon the road to truth. In every court there are likely to be as many estimates of the "Zeitgeist" as there are judges on its bench. Of the power of favor or prejudice in any sordid or vulgar or evil sense, I have found no trace, not even the faintest, among the judges whom I have known. But every day there is borne in on me a new conviction of the inescapable relation between the truth without us and the truth within. The spirit of the age, as it is revealed to each of us, is too often only the spirit of the group in which the accidents of birth or education or occupation or fellowship have given us a place. No effort or revolution of the mind will overthrow utterly and at all times the empire of these subconscious loyalties. "Our beliefs and opinions," says James Harvey Robinson, "like our standards of conduct come to us insensibly as products of our companionship with our fellow men, not as results of our personal experience and the inferences we individually make from our own observations. We are constantly misled by our extraordinary faculty of "rationalizing"—that is, of devising plausible arguments for accepting what is imposed upon us by the traditions of the group to which we belong. We are abjectly credulous by nature, and instinctively accept the verdicts of the group. We are suggestible not merely when under the spell of an excited mob or a fervent revival, but we are ever and always listening to the still small voice of the herd, and are ever ready to defend and justify its instructions and warnings, and accept them as the mature results of our own reasoning." This was written, not of judges specially, but of men and women of all classes. The training of the judge, if coupled with what is styled the judicial temperament, will help in some degree to emancipate him from the suggestive power of individual dislikes and prepossessions. It will help to broaden the group to which his subconscious loyalties are due. Never will these loyalties be utterly extinguished while human nature is what it is. We may wonder sometimes how from the play of all these forces of individualism, there can come anything coherent, anything but chaos and the void. Those are the moments in which we exaggerate the elements of difference. In the end there emerges something which has a composite shape and truth and order. It has been said that "History, like mathematics, is obliged to assume that eccentricities more or less balance each other, so that something remains constant at last." The like is true of the work of courts. The eccentricities of judges balance one another. One judge looks at problems from the point of view of history, another from that of philosophy, another from that of social utility, one is a formalist, another a latitudinarian, one is timorous of change, another dissatisfied with the present; out of the attrition of diverse minds there is beaten something which has a constancy and uniformity and average value greater than its component elements. The same thing is true of the work of juries. I do not mean to suggest that the product in either case does not betray the flaws inherent in its origin. The flaws are there as in every human institution. Because they are not only there but visible, we have faith that they will be corrected. There is no assurance that the rule of the majority will be the expression of perfect reason when embodied in constitution or in statute. We ought not to expect more of it when embodied in the judgments of the courts. The tide rises and falls, but the sands of error crumble.

David Mamet

from THE VERDICT

Playwright and screenwriter David Mamet wrote the screenplay for The Verdict *(1982), a film directed by Sidney Lumet and starring Paul Newman as broken-down, ambulance-chasing attorney Frank Galvin. In this scene from a trial involving a negligence suit against two doctors who rendered Galvin's client brain-dead, Galvin, in his summation, invokes the principle of religious faith as a way to persuade the jury to ignore the moral corruption of the trial and do the right thing by reaching a verdict for his client.*

FRANK GALVIN'S SUMMATION

You know, so much of the time, we're just lost. We say, "Please, God . . . tell us what is right. Tell us what is true." And there is no justice. The rich win, the poor are powerless. We become . . . tired of hearing people lie. And after a time, we become dead. A little dead. We think of ourselves . . . as victims. And we become victims. We become . . . we become weak. We doubt ourselves, we doubt our beliefs. We doubt our institutions. And we doubt the law. But today, you are the law. You are the law. Not some book. Not the lawyers. Not the, the marble statue . . . or the trappings of the court. See, those are just symbols . . . of our desire . . . to be just. But they are . . . they are, in fact, a prayer, I mean, a fervent and frightened prayer. In my religion . . . they say, "Act as if ye had faith . . . and faith will be given to you." If . . . if we are to have faith in justice . . . we need only to believe in ourselves . . . and act with justice. And I believe that there is justice in our hearts. Thank you.

Judge Learned Hand

OPINION FROM

SCHMIDT v. UNITED STATES

Judge Learned Hand served on the U.S. Court of Appeals for the Second Circuit from 1924 to 1951. He was a wonderful writer whose opinions often reflected the emotional honesty of a judge who remembered that he was also a human being. In his opinion in Schmidt v. United States, *a case involving a man who was denied U.S. citizenship because he admitted to having had sex with unmarried women, Judge Hand acknowledges that sometimes too much truth is not such a good thing, and that judges are not necessarily better at judging moral character than anyone else.*

United States Court of Appeals, Second Circuit.

SCHMIDT

v.

UNITED STATES.
No. 15, Docket 21325.
Argued Oct. 6, 1949.
Decided Oct. 24, 1949.

177 F.2d 450

L. HAND, Chief Judge.

The petitioner has appealed from an order denying his petition for naturalization on the ground that he had failed to establish that he was a person of "good moral character" for the five years preceding the filing of the petition on July 5, 1944. He was a native of Germany, at that time thirty-nine years old, who had been admitted to the United States for permanent residence on January 17, 1939. He was a teacher of French and German in the College of the City of New York and was in every way qualified as a citizen, except that, in a moment of what may have been unnecessary frankness, he verified an affidavit before the examiner, which contained the following passage. "Now and then I engaged in an act in sexual intercourse with women. These women have been single and unmarried women. As to the frequency of these acts I can only state that they occurred now and then. My last such act took place about half a year ago with an unmarried woman." The only question in the case is whether by this admission the alien showed that he was not a person of "good moral character."

In United States ex rel. *Iorio v. Day*, a deportation case where the Commissioner of Immigration had held that a violation of the Prohibition Law was "a crime involving moral turpitude," we said that it was "impossible to decide at all without some estimate, necessarily based on conjecture, as to what people generally feel." The phrase, "good moral character," in the Naturalization Law 8 U.S.C.A. 155, is of the same kind, and makes the same demand. It is true that in *Estrin v. United States* we held that a single act of adultery, unexplained and unpalliated, was alone enough to prevent the alien's naturalization; but we refused to say whether under the "common standards of morality" there might not be "extenuating circumstances" for such a single lapse. In Petitions of Ruder et al. the question arose as to what those circumstances might be. Each of several aliens had been living for years with a single woman in an adulterous union, which apparently had not been concupiscent. Either the alien or the woman had been unable, for one reason or another, to get a divorce. We admitted them all because we did not "believe that the present sentiment of the community views as morally reprehensible such faithful and long continued relationships under the circumstances here disclosed." In *United States v. Rubia* the alien was admitted upon substantially the same facts, save that he had had a good war record. In *United States v. Francioso* we admitted an alien who had married, and was living with his niece under circumstances where we thought that "the moral feelings, now prevalent generally in this country" would not "be outraged because Francioso continued to live" with his wife and with four children whom he had had by her. The last case in which we passed on the clause was *Repouille v. United States* where the alien, in order to relieve his family of crushing expense, had killed his child who was a hopeless bed-ridden idiot. We thought that such conduct did not conform to "the generally accepted moral conventions current at the time;" but we added: "Left at large as we are, without means of verifying our conclusion, and without authority to substitute our individual beliefs, the outcome must needs be tentative; and not much is gained by discussion." In two very recent cases the Third Circuit by an equally divided court of all six judges, affirmed orders admitting two aliens in the following circumstances. In the first case, an unmarried man admitted that he had had occasional meretricious relations with a single woman for pay; in the second case, the facts were the same, except that the alien had a wife and children in Italy, from whom he had apparently not been legally separated.

The foregoing are the only cases that we have discovered in Courts of Appeal which touch nearly enough upon the case at bar to be important; and it must be owned that the law upon the subject is not free from doubt. We do not see how we can get any help from outside. It would not be practicable—even if the parties had asked for it, which they did not—to conduct an inquiry as to what is the common conscience on the point. Even though we could take a poll, it would not be enough merely to count heads, without any appraisal of the voters. A majority of the votes of those in prisons and brothels, for instance, ought scarcely to outweigh the votes of accredited churchgoers. Nor can we see any reason to suppose that the opinion of clergymen would be a more reliable estimate than our own. The situation is one in which to proceed by any available method would not be more likely to satisfy the impalpable standard, deliberately chosen, than that we adopted in the foregoing cases: that is, to resort to our own conjecture, fallible as we recognize it to be. It is true that recent investigations have attempted to throw light upon the actual habits of men in the petitioner's position, and they have disclosed—what few people would have doubted in any event—that his practice is far from uncommon; but it does not follow that on this point common practice may not have diverged as much from precept as it often does. We have answered in the negative the question whether an unmarried man must live completely celibate, or forfeit his claim to a "good moral character"; but, as we have said, those were cases of continuous, though adulterous, union. We have now to say whether it makes a critical difference that the alien's lapses are casual, concupiscent and promiscuous, but not adulterous. We do not believe that discussion will make our conclusion more persuasive; but, so far as we can divine anything so tenebrous and impalpable as the common conscience, these added features do not make a critical difference.

Order reversed; petition granted.

Émile Zola

from "J'ACCUSE"

In what is perhaps the most righteous of all legal writings, French novelist and playwright Émile Zola published a front-page article in the newspaper L'Aurore on January 13, 1898, as an open letter to the president of France, accusing the government of anti-Semitism in having wrongfully convicted Alfred Dreyfus, a Jewish captain in the French military, of espionage. France was deeply divided in what became known as the Dreyfus Affair, and Zola placed himself at considerable risk—in both his career and his life—by defending Dreyfus in an era of such inflamed passions and prejudice. Zola, in fact, was convicted of libel and fled to England. Later, after spending many years in prison, Captain Dreyfus was freed, pardoned, and eventually exonerated.

Sir,

Would you allow me, grateful as I am for the kind reception you once extended to me, to show my concern about maintaining your well-deserved prestige and to point out that your star which, until now, has shone so brightly, risks being dimmed by the most shameful and indelible of stains?

Unscathed by vile slander, you have won the hearts of all. You are radiant in the patriotic glory of our country's alliance with Russia, you are about to preside over the solemn triumph of our World Fair, the jewel that crowns this great century of labour, truth, and freedom. But what filth this wretched Dreyfus affair has cast on your name—I wanted to say "reign"—. A court martial, under orders, has just dared to acquit a certain Esterhazy, a supreme insult to all truth and justice. And now the image of France is sullied by this filth, and history shall record that it was under your presidency that this crime against society was committed.

As they have dared, so shall I dare. Dare to tell the truth, as I have pledged to tell it, in full, since the normal channels of justice have failed to do so. My duty is to speak out; I do not wish to be an accomplice in this travesty. My nights would otherwise be haunted by the spectre of the innocent man, far away, suffering the most horrible of tortures for a crime he did not commit.

And it is to you, Sir, that I shall proclaim this truth, with all the force born of the revulsion of an honest man. Knowing your integrity, I am convinced that you do not know the truth. But to whom if not to you, the first magistrate of the country, shall I reveal the vile baseness of the real guilty parties?

The truth, first of all, about Dreyfus' trial and conviction:

* * *

So an internal search was conducted. Handwriting samples were compared, as if this were some family affair, a traitor to be sniffed out and expelled from within the War Office. And, although I have no desire to dwell on a story that is only partly known, Major du Paty de Clam entered on the scene as soon as the slightest suspicion fell upon Dreyfus. From that moment on, he was the one who "invented" Dreyfus the traitor, the one who orchestrated the whole affair and made it his own. He boasted that he would confuse him and make him confess all. Oh, yes, there was of course the Minister of War, General Mercier, a man of apparently mediocre intellect; and there were also the Chief of Staff, General de Boisdeffre, who appears to have yielded to his own religious bigotry, and the Deputy Chief of Staff, General Gonse, whose conscience allowed for many accommodations. But, at the end of the day, it all started with Major du Paty de Clam, who led them on, hypnotized them, for, as an adept of spiritualism and the occult, he conversed with spirits. Nobody would ever believe the experiments to which he subjected the unfortunate Dreyfus, the traps he set for him, the wild investigations, the monstrous fantasies, the whole demented torture.

Ah, that first trial! What a nightmare it is for all who know it in its true details. Major du Paty de Clam had Dreyfus arrested and placed in solitary confinement. He ran to Mme Dreyfus, terrorised her, telling her that, if she talked, that was it for her husband. Meanwhile, the unfortunate Dreyfus was tearing his hair out and proclaiming his innocence. And this is how the case proceeded, like some fifteenth century chronicle, shrouded in mystery, swamped in all manner of nasty twists and turns, all stemming from one trumped-up charge, that stupid *bordereau*. This was not only a bit of cheap trickery but also the most outrageous fraud imaginable, for almost all of these notorious secrets turned out in fact to be worthless. I dwell on this, because this is the germ of it all, whence the true crime would emerge, that horrifying miscarriage of justice that has blighted France. I would like to point out how this travesty was made possible, how it sprang out of the machinations of Major du Paty de Clam, how Generals Mercier, de Boisdeffre and Gonse became so ensnared in this falsehood that they would later feel compelled to impose it as holy and indisputable truth. Having set it all in motion merely by carelessness and lack of intelligence, they seem at worst to have given in to the religious bias of their milieu and the prejudices of their class. In the end, they allowed stupidity to prevail.

But now we see Dreyfus appearing before the court martial. Behind the closed doors, the utmost secrecy is demanded. Had a traitor opened the border to the enemy and driven the Kaiser straight to Notre-Dame the measures of secrecy and silence could not have been more stringent. The public was astounded; rumors flew of the most horrible acts, the most monstrous deceptions, lies that were an affront to our history. The public, naturally, was taken in. No punishment could be too harsh. The people clamored for the traitor to be publicly stripped of his rank and demanded to see him writhing with remorse on his rock of infamy. Could these things be true, these unspeakable acts, these deeds so dangerous that they must be carefully hidden behind closed doors to keep Europe from going up in flames? No! They were nothing but the demented fabrications of Major du Paty de Clam, a cover-up of the most preposterous fantasies imaginable. To be convinced of this one need only read carefully the accusation as it was presented before the court martial.

How flimsy it is! The fact that someone could have been convicted on this charge is the ultimate iniquity. I defy decent men to read it without a stir of indignation in their hearts and a cry of revulsion, at the thought of the undeserved punishment being meted out there on Devil's Island. He knew several languages: a crime! He carried no compromising papers: a crime! He would occasionally visit his country of origin: a crime! He was hard-working, and strove to be well informed: a crime! He did not become confused: a crime! He became confused: a crime! And how childish the language is, how groundless the accusation! We also heard talk of fourteen charges but we found only one, the one about the *bordereau*, and we learn that even there the handwriting experts could not agree. One of them, Mr. Gobert, faced military pressure when he dared to come to a conclusion other than the desired one. We were told also that twenty-three officers had testified against Dreyfus. We still do not know what questions they were asked, but it is certain that not all of them implicated him. It should be noted, furthermore, that all of them came from the War Office. The whole case had been handled as an internal affair, among insiders. And we must not forget this: members of the General Staff had sought this trial to begin with and had passed judgment. And now they were passing judgment once again.

So all that remained of the case was the *bordereau*, on which the experts had not been able to agree. It is said that within the council chamber the judges were naturally leaning toward acquittal. It becomes clear why, at that point, as justification for the verdict, it became vitally important to turn up some damning evidence, a secret document that, like God, could not be shown, but which explained everything, and was invisible, unknowable, and incontrovertible. I deny the existence of that document. With all my strength, I deny it! Some trivial note, maybe, about some easy women, wherein a certain D . . . was becoming too insistent, no doubt some demanding husband who felt he wasn't getting a good enough price for the use of his wife. But a document concerning national defense that could not be produced without sparking an immediate declaration of war tomorrow? No! No! It is a lie, all the more odious and cynical in that its perpetrators are getting off free without even admitting it. They stirred up all of France, they hid behind the understandable commotion they had set off, they sealed their lips while troubling our hearts and perverting our spirit. I know of no greater crime against the state.

These, Sir, are the facts that explain how this miscarriage of justice came about; The evidence of Dreyfus's character, his affluence, the lack of motive and his continued affirmation of innocence combine to show that he is the victim of the lurid imagination of Major du Paty de Clam, the religious circles surrounding him, and the "dirty Jew" obsession that is the scourge of our time.

* * *

So they rendered an iniquitous verdict that will forever weigh upon our courts martial and will henceforth cast a shadow of suspicion on all their decrees. The first court martial was perhaps unintelligent; the second one is inescapably criminal. Their excuse, I repeat, is that the supreme chief had spoken, declaring the previous judgment incontrovertible, holy and above mere mortals. How, then, could subordinates contradict it? We are told of the honor of the army; we are supposed to love and respect it. Ah, yes, of course, an army that would rise to the first threat, that would defend French soil, that army is the nation itself, and for that army we have nothing but devotion and respect. But this is not about that army, whose dignity we are seeking, in our cry for justice. What is at stake is the sword, the master that will one day, perhaps, be forced upon us. Bow and scrape before that sword, that god? No!

As I have shown, the Dreyfus case was a matter internal to the War Office: an officer of the General Staff, denounced by his co-officers of the General Staff, sentenced under pressure by the Chiefs of Staff. Once again, he could not be found innocent without the entire General Staff being guilty. And so, by all means imaginable, by press campaigns, by official communications, by influence, the War Office covered up for Esterhazy only to condemn Dreyfus once again. Ah, what a good sweeping out the government of this Republic should give to that Jesuit-lair, as General Billot himself calls it. Where is that truly strong, judiciously patriotic administration that will dare to clean house and start afresh? How many people I know who, faced with the possibility of war, tremble in anguish knowing to what hands we are entrusting our nation's defense! And what a nest of vile intrigues, gossip, and destruction that sacred sanctuary that decides the nation's fate has become! We are horrified by the terrible light the Dreyfus affair has cast upon it all, this human sacrifice of an unfortunate man, a "dirty Jew." Ah, what a cesspool of folly and foolishness, what preposterous fantasies, what corrupt police tactics, what inquisitorial, tyrannical practices! What petty whims of a few higher-ups trampling the nation under their boots, ramming back down their throats the people's cries for truth and justice, with the travesty of state security as a pretext.

Indeed, it is a crime to have relied on the most squalid elements of the press, and to have entrusted Esterhazy's defense to the vermin of Paris, who are now gloating over the defeat of justice and plain truth. It is a crime that those people who wish to see a generous France take her place as leader of all the free and just nations are being accused of fomenting turmoil in the country, denounced by the very plotters who are conniving so shamelessly to foist this miscarriage of justice on the entire world. It is a crime to lie to the public, to twist public opinion to insane lengths in the service of the vilest death-dealing machinations. It is a crime to poison the minds of the meek and the humble, to stoke the passions of reactionism and intolerance, by appealing to that odious anti-Semitism that, unchecked, will destroy the freedom-loving France of Human Rights. It is a crime to exploit patriotism in the service of hatred, and it is, finally, a crime to ensconce the sword as the modern god, whereas all science is toiling to achieve the coming era of truth and justice.

* * *

This is the plain truth, Mr. President, and it is terrifying. It will leave an indelible stain on your presidency. I realize that you have no power over this case, that you are limited by the Constitution and your entourage. You have, nonetheless, your duty as a man, which you will recognize and fulfill. As for myself, I have not despaired in the least, of the triumph of right. I repeat with the most vehement conviction: truth is on the march, and nothing will stop it. Today is only the beginning, for it is only today that the positions have become clear: on one side, those who are guilty, who do not want the light to shine forth, on the other, those who seek justice and who will give their lives to attain it. I said it before and I repeat it now: when truth is buried underground, it grows and it builds up so much force that the day it explodes it blasts everything with it. We shall see whether we have been setting ourselves up for the most resounding of disasters, yet to come.

* * *

In making these accusations I am aware that I am making myself liable to articles 30 and 31 of the law of 29/7/1881 regarding the press, which make libel a punishable offence. I expose myself to that risk voluntarily.

As for the people I am accusing, I do not know them, I have never seen them, and I bear them neither ill will nor hatred. To me they are mere entities, agents of harm to society. The action I am taking is no more than a radical measure to hasten the explosion of truth and justice.

I have but one passion: to enlighten those who have been kept in the dark, in the name of humanity which has suffered so much and is entitled to happiness. My fiery protest is simply the cry of my very soul. Let them dare, then, to bring me before a court of law and let the inquiry take place in broad daylight! I am waiting.

With my deepest respect, Sir.
Émile Zola, 13th January 1898

PART II

Lawless Law

Sometimes justice is best served, and makes the most moral sense, when the law is not even resorted to. The relief of injustice is, in some instances, beyond the capacity of law. Access to the law is arguably there, but the desire to pursue it, to seek a legal vindication, is not. This is the absence of law—the tendency toward lawlessness—which offers its own appeal. Individuals take matters into their own hands rather than avail themselves of the grinding machinery of justice. It is faster, after all, and often more just, and surely more final. And the impulse for revenge runs deeper, and can be more personally satisfying than a court-imposed judgment.

Guy de Maupassant

from "A VENDETTA"

Perhaps France's greatest short-story writer, Guy de Maupassant wrote darkly pessimistic stories in the aftermath of the Franco-Prussian War of the 1870s that borrowed heavily from the peasant life of his native Normandy. In "A Vendetta," we see the moral anguish of a mother whose son is murdered and who, in the absence of a legal system's righteous response, takes matters into her own hands, with the aid of a famished dog.

The widow of Paolo Saverini lived alone with her son in a poor little house on the outskirts of Bonifacio. The town, built on an outjutting part of the mountain, in places even overhanging the sea, looks across the straits, full of sandbanks, towards the southernmost coast of Sardinia. Beneath it, on the other side and almost surrounding it, is a cleft in the cliff like an immense corridor which serves as a harbor, and along it the little Italian and Sardinian fishing boats come by a circuitous route between precipitous cliffs as far as the first houses, and every two weeks the old, wheezy steamer which makes the trip to Ajaccio.

* * *

The house of widow Saverini, clinging to the very edge of the precipice, looks out, through its three windows, over this wild and desolate picture.

She lived there alone, with her son Antoine and their dog "Semillante," a big, thin beast, with a long rough coat, of the sheep-dog breed. The young man took her with him when out hunting.

One night, after some kind of a quarrel, Antoine Saverini was treacherously stabbed by Nicolas Ravolati, who escaped the same evening to Sardinia.

When the old mother received the body of her child, which the neighbors had brought back to her, she did not cry, but she stayed there for a long time motionless, watching him. Then, stretching her wrinkled hand over the body, she promised him a vendetta. She did not wish anybody near her, and she shut herself up beside the body with the dog, which howled continuously, standing at the foot of the bed, her head stretched towards her master and her tail between her legs. She did not move any more than did the mother, who, now leaning over the body with a blank stare, was weeping silently and watching it.

The young man, lying on his back, dressed in his jacket of coarse cloth, torn at the chest, seemed to be asleep. But he had blood all over him; on his shirt, which had been torn off in order to administer the first aid; on his vest, on his trousers, on his face, on his hands. Clots of blood had hardened in his beard and in his hair.

His old mother began to talk to him. At the sound of this voice the dog quieted down.

"Never fear, my boy, my little baby, you shall be avenged. Sleep, sleep; you shall be avenged. Do you hear? It's your mother's promise! And she always keeps her word, your mother does, you know she does."

Slowly she leaned over him, pressing her cold lips to his dead ones.

Then Semillante began to howl again with a long, monotonous, penetrating, horrible howl.

The two of them, the woman and the dog, remained there until morning.

Antoine Saverini was buried the next day and soon his name ceased to be mentioned in Bonifacio.

He had neither brothers nor cousins. No man was there to carry on the vendetta. His mother, the old woman, alone pondered over it.

On the other side of the straits she saw, from morning until night, a little white speck on the coast. It was the little Sardinian village Longosardo, where Corsican criminals take refuge when they are too closely pursued. They compose almost the entire population of this hamlet, opposite their native island, awaiting the time to return, to go back to the "maquis." She knew that Nicolas Ravolati had sought refuge in this village.

All alone, all day long, seated at her window, she was looking over there and thinking of revenge. How could she do anything without help—she, an invalid and so near death? But she had promised, she had sworn on the body. She could not forget, she could not wait. What could she do? She no longer slept at night; she had neither rest nor peace of mind; she thought persistently. The dog, dozing at her feet, would sometimes lift her head and howl. Since her master's death she often howled thus, as though she were calling him, as though her beast's soul, inconsolable too, had also retained a recollection that nothing could wipe out.

One night, as Semillante began to howl, the mother suddenly got hold of an idea, a savage, vindictive, fierce idea. She thought it over until morning. Then, having arisen at daybreak she went to church. She prayed, prostrate on the floor, begging the Lord to help her, to support her, to give to her poor, broken-down body the strength which she needed in order to avenge her son.

She returned home. In her yard she had an old barrel, which acted as a cistern. She turned it over, emptied it, made it fast to the ground with sticks and stones. Then she chained Semillante to this improvised kennel and went into the house.

She walked ceaselessly now, her eyes always fixed on the distant coast of Sardinia. He was over there, the murderer.

All day and all night the dog howled. In the morning the old woman brought her some water in a bowl, but nothing more; no soup, no bread.

Another day went by. Semillante, exhausted, was sleeping. The following day her eyes were shining, her hair on end and she was pulling wildly at her chain.

All this day the old woman gave her nothing to eat. The beast, furious, was barking hoarsely. Another night went by.

Then, at daybreak, Mother Saverini asked a neighbor for some straw. She took the old rags which had formerly been worn by her husband and stuffed them so as to make them look like a human body.

Having planted a stick in the ground, in front of Semillante's kennel, she tied to it this dummy, which seemed to be standing up. Then she made a head out of some old rags.

The dog, surprised, was watching this straw man, and was quiet, although famished. Then the old woman went to the store and bought a piece of black sausage. When she got home she started a fire in the yard, near the kennel, and cooked the sausage. Semillante, frantic, was jumping about, frothing at the mouth, her eyes fixed on the food, the odor of which went right to her stomach.

Then the mother made of the smoking sausage a necktie for the dummy. She tied it very tight around the neck with string, and when she had finished she untied the dog.

With one leap the beast jumped at the dummy's throat, and with her paws on its shoulders she began to tear at it. She would fall back with a piece of food in her mouth, then would jump again, sinking her fangs into the string, and snatching a few pieces of meat she would fall back again and once more spring forward. She was tearing up the face with her teeth and the whole neck was in tatters.

The old woman, motionless and silent, was watching eagerly. Then she chained the beast up again, made her fast for two more days and began this strange performance again.

For three months she accustomed her to this battle, to this meal conquered by a fight. She no longer chained her up, but just pointed to the dummy.

She had taught her to tear him up and to devour him without even leaving any traces in her throat.

Then, as a reward, she would give her a piece of sausage.

As soon as she saw the man, Semillante would begin to tremble. Then she would look up to her mistress, who, lifting her finger, would cry, "Go!" in a shrill tone.

When she thought that the proper time had come, the widow went to confession and, one Sunday morning she partook of communion with an ecstatic fervor. Then, putting on men's clothes and looking like an old tramp, she struck a bargain with a Sardinian fisherman who carried her and her dog to the other side of the straits.

In a bag she had a large piece of sausage. Semillante had had nothing to eat for two days. The old woman kept letting her smell the food and whetting her appetite.

They got to Longosardo. The Corsican woman walked with a limp. She went to a baker's shop and asked for Nicolas Ravolati. He had taken up his old trade, that of carpenter. He was working alone at the back of his store.

The old woman opened the door and called:

"Hallo, Nicolas!"

He turned around. Then releasing her dog, she cried:

"Go, go! Eat him up! Eat him up!"

The maddened animal sprang for his throat. The man stretched out his arms, clasped the dog and rolled to the ground. For a few seconds he squirmed, beating the ground with his feet. Then he stopped moving, while

Semillante dug her fangs into his throat and tore it to ribbons. Two neighbors, seated before their door, remembered perfectly having seen an old beggar come out with a thin, black dog which was eating something that its master was giving him.

At nightfall the old woman was at home again. She slept well that night.

Alexandre Dumas

from THE COUNT OF MONTE CRISTO

Alexandre Dumas's The Count of Monte Cristo *(1846), the greatest of all revenge novels, invoked even in feature films of revenge such as* The Shawshank Redemption *and* Sleepers, *reminds us of what can happen when the legal system
fails to do what's right, when, through corruption or neglect or self-interest, it becomes complicit in aggravating the very injustice that it was charged to remedy.
Edmond Dantes is imprisoned for a crime he did not commit (being a loyalist to
Napoleon and a traitor to the crown), and the chief prosecutor, who knows the
truth, destroys the evidence that would incriminate his own father and exonerate
Dantes. Dantes is transformed by his imprisonment and emerges as the Count of
Monte Cristo. In this section, he elaborates to two young men, who are unaware of
his true identity and the motives for why he has befriended them, on his preference
for a form of revenge that is gradual rather than immediate and final.*

"Why so? In life, our greatest preoccupation is death; is it not then, curious to
study the different ways by which the soul and body can part; and how, according to their different characters, temperaments, and even the different
customs of their countries, different persons bear the transition from life to
death, from existence to annihilation? As for myself, I can assure you of one
thing,—the more men you see die, the easier it becomes to die yourself; and
in my opinion, death may be a torture, but it is not an expiation."

"I do not quite understand you," replied Franz; "pray explain your meaning, for you excite my curiosity to the highest pitch."

"Listen," said the count, and deep hatred mounted to his face, as the blood
would to the face of any other. "If a man had by unheard-of and excruciating
tortures destroyed your father, your mother, your betrothed,—a being who,
when torn from you, left a desolation, a wound that never closes, in your
breast,—do you think the reparation that society gives you is sufficient when

it interposes the knife of the guillotine between the base of the occiput and the trapezal muscles of the murderer, and allows him who has caused us years of moral sufferings to escape with a few moments of physical pain?"

"Yes, I know," said Franz, "that human justice is insufficient to console us; she can give blood in return for blood, that is all; but you must demand from her only what it is in her power to grant."

"I will put another case to you," continued the count; "that where society, attacked by the death of a person, avenges death by death. But are there not a thousand tortures by which a man may be made to suffer without society taking the least cognizance of them, or offering him even the insufficient means of vengeance, of which we have just spoken? Are there not crimes for which the impalement of the Turks, the augers of the Persians, the stake and the brand of the Iroquois Indians, are inadequate tortures, and which are unpunished by society? Answer me, do not these crimes exist?"

"Yes," answered Franz; "and it is to punish them that dueling is tolerated."

"Ah, dueling," cried the count; "a pleasant manner, upon my soul, of arriving at your end when that end is vengeance! A man has carried off your mistress, a man has seduced your wife, a man has dishonored your daughter; he has rendered the whole life of one who had the right to expect from heaven that portion of happiness God his promised to every one of his creatures, an existence of misery and infamy; and you think you are avenged because you send a ball through the head, or pass a sword through the breast, of that man who has planted madness in your brain, and despair in your heart. And remember, moreover, that it is often he who comes off victorious from the strife, absolved of all crime in the eyes of the world. No, no," continued the count, "had I to avenge myself, it is not thus I would take revenge."

"Then you disapprove of dueling? You would not fight a duel?" asked Albert in his turn, astonished at this strange theory.

"Oh, yes," replied the count; "understand me, I would fight a duel for a trifle, for an insult, for a blow; and the more so that, thanks to my skill in all bodily exercises, and the indifference to danger I have gradually acquired, I should be almost certain to kill my man. Oh, I would fight for such a cause; but in return for a slow, profound, eternal torture, I would give back the same, were it possible; an eye for an eye, a tooth for a tooth, as the Orientalists say,— our masters in everything,—those favored creatures who have formed for themselves a life of dreams and a paradise of realities."

"But," said Franz to the count, "with this theory, which renders you at once judge and executioner of your own cause, it would be difficult to adopt a course that would forever prevent your falling under the power of the law. Hatred is blind, rage carries you away; and he who pours out vengeance runs the risk of tasting a bitter draught."

"Yes, if he be poor and inexperienced, not if he be rich and skilful; besides, the worst that could happen to him would be the punishment of which we have already spoken, and which the philanthropic French Revolution has substituted for being torn to pieces by horses or broken on the wheel. What matters this punishment, as long as he is avenged? On my word, I almost regret that in all probability this miserable Peppino will not be beheaded, as you might have had an opportunity then of seeing how short a time the punishment lasts, and whether it is worth even mentioning; but, really this is a most singular conversation for the Carnival, gentlemen; how did it arise? Ah, I recollect, you asked for a place at my window; you shall have it; but let us first sit down to table, for here comes the servant to inform us that breakfast is ready." As he spoke, a servant opened one of the four doors of the apartment, saying—*"Al suo commodo!"* The two young men arose and entered the breakfast-room.

Akiva Goldsman

from A TIME TO KILL

(based on the novel by John Grisham)

In Akiva Goldsman's 1996 film adaptation of John Grisham's first novel, A Time
to Kill, *a story about race, justice, and revenge in Mississippi, defense attorney Jake
Brigance must convince the jury that although his client, Carl Lee Haley, committed the murders for which he is charged, he did so in retaliation against the men
who brutally raped, beat, and nearly killed his nine-year-old daughter. In this
iconic trial scene, the reader is left to ponder the legitimacy of self-help, or whether
there is ever such a thing as a time to kill.*

JAKE BRIGANCE'S SUMMATION

Now, I had a great summation all worked out, full of some sharp lawyering,
but I am not going to read it. I'm here to apologize. I am young, and I am
inexperienced. But you cannot hold Carl Lee Hailey responsible for my
shortcomings.

Do you see? In all this legal maneuvering something has gotten lost. That
something is the truth. Now, it is incumbent upon us lawyers . . . not to just
talk about the truth . . . but to actually seek it . . . to find it, to live it.

My teacher taught me that.

Let's take Dr. Bass, for example. Now, obviously, I would have never knowingly put a convicted felon on the stand. I hope you can believe that. But what
is the truth? That he's a disgraced liar? What if I told you the woman he was
accused of raping was seventeen . . . he was twenty-three . . . that she became
his wife . . . bore his child . . . and is still married to the man today? Does that
make his testimony more or less true?

What is it in us that seeks the truth? Is it our minds . . . or is it our hearts?

I set out to prove a black man could get a fair trial in the South, that we are
all equal in the eyes of the law.

That's not the truth.

Because the eyes of the law are human eyes . . . yours and mine, and until we can see each other as equals . . . justice is never going to be evenhanded. It will remain nothing more than a reflection of our own prejudices.

So until *that* day . . . we have a duty under God to seek the truth . . . not with our eyes . . . and not with our minds . . . where fear and hate turn commonality into prejudice . . . but with our hearts . . . but we don't know better.

I want to tell you a story. I'm going to ask you all to close your eyes while I tell you this story. I want you to listen to me. I want you to listen to yourselves. Go ahead. Close your eyes, please. This is a story about a little girl . . . walking home from the grocery store one sunny afternoon. I want you to picture this little girl. Suddenly a truck races up. Two men jump out and grab her. They drag her into a nearby field . . . and they tie her up . . . then rip the clothes from her body. They climb on. First one, then the other . . . raping her . . . shattering everything innocent and pure . . . with a vicious thrust . . . in a fog of drunken breath and sweat. And when they're done . . . after they've killed her tiny womb . . . murdered any chance for her to bear children . . . to have life . . . beyond her own . . . they decide to use her for target practice. So they start throwing full beer cans at her. They throw them so hard . . . that it tears the flesh all the way to her bones. Then they urinate on her. Now comes the hanging. They have a rope. They tie a noose. Imagine the noose coiling tight around her neck . . . and a sudden blinding jerk. She's pulled into the air and her feet and legs go kicking. . . . They don't find the ground. The hanging branch . . . isn't strong enough. It snaps and she falls back to earth. So they pick her up . . . throw her in the back of the truck . . . drive out to Foggy Creek Bridge . . . pitch her over the edge. And she drops some thirty feet . . . down to the creek bottom below.

Can you see her? Her raped . . . beaten . . . broken body . . . soaked in their urine . . . soaked in their semen . . . soaked in her blood . . . left to die.

Can you see her? I want you to picture . . . that little girl. . . .

Now, imagine she's white.

The defense rests, your Honor.

PART III

The Law and Liberty

Human freedom sometimes requires that individuals simply remain aloof from the law, indifferent to its misapplied rules, disobedient and dissenting—right to the bitter end. In the face of injustice, human beings must retain their humanity, refusing to allow, as Margaret Atwood remarks, the "bastards to grind [them] down." They must shake off the stigma of court-ordered scarlet letters even though scars inevitably will remain. And the human spirit must be allowed to flourish despite the many legal impediments to doing so. With all the rules and warnings surrounding us, individuals must gain the confidence to know which doors to walk through and which doors to walk away from.

Franz Kafka

from THE TRIAL

Frank Kafka, the ambivalent Czech lawyer who became a literary rock star, but not in his own lifetime, was known for creating nightmarishly surreal, allegorical tales of individuals rendered helpless by large forces that refuse either safe harbor or easy entry. In The Trial *(1925), Joseph K. is accused of a nameless crime and is arrested, although he is seemingly free to roam about Prague desperately seeking ways to exonerate himself. Caught within the bureaucratic machinery of justice, he enters a cathedral and speaks with a priest, who is of no help but offers K. some advice that he isn't able to follow or even comprehend.*

"You're Joseph K.," said the priest, and lifted one hand from the balustrade in a vague gesture. "Yes," said K.; he recalled how openly he had always said his name; for some time now it had been a burden, and people he met for the first time already knew his name; how good it felt to introduce oneself first and only then be known. "You stand accused," said the priest in a very low voice. "Yes," said K. "I've been notified about it." "Then you're the one I'm seeking," said the priest. "I'm the prison chaplain." "I see," said K. "I had you brought here," said the priest, "so I could speak with you." "I didn't know that," said K. "I came here to show the cathedral to an Italian." "Forget such irrelevancies," said the priest. "What's that in your hand? Is it a prayer book?" "No," replied K., "it's an album of city sights." "Put it aside," said the priest. K. threw it down so violently that it flew open and skidded some distance across the floor, its pages crushed. "Do you realize your trial is going badly?" asked the priest. "It seems that way to me too," said K. "I've tried as hard as I can, but without any success so far. Of course I haven't completed my petition yet." "How do you imagine it will end," asked the priest. "At first I thought it would surely end well," said K., "now sometimes I even have doubts myself. I don't know how it will end. Do you?" "No," said the priest, "but I fear it will end badly. They think you're guilty. Your trial may never move beyond the lower courts. At least for the moment, your guilt is assumed proved." "But I'm not guilty," said K. "It's a mistake. How can any person in general be guilty? We're all human after all, each and every one of us." "That's right," said the priest, "but that's how guilty people always talk." "Are you prejudiced against me too?" asked K. "I'm not prejudiced against you," said the priest. "Thank you," said K. "But everyone else involved with the proceedings is prejudiced against me. And they instill it in those who aren't involved. My position is becoming increasingly difficult." "You misunderstand the facts of the matter," said the priest. "The judgment isn't simply delivered at some point; the proceedings gradually merge into the judgment." "So that's how it is," said K. and bowed his head. "What will you do next in your case?" asked the priest. "I intend to seek additional help," said K., and raised his head to see how the priest judged this. "There are still certain possibilities I haven't taken advantage of." "You seek too much outside help," the priest said disapprovingly, "particularly from women. Haven't you noticed that it isn't true help?" "Sometimes, often even, I'd have to say you're right," said K., "but not always. Women have great power. If I could get a few of the women 1 know to join forces and work for me, I could surely make it through. Particularly with this court, which consists almost entirely of skirt chasers. Show the examining magistrate a woman, even at a distance, and he'll knock over the courtroom table and the defendant to get to her first." The priest lowered his head to the balustrade; only now did the pulpit's roof seem to weigh down upon him. What sort of a storm could there be outside? It was no longer a dull day, it was already deep night. No pane of stained glass within the great window emitted even a shimmer of light to interrupt the wall's darkness. And this was the moment the sexton chose to start extinguishing the candles on the main altar one by one. "Are you angry with me?" K. asked the priest. "Perhaps you don't know the sort of court you serve." He received no reply. "Of course that's just my own personal experience," said K. Still only silence from above. "I didn't mean to insult you," said K. Then the priest screamed down at K.: "Can't you see two steps in front of you?" It was a cry of rage, but at the same time it was the cry of someone who, seeing a man falling, shouts out in shock, involuntarily, without thinking.

Now both were silent for a long time. Of course the priest could barely distinguish K. in the darkness reigning below, while K. could see the priest clearly by the light of the little lamp. Why didn't the priest come down? He hadn't de-

livered a sermon, but instead merely told K. a few things that would probably
harm him more than help if he paid any attention to them. Nevertheless, the
priest's good intentions seemed clear to K.; it was not impossible that they
might come to terms if he would come down, it was not impossible that he
might receive some form of decisive and acceptable advice from him, something that might show him, for example, not how to influence the trial, but
how to break out of it, how to get around it, how to live outside the trial.
Surely that possibility existed; K. had thought about it often in the recent past.
If the priest knew of such a possibility, he might reveal it if asked, even though
he himself was part of the court, and even though when K. attacked the court,
he had suppressed his gentle nature and actually shouted at K.

"Won't you come down now?" asked K. "There's no sermon to deliver.
Come down to me." "Now I can come," said the priest, perhaps regretting
having yelled at him. As he removed the lamp from its hook, he said: "I had to
speak to you first from a distance. Otherwise I'm too easily influenced and forget my position."

K. awaited him at the bottom of the steps. The priest stretched out his hand
to him while still on the upper steps as he descended. "Do you have a little
time for me?" asked K. "As much time as you need," said the priest, and
handed the little lamp to K. for him to carry. Even up close, there was still a
certain aura of solemnity about him. "You're very friendly toward me," said K.
They walked side by side up and down the dark side aisle. "You're an exception among those who belong to the court. I trust you more than I do any of
them I've met so far. I can speak openly with you." "Don't deceive yourself,"
said the priest. "How am I deceiving myself?" asked K. "You're deceiving yourself about the court," said the priest, "in the introductory texts to the Law it
says of this deception: Before the Law stands a doorkeeper. A man from the
country comes to this doorkeeper and requests admittance to the Law. But the
doorkeeper says that he can't grant him admittance now. The man thinks it
over and then asks if he'll be allowed to enter later. 'It's possible,' says the doorkeeper, 'but not now.' Since the gate to the Law stands open as always, and the
doorkeeper steps aside, the man bends down to look through the gate into the
interior. When the doorkeeper sees this he laughs and says: 'If you're so drawn
to it, go ahead and try to enter, even though I've forbidden it. But bear this in
mind: I'm powerful. And I'm only the lowest doorkeeper. From hall to hall,
however, stand doorkeepers each more powerful than the one before. The

mere sight of the third is more than even I can bear.' The man from the country has not anticipated such difficulties; the Law should be accessible to anyone at any time, he thinks, but as he now examines the doorkeeper in his fur coat more closely, his large, sharply pointed nose, his long, thin, black tartar's beard, he decides he would prefer to wait until he receives permission to enter. The doorkeeper gives him a stool and lets him sit down at the side of the door. He sits there for days and years. He asks time and again to be admitted and wearies the doorkeeper with his entreaties. The doorkeeper often conducts brief interrogations, inquiring about his home and many other matters, but he asks such questions indifferently, as great men do, and in the end he always tells him he still can't admit him. The man, who has equipped himself well for his journey, uses everything he has, no matter how valuable, to bribe the doorkeeper. And the doorkeeper accepts everything, but as he does so he says: 'I'm taking this just so you won't think you've neglected something.' Over the many years, the man observes the doorkeeper almost incessantly. He forgets the other doorkeepers and this first one seems to him the only obstacle to his admittance to the Law. He curses his unhappy fate, loudly during the first years, later, as he grows older, merely grumbling to himself. He turns childish, and since he has come to know even the fleas in the doorkeeper's collar over his years of study, he asks the fleas too to help him change the doorkeeper's mind. Finally his eyes grow dim and he no longer knows whether it's really getting darker around him or if his eyes are merely deceiving him. And yet in the darkness he now sees a radiance that streams forth inextinguishably from the door of the Law. He doesn't have much longer to live now. Before he dies, everything he has experienced over the years coalesces in his mind into a single question he has never asked the doorkeeper. He motions to him, since he can no longer straighten his stiffening body. The doorkeeper has to bend down to him, for the difference in size between them has altered greatly to the man's disadvantage. 'What do you want to know now,' asks the doorkeeper, 'you're insatiable.' 'Everyone strives to reach the Law,' says the man, 'how does it happen, then, that in all these years no one but me has requested admittance.' The doorkeeper sees that the man is nearing his end, and in order to reach his failing hearing, he roars at him: 'No one else could gain admittance here, because this entrance was meant solely for you. I'm going to go and shut it now.'"

Henry David Thoreau

from CIVIL DISOBEDIENCE

In this excerpt from nineteenth-century American writer Henry David Thoreau's Civil Disobedience, *the reader is treated to the moral justification for disobeying unjust laws and the grim consequences when majority rule trumps individual freedom. The man who wrote "that government is best which governs least" and who influenced thinkers such as Gandhi and Martin Luther King Jr. set forth the idea that disobedience, peacefully performed, is always an appropriate response to injustice and governmental abuse.*

Unjust laws exist: shall we be content to obey them, or shall we endeavor to amend them, and obey them until we have succeeded, or shall we transgress them at once? Men, generally, under such a government as this, think that they ought to wait until they have persuaded the majority to alter them. They think that, if they should resist, the remedy would be worse than the evil. But it is the fault of the government itself that the remedy is worse than the evil. It makes it worse. Why is it not more apt to anticipate and provide for reform? Why does it not cherish its wise minority? Why does it cry and resist before it is hurt? Why does it not encourage its citizens to put out its faults, and do better than it would have them? Why does it always crucify Christ and excommunicate Copernicus and Luther, and pronounce Washington and Franklin rebels?

One would think, that a deliberate and practical denial of its authority was the only offense never contemplated by its government; else, why has it not assigned its definite, its suitable and proportionate, penalty? If a man who has no property refuses but once to earn nine shillings for the State, he is put in prison for a period unlimited by any law that I know, and determined only by the discretion of those who put him there; but if he should steal ninety times nine shillings from the State, he is soon permitted to go at large again.

If the injustice is part of the necessary friction of the machine of government, let it go, let it go: perchance it will wear smooth—certainly the machine will wear out. If the injustice has a spring, or a pulley, or a rope, or a crank, exclusively for itself, then perhaps you may consider whether the remedy will not be worse than the evil; but if it is of such a nature that it requires you to be the agent of injustice to another, then I say, break the law. Let your life be a counter-friction to stop the machine. What I have to do is to see, at any rate, that I do not lend myself to the wrong which I condemn.

As for adopting the ways which the State has provided for remedying the evil, I know not of such ways. They take too much time, and a man's life will be gone. I have other affairs to attend to. I came into this world, not chiefly to make this a good place to live in, but to live in it, be it good or bad. A man has not everything to do, but something; and because he cannot do everything, it is not necessary that he should be petitioning the Governor or the Legislature any more than it is theirs to petition me; and if they should not hear my petition, what should I do then? But in this case the State has provided no way: its very Constitution is the evil. This may seem to be harsh and stubborn and unconcilliatory; but it is to treat with the utmost kindness and consideration the only spirit that can appreciate or deserves it. So is all change for the better, like birth and death, which convulse the body.

Marquis de Sade

from "THE GRANDE LETTRE"

The eighteenth-century French novelist the Marquis de Sade, best known as a cliché for his own debauchery and pornographic writings—and as the inspiration for the clinical term "sadism"—spent much of his adult life in prison and asylums. In this letter to his wife, written while he was in prison, de Sade addresses the dehumanization of a criminal justice system that taunts a prisoner with the anticipation of freedom that never comes, and the futility of believing that prison will lead to reform.

Sade to his wife.
[February 20, 1781]

> *Despite my chains, I have never adopted the heart of a slave.*
> *(Les Arsacides)*

And I never will. These wretched chains, yes, were they to drag me into the grave, you would still find me exactly the same. I have the misfortune to have received from heaven a strong soul that has never known how to stoop and never will. I have not the slightest fear of offending anyone at all. You give me too many proofs that my sentence is fixed for me to doubt it: therefore, it is not up to anyone to increase it or to reduce it. Moreover, even were this not so, these fellows here that hold me in thrall would not be the ones to do it: this would be a matter for the king, and he is the only person in the entire kingdom that I respect—he and the princes of his blood. Beneath them, I regard everyone else as so completely undifferentiated, as so utterly on a par that, given the circumstances, I do not want to look too closely into even the most well-born of them because, the superiority then falling on my side, it would only all the more strengthen my profound contempt.

You well imagine that it is absurd to try to treat me as they do and yet demand that I do not complain about it. Once and for all, let us think about this reasonably: when an imprisonment must be as long as mine, is there no more absolute wickedness than to try to increase the horror by all that it pleased your mother to invent in order to torture me here? What! Is it not enough to be deprived of everything that makes life pleasant and agreeable, is it not enough to be deprived even of breathing God's air, to constantly witness all one's wishes shattered against the four walls and to see one's days go by merely like those that await us in our tombs? But this hideous torture is not enough for that horrible creature: it is necessary to aggravate it further with whatever else she can conceive to double all the infamy. You will admit that there is only one monster capable of carrying vengeance to that height . . . *But it is all in your imagination,* you are going to tell me; *they are not doing that at all; these are fantasies that naturally develop in your situation.* Fantasies, you say? Very well! I am going to look at my journal, where are laid out today 56 proofs of the sort that I am about to indicate to you by extracting only one, and you will see if it is not poisonous rage that dictated all the maneuvers that this hateful vixen sets into motion here, and if that can properly be called fantasies.

One ought not doubt for an instant that whatever reasons a prisoner might have for believing in a far distant release, the slightest action that might appear to him to support an earlier release would be clutched by him with incredible eagerness: that is exactly in accord with human nature, and it is not wrong to do; so it ought not be punished, it ought rather to be pitied. There is, then, a no more patent cruelty than to incite, instigate, put into action those procedures that propel him into error. One should rather take the greatest care to do the opposite, and humanity (if there were any here) constantly ought to dictate to the core of their souls not to [aggravate] in that way the most painful feeling of the unfortunates; because it is clear in the end that all the suicides come from nothing but blasted hope. One ought not, therefore, encourage this hope when there is no reason for it, and anyone who does it is manifestly a monster. Hope is the most sensitive part of an unfortunate victim's soul; anyone who gives hope only to blast it imitates the torturers of hell who, it is said, ceaselessly renew wound upon wound and will aim, even more fiercely than anywhere else, at the part already lacerated. But even so, that is exactly what your mother has been doing to me for the past four years: a multitude of hopes raised month by month. To listen to these fellows here, to examine your letters, etc., I was always on the eve of my release. Then, when this eve finally comes, there is suddenly a fine thrust of the dagger and *a nice big laugh.* It seems that this despicable woman amuses herself by trying to make me build paper castles in order to have the pleasure of destroying them as soon as they are built. Over and above all the risks in all of that to one's optimism, to the great likelihood of destroying it, and to the certainty of making it untrustworthy for the rest of one's life, there is, you will admit, the much greater risk of the fatal excess of despair; and I now have no reason to doubt for a second that this is not the sole purpose of it all, and that not having been able to succeed in having me killed by leaving me for five years in the hideous situation I was in before prison, she imagined she would perhaps accomplish it in another five years by more certain means.

* * *

Oh! you do not get it, you add; *all of that was necessary; that is what rehabilitates us!*—To rehabilitate! Honestly, suppose I were to leave here tomorrow, would you dare say that I was rehabilitated, without being afraid that I should accuse you of an outrageous impudence? To rehabilitate! to put someone in prison for four or five years *over a party with some girls* [the Marseilles prostitutes] which happens eighty times a day every day in Paris! And then to come tell him that he is indeed fortunate to be released after five years in prison and that if they had vexed him as they did, it was only to *rehabilitate him*! No, I reject this idea, because it revolts me too much, and I am quite sure that you will never have the audacity to claim that to me.

E.L. Doctorow

from THE BOOK OF DANIEL

In this excerpt from E.L. Doctorow's The Book of Daniel *(1971), a novel about the moral, political, and psychological consequences of the cold war, we are introduced to Artie Sternlicht, an acidhead, 1960s radical from the East Village who regales Daniel, the surviving son of the Isaacsons, who were prosecuted and executed for espionage (a fictionalized treatment of the Rosenbergs), about his parents' failure to defy a courtroom that was already prejudged to find them guilty.*

"It's too fucking hot," Artie says. "This fucking city is like an oven." He stands up and starts to pace the room. "You want to know what was wrong with the old American Communists? They were into the system. They wore ties. They held down jobs. They put people up for President. They thought politics is something you do at a meeting. When they got busted they called it tyranny. They were Russian tit suckers. Russia! Who's free in Russia? All the Russians want is steel up everyone's ass. Where's the Revolution in Russia?"

He looks at me as if he really expects an answer. He paces. "The American Communist Party set the Left back fifty years. I think they worked for the FBI. That's the only explanation. They were conspiratorial. They were invented by J. Edgar Hoover. They were his greatest invention."

"How do you know Susan?"

"Baby, how do we know Susan? I think we met her in Boston when I was up there to rap."

"That's when it was," Baby calls in.

"She was into this thing about your parents," Sternlicht says.

"Right."

"Well, man, I mean can I tell it to you straight or are you gonna trip out the minute I open my mouth?"

"Go ahead."

"Your folks didn't know shit. The way they handled themselves at their trial was pathetic. I mean they played it by *their* rules. The government's rules. You know what I mean? Instead of standing up and saying fuck you, do what you want, I can't get an honest trial anyway with you fuckers—they made motions, they pleaded innocent, they spoke only when spoken to, they played the game. All right? The whole frame of reference brought them down because they acted like defendants at a trial. You dig?"

"Yeah."

"I mean someday they're gonna really off me. When the Federales wake up and they see I'm not just some crazy acid head, when they see that all the freaks are together and putting it together we will be set up for the big hit or the big bust or both, which is all right because I don't give a shit about dying, when you're into revolution you have to die, and you can't be a revolution unless you're willing to die. But man, if they ever put me on trial my action will be to show them up for the corrupt fuckers they really are. That trial will be my chance. I will turn that courtroom on, and what I say and do in that court-room will go out on the wire, and the teletype, and kids all over the world will be at that trial and say, 'Man, who is that dude, dig the way he's got his shit to-gether!' And if they find me guilty I will find them guilty, and if they find me innocent I will still find them guilty. And I won't come on except as a judge of them, a new man, like a new nation with new laws of life. And they will be on trial, not me. You see? They blew the whole goddamn thing!"

Dr. Martin Luther King Jr.

from "LETTER FROM A BIRMINGHAM JAIL"

Dr. Martin Luther King Jr., the leader of the American civil rights movement and the primary author of its call for peaceful, nonviolent resistance, composed this letter while incarcerated in a Birmingham, Alabama, prison. The letter is a manifesto for civil disobedience in response to injustice, as well as an intellectually grounded attack against local government's efforts to deprive southern blacks of due process under the law.

April 16, 1963

My Dear Fellow Clergymen:

While confined here in the Birmingham City Jail, I came across your recent statement calling our present activities "unwise and untimely." Seldom, if ever, do I pause to answer criticism of my work and ideas. If I sought to answer all the criticisms that cross my desk, my secretaries would be engaged in little else in the course of the day, and I would have no time for constructive work. But since I feel that you are men of genuine goodwill and your criticisms are sincerely set forth, I would like to answer your statement in what I hope will be patient and reasonable terms.

I think I should give the reason for my being in Birmingham, since you have been influenced by the argument of "outsiders coming in." I have the honor of serving as president of the Southern Christian Leadership Conference, an organization operating in every Southern state, with headquarters in Atlanta, Georgia. We have some eighty-five affiliate organizations all across the South—one being the Alabama Christian Movement for Human Rights. Whenever necessary and possible we share staff, educational and financial resources with our affiliates. Several months ago our local affiliate here in Birmingham invited us to be on call to engage in a nonviolent direct action program if such were deemed necessary. We readily consented and when the hour came we lived up to our promises. So I am here, along with several members of my staff, because I have basic organizational ties here.

Beyond this, I am in Birmingham because injustice is here. . . .

* * *

You deplore the demonstrations that are presently taking place in Birmingham. But I am sorry that your statement did not express a similar concern for the conditions that brought the demonstrations into being. I am sure that each of you would want to go beyond the superficial social analyst who looks merely at effects, and does not grapple with underlying causes. I would not hesitate to say that it is unfortunate that so-called demonstrations are taking place in Birmingham at this time, but I would say in more emphatic terms that it is even more unfortunate that the white power structure of this city left the Negro community with no other alternative.

* * *

You may well ask: "Why direct action? Why sit-ins, marches, etc.? Isn't negotiation a better path?" You are exactly right in your call for negotiation. Indeed, this is the purpose of direct action. Nonviolent direct action seeks to create such a crisis and establish such creative tension that a community that has constantly refused to negotiate is forced to confront the issue. It seeks so to dramatize the issue that it can no longer be ignored. I just referred to the creation of tension as a part of the work of the nonviolent resister. This may sound rather shocking. But I must confess that I am not afraid of the word tension. I have earnestly worked and preached against violent tension, but there is a type of constructive nonviolent tension that is necessary for growth. Just as Socrates felt that it was necessary to create a tension in the mind so that individuals could rise from the bondage of myths and half-truths to the unfettered realm of creative analysis and objective appraisal, we must see the need of having nonviolent gadflies to create the kind of tension in society that will help men to rise from the dark depths of prejudice and racism to the majestic heights of understanding and brotherhood. So the purpose of the direct action is to create a situation so crisis-packed that it will inevitably open the door to negotiation. We, therefore, concur with you in your call for negotiation. Too long has our beloved Southland been bogged down in the tragic attempt to live in monologue rather than dialogue.

* * *

We know through painful experience that freedom is never voluntarily given by the oppressor; it must be demanded by the oppressed. Frankly, I have never yet engaged in a direct action movement that was "well timed," according to the timetable of those who have not suffered unduly from the disease of segregation. For years now I have heard the words "Wait!" It rings in the ear of every Negro with a piercing familiarity. This "Wait" has almost always meant "Never." We must come to see with the distinguished jurist of yesterday that "justice too long delayed is justice denied."

We have waited for more than three hundred and forty years for our constitutional and God-given rights. The nations of Asia and Africa are moving with jet-like speed toward the goal of political independence, and we still creep at horse and buggy pace toward the gaining of a cup of coffee at a lunch counter. I guess it is easy for those who have never felt the stinging darts of segregation to say, "Wait." But when you have seen vicious mobs lynch your mothers and fathers at will and drown your sisters and brothers at whim; when you have seen hate filled policemen curse, kick, brutalize and even kill your black brothers and sisters with impunity; when you see the vast majority of your twenty million Negro brothers smothering in an airtight cage of poverty in the midst of an affluent society; when you suddenly find your tongue twisted and your speech stammering as you seek to explain to your six-year-old daughter why she can't go to the public amusement park that has just been advertised on television, and see tears welling up in her eyes when she is told that Funtown is closed to colored children, and see the depressing clouds of inferiority begin to form in her little mental sky, and see her begin to distort her little personality by unconsciously developing a bitterness toward white people; when you have to concoct an answer for a five-year-old son asking in agonizing pathos: "Daddy, why do white people treat colored people so mean?"; when you take a cross-country drive and find it necessary to sleep night after night in the uncomfortable corners of your automobile because no motel will accept you; when you are humiliated day in and day out by nagging signs reading "white" and "colored"; when your first name becomes "nigger," your middle name becomes "boy" (however old you are) and your last name becomes "John," and your wife and mother are never given the respected title "Mrs."; when you are harried by day and haunted by night by the fact that you are a Negro, living constantly at tip-toe stance never quite knowing what to expect next, and plagued with inner fears and outer resentments; when you are forever fighting a degenerating sense of "nobodiness"; then you will understand why we find it difficult to wait. There comes a time when the cup of endurance runs over, and men are no longer willing to be plunged into an abyss of despair. I hope, sirs, you can understand our legitimate and unavoidable impatience.

You express a great deal of anxiety over our willingness to break laws. This is certainly a legitimate concern. Since we so diligently urge people to obey the Supreme Court's decision of 1954 outlawing segregation in the public schools, it is rather strange and paradoxical to find us consciously breaking laws. One may well ask: "How can you advocate breaking some laws and obeying others?" The answer is found in the fact that there are two types of laws: There are *just* and there are *unjust* laws. I would agree with Saint Augustine that "An unjust law is no law at all."

Now, what is the difference between the two? How does one determine when a law is just or unjust? A just law is a man-made code that squares with the moral law or the law of God. An unjust law is a code that is out of harmony with the moral law. To put it in the terms of Saint Thomas Aquinas, an unjust law is a human law that is not rooted in eternal and natural law. Any law that uplifts human personality is just. Any law that degrades human personality is unjust. All segregation statutes are unjust because segregation distorts the soul and damages the personality. It gives the segregator a false sense of superiority, and the segregated a false sense of inferiority. To use the words of Martin Buber, the Jewish philosopher, segregation substitutes and "I-it" relationship for an "I-thou" relationship, and ends up relegating persons to the status of things. So segregation is not only politically, economically and sociologically unsound, but it is morally wrong and sinful. Paul Tillich has said that sin is separation. Isn't segregation an existential expression of man's tragic separation, an expression of his awful estrangement, his terrible sinfulness? So I can urge men to disobey segregation ordinances because they are morally wrong.

* * *

I must make two honest confessions to you, my Christian and Jewish brothers. First, I must confess that over the last few years I have been gravely disappointed with the white moderate. I have almost reached the regrettable conclusion that the Negro's great stumbling block in the stride toward freedom is not the White Citizen's Counciler or the Ku Klux Klanner, but the white moderate who is more devoted to "order" than to justice; who prefers a negative peace which is the absence of tension to a positive peace which is the presence of justice; who constantly says "I agree with you in the goal you seek, but I can't agree with your methods of direct action"; who paternalistically feels he can set the timetable for another man's freedom; who lives by the myth of time and who constantly advises the Negro to wait until a "more convenient season." Shallow understanding from people of goodwill is more frustrating than absolute misunderstanding from people of ill will. Lukewarm acceptance is much more bewildering than outright rejection.

* * *

More and more I am coming to feel that the people of ill-will have used time much more effectively than the people of goodwill. We will have to repent in this generation not merely for the vitriolic words and actions of the bad people, but for the appalling silence of the good people. We must come to see that human progress never rolls in on wheels of inevitability. It comes through the tireless efforts and persistent work of men willing to be co-workers with God, and without this hard work time itself becomes an ally of the forces of social stagnation. We must use time creatively, and forever realize that the time is always ripe to do right. Now is the time to make real the promise of democracy, and transform our pending national elegy into a creative psalm of brotherhood. Now is the time to lift our national policy from the quicksand of racial injustice to the solid rock of human dignity.

Nathaniel Hawthorne

from THE SCARLET LETTER

In Nathaniel Hawthorne's masterpiece, The Scarlet Letter *(1850), the religious tyranny and intolerance of a New England Puritan community, and the manipulation and harshness of its laws, lead to the moral censure of Hester Prynne. But in this excerpt, after years of legal punishment and banishment, Hester finally experiences the exhilaration of a freedom that comes simply from tearing away the stigma of her shame.*

Arthur Dimmesdale gazed into Hester's face with a look in which hope and joy shone out, indeed, but with fear betwixt them, and a kind of horror at her boldness, who had spoken what he vaguely hinted at, but dared not speak.

But Hester Prynne, with a mind of native courage and activity, and for so long a period not merely estranged, but outlawed from society, had habituated herself to such latitude of speculation as was altogether foreign to the clergyman. She had wandered, without rule or guidance, in a moral wilderness, as vast, as intricate, and shadowy as the untamed forest, amid the gloom of which they were now holding a colloquy that was to decide their fate. Her intellect and heart had their home, as it were, in desert places, where she roamed as freely as the wild Indian in his woods. For years past she had looked from this estranged point of view at human institutions, and whatever priests or legislators had established; criticising all with hardly more reverence than the Indian would feel for the clerical band, the judicial robe, the pillory, the gallows, the fireside, or the church. The tendency of her fate and fortunes had been to set her free. The scarlet letter was her passport into regions where other women dared not tread. Shame, Despair, Solitude! These had been her teachers—stern and wild ones—and they had made her strong, but taught her much amiss.

The minister, on the other hand, had never gone through an experience calculated to lead him beyond the scope of generally received laws; although, in a single instance, he had so fearfully transgressed one of the most sacred of them. But this had been a sin of passion, not of principle, nor even purpose. Since that wretched epoch, he had watched with morbid zeal and minuteness, not his acts—for those it was easy to arrange—but each breath of emotion, and his every thought. At the head of the social system, as the clergymen of that day stood, he was only the more trammeled by its regulations, its principles, and even its prejudices. As a priest, the framework of his order inevitably hemmed him in. As a man who had once sinned, but who kept his conscience all alive and painfully sensitive by the fretting of an unhealed wound, he might have been supposed safer within the line of virtue than if he had never sinned at all.

Thus we seem to see that, as regarded Hester Prynne, the whole seven years of outlaw and ignominy had been little other than a preparation for this very hour. But Arthur Dimmesdale! Were such a man once more to fall, what plea could be urged in extenuation of his crime? None; unless it avail him somewhat that he was broken down by long and exquisite suffering; that his mind was darkened and confused by the very remorse which harrowed it; that, between fleeing as an avowed criminal, and remaining as a hypocrite, conscience might find it hard to strike the balance; that it was human to avoid the peril of death and infamy, and the inscrutable machinations of an enemy; that, finally, to this poor pilgrim, on his dreary and desert path, faint, sick, miserable, there appeared a glimpse of human affection and sympathy, a new life, and a true one, in exchange for the heavy doom which he was now expiating. And be the stern and sad truth spoken, that the breach which guilt has once made into the human soul is never, in this mortal state, repaired. It may be watched and guarded, so that the enemy shall not force his way again into the citadel, and might even in his subsequent assaults, select some other avenue, in preference to that where he had formerly succeeded. But there is still the ruined wall, and near it the stealthy tread of the foe that would win over again his unforgotten triumph.

The struggle, if there were one, need not be described. Let it suffice that the clergyman resolved to flee, and not alone.

"If in all these past seven years," thought he, "I could recall one instant of peace or hope, I would yet endure, for the sake of that earnest of Heaven's mercy. But now—since I am irrevocably doomed—wherefore should I not snatch the solace allowed to the condemned culprit before his execution? Or, if this be the path to a better life, as Hester would persuade me, I surely give up no fairer prospect by pursuing it! Neither can I any longer live without her companionship; so powerful is she to sustain—so tender to soothe! O Thou to whom I dare not lift mine eyes, wilt Thou yet pardon me?"

"Thou wilt go!" said Hester calmly, as he met her glance.

The decision once made, a glow of strange enjoyment threw its flickering brightness over the trouble of his breast. It was the exhilarating effect—upon a prisoner just escaped from the dungeon of his own heart—of breathing the wild, free atmosphere of an unredeemed, unchristianised, lawless region. His spirit rose, as it were, with a bound, and attained a nearer prospect of the sky, than throughout all the misery which had kept him groveling on the earth. Of a deeply religious temperament, there was inevitably a tinge of the devotional in his mood.

"Do I feel joy again?" cried he, wondering at himself. "Methought the germ of it was dead in me! Oh, Hester, thou art my better angel! I seem to have flung myself—sick, sin-stained, and sorrow-blackened—down upon these forest leaves, and to have risen up all made anew, and with new powers to glorify Him that hath been merciful! This is already the better life! Why did we not find it sooner?"

"Let us not look back," answered Hester Prynne. "The past is gone! Wherefore should we linger upon it now? See! With this symbol I undo it all, and make it as if it had never been!"

So speaking, she undid the clasp that fastened the scarlet letter, and, taking it from her bosom, threw it to a distance among the withered leaves. The mystic token alighted on the hither verge of the stream. With a hand's-breadth further flight, it would have fallen into the water, and have given the little brook another woe to carry onward, besides the unintelligible tale which it still kept murmuring about. But there lay the embroidered letter, glittering like a lost jewel, which some ill-fated wanderer might pick up, and thenceforth be haunted by strange phantoms of guilt, sinkings of the heart, and unaccountable misfortune.

The stigma gone, Hester heaved a long, deep sigh, in which the burden of shame and anguish departed from her spirit. O exquisite relief! She had not known the weight until she felt the freedom! By another impulse, she took off the formal cap that confined her hair, and down it fell upon her shoulders, dark and rich, with at once a shadow and a light in its abundance, and imparting the charm of softness to her features. There played around her mouth, and beamed out of her eyes, a radiant and tender smile, that seemed gushing from the very heart of womanhood. A crimson flush was glowing on her cheek, that had been long so pale. Her sex, her youth, and the whole richness of her beauty, came back from what men call the irrevocable past, and clustered themselves with her maiden hope, and a happiness before unknown, within the magic circle of this hour. And, as if the gloom of the earth and sky had been but the effluence of these two mortal hearts, it vanished with their sorrow. All at once, as with a sudden smile of heaven, forth burst the sunshine, pouring a very flood into the obscure forest, gladdening each green leaf, transmuting the yellow fallen ones to gold, and gleaming adown the gray trunks of the solemn trees. The objects that had made a shadow hitherto, embodied the brightness now. The course of the little brook might be traced by its merry gleam afar into the wood's heart of mystery, which had become a mystery of joy.

Such was the sympathy of Nature—that wild, heathen Nature of the forest, never subjugated by human law, nor illumined by higher truth—with the bliss of these two spirits! Love, whether newly-born, or aroused from a death-like slumber, must always create a sunshine, filling the heart so full of radiance, that it overflows upon the outward world. Had the forest still kept its gloom, it would have been bright in Hester's eyes, and bright in Arthur Dimmesdale's!

William Faulkner

from INTRUDER IN THE DUST

*One of southern writer and Nobel Prize–winner William Faulkner's finest novels,
although not among his best known,* Intruder in the Dust *(1948), set in the
post–World War II American South, is a story of racial injustice in which a black
farmer, Lucas Beauchamp, is on trial for the murder of a white man. In the novel,
a southern white teenager, his black friend, and an elderly white woman rally to
rescue the falsely accused Beauchamp and prevent a lynching. The sense of moral
responsibility that the South must share for the inhumane treatment of its black
neighbors is revealed by a cynical attorney, the uncle of the white teenager, who is
representing the accused.*

"Yes," his uncle said. "*Thou shalt not kill* in precept and even when you do,
precept still remains unblemished and scarless: *Thou shalt not kill* and who
knows, perhaps next time maybe you won't. But *Gowrie must not kill Gowrie's
brother:* no maybe about it, no next time to maybe not Gowrie kill Gowrie because there must be no first time. And not just for Gowrie but for all: Stevens
and Mallison and Edmonds and McCaslin too; if we are not to hold to the belief that that point not just shall not but must not and *can*not come at which
Gowrie or Ingrum or Stevens or Mallison may shed Gowrie or Ingrum or
Stevens or Mallison blood, how hope ever to reach that one where *Thou shalt
not kill at all*, where Lucas Beauchamp's life will be secure not despite the fact
that he is Lucas Beauchamp but because he is?"

"So they ran to keep from having to lynch Crawford Gowrie," he said.

"They wouldn't have lynched Crawford Gowrie," his uncle said. "There
were too many of them. Don't you remember, they packed the street in front
of the jail and the Square too all morning while they still believed Lucas had
shot Vinson Gowrie in the back without bothering him at all?"

"They were waiting for Beat Four to come in and do it."

"Which is exactly what I am saying—granted for the moment that that's true. That part of Beat Four composed of Gowries and Workitts and the four or five others who wouldn't have given a Gowrie or Workitt either a chew of tobacco and who would have come along just to see the blood, is small enough to produce a mob. But not all of them together because there is a simple numerical point at which a mob cancels and abolishes itself, maybe because it has finally got too big for darkness, the cave it was spawned in is no longer big enough to conceal it from light and so at last whether it will or no it has to look at itself, or maybe because the amount of blood in one human body is no longer enough, as one peanut might titillate one elephant but not two or ten. Or maybe it's because man having passed into mob passes then into mass which abolishes mob by absorption, metabolism, then having got too large even for mass becomes man again conceptible of pity and justice and conscience even if only in the recollection of his long painful aspiration toward them, toward that something anyway of one serene universal light."

"So man is always right," he said.

"No," his uncle said. "He tries to be if they who use him for their own power and aggrandizement let him alone. Pity and justice and conscience too—that belief in more than the divinity of individual man (which we in America have debased into a national religion of the entrails in which man owes no duty to his soul because he has been absolved of soul to owe duty to and instead is static heir at birth to an inevictible quit-claim on a wife a car a radio and an old-age pension) but in the divinity of his continuity as Man; think how easy it would have been for them to attend to Crawford Gowrie: no mob moving fast in darkness watching constantly over its shoulder but one indivisible public opinion: that peanut vanishing beneath a whole concerted trampling herd with hardly one elephant to really know the peanut had even actually been there since the main reason for a mob is that the individual red hand which actually snapped the thread may vanish forever into one inviolable confraternity of namelessness: where in this case that one would have had no more reason to lie awake at night afterward than a paid hangman. They didn't want to destroy Crawford Gowrie. They repudiated him. If they had lynched him they would have taken only his life. What they really did was worse: they deprived him to the full extent of their capacity of his citizenship in man."

He didn't move yet. "You're a lawyer." Then he said, "They were not running from Crawford Gowrie or Lucas Beauchamp either. They were running from themselves. They ran home to hide their heads under the bedclothes from their own shame."

"Exactly correct," his uncle said. "Haven't I been saying that all the time? There were too many of them. This time there were enough of them to be able to run from shame, to have found unbearable the only alternative which would have been the mob's: which (the mob) because of its smallness and what it believed was its secretness and tightness and what it knew to be its absolute lack of trust in one another, would have chosen the quick and simple alternative of abolishing knowledge of the shame by destroying the witness to it. So as you like to put it they ran."

* * *

"Nobody lynched anybody to be defended from it," his uncle said.

"All right," he said. "Excuse them then."

"Nor that either," his uncle said. "I'm defending Lucas Beauchamp. I'm defending Sambo from the North and East and West—the outlanders who will fling him decades back not merely into injustice but into grief and agony and violence too, by forcing on us laws based on the idea that man's injustice to man can be abolished overnight by police. Sambo will suffer it of course; there are not enough of him yet to do anything else. And he will endure it, absorb it and survive because he is Sambo and has that capacity; he will even beat us there because he has the capacity to endure and survive but he will be thrown back decades and what he survives to may not be worth having because by that time divided we may have lost America."

"But you're still excusing it."

"No," his uncle said. "I only say that the injustice is ours, the South's. We must expiate and abolish it ourselves, alone and without help nor even (with thanks) advice. We owe that to Lucas whether he wants it or not (and this Lucas anyway wont) not because of his past since a man or a race either if he's any good can survive his past without even needing to escape from it and not because of the high quite often only too rhetorical rhetoric of humanity but for the simple indubitable practical reason of his future: that capacity to survive and absorb and endure and still be steadfast."

"All right," he said again. "You're still a lawyer and they still ran. Maybe they intended for Lucas to clean it up since he came from a race of floor-moppers. Lucas and Hampton and you since Hampton ought to do something now and then for his money and they even elected you to a salary too. Did they think to tell you how to do it? what to use for bait to get Crawford Gowrie to come in and say All right, boys, I pass. Deal them again. Or were they too busy being—being. . . ."

His uncle said quietly: "Righteous?"

* * *

"Yes?" his uncle said. Then his uncle said. "Yes. Some things you must always be unable to bear. Some things you must never stop refusing to bear. Injustice and outrage and dishonor and shame. No matter how young you are or how old you have got. Not for kudos and not for cash: your picture in the paper nor money in the bank either. Just refuse to bear them. That it?"

"Who, me," he said, moving now already crossing the room, not even waiting for the slippers. "I haven't been a Tenderfoot scout since I was twelve years old."

"Of course not," his uncle said. "But just regret it: don't be ashamed."

Margaret Atwood

from THE HANDMAID'S TALE

Canadian author Margaret Atwood's The Handmaid's Tale *(1985) is a caution-
ary novel of what happens in societies that are no longer governed by constitutional
rights, civil liberties, and the rule of law. In this excerpt, the reader is reminded
that storytelling and memory are crucial to moral survival when the law has abandoned its citizens, and that individuals must muster the courage and resilience to
fight against oppression that is intended to break the human spirit.*

Or in a park somewhere, with my mother. How old was I? It was cold, our
breaths came out in front of us, there were no leaves on the trees; gray sky, two
ducks in the pond, disconsolate. Bread crumbs under my fingers, in my
pocket. That's it: she said we were going to feed the ducks.

But there were some women burning books, that's what she was really there
for. To see her friends; she'd lied to me, Saturdays were supposed to be my day.
I turned away from her, sulking, towards the ducks, but the fire drew me back.

There were some men, too, among the women, and the books were magazines. They must have poured gasoline, because the flames shot high, and then
they began dumping the magazines, from boxes, not too many at a time. Some
of them were chanting; onlookers gathered.

Their faces were happy, ecstatic almost. Fire can do that. Even my mother's
face, usually pale, thinnish, looked ruddy and cheerful, like a Christmas card;
and there was another woman, large, with a soot smear down her cheek and
an orange knitted cap, I remember her.

You want to throw one on, honey? she said. How old was I?

Good riddance to bad rubbish, she said, chuckling. It okay? she said to my
mother.

If she wants to, my mother said; she had a way of talking about me to others as if I couldn't hear.

The woman handed me one of the magazines. It had a pretty woman on it, with no clothes on, hanging from the ceiling by a chain wound around her hands. I looked at it with interest. It didn't frighten me. I thought she was swinging, like Tarzan from a vine, on the TV.

Don't let her *see* it, said my mother. Here, she said to me, toss it in, quick.

I threw the magazine into the flames. It riffled open in the wind of its burning; big flakes of paper came loose, sailed into the air, still on fire, parts of women's bodies, turning to black ash, in the air, before my eyes.

But then what happens, but then what happens?

I know I lost time.

There must have been needles, pills, something like that. I couldn't have lost that much time without help. You have had a shock, they said.

I would come up through a roaring and confusion, like surf boiling. I can remember feeling quite calm, I can remember screaming, it felt like screaming though it may have been only a whisper, *Where is she? What have you done with her?*

There was no night or day; only a flickering. After a while there were chairs again, and a bed, and after that a window.

She's in good hands, they said. With people who are fit. You are unfit, but you want the best for her. Don't you?

They showed me a picture of her, standing outside on a lawn, her face a closed oval. Her light hair was pulled back tight behind her head. Holding her hand was a woman I didn't know. She was only as tall as the woman's elbow.

You've killed her, I said. She looked like an angel, solemn, compact, made of air.

She was wearing a dress I'd never seen, white and down to the ground.

* * *

I would like to believe this is a story I'm telling. I need to believe it. I must believe it. Those who can believe that such stories are only stories have a better chance.

If it's a story I'm telling, then I have control over the ending. Then there will be an ending, to the story, and real life will come after it. I can pick up where I left off.

It isn't a story I'm telling.

It's also a story I'm telling, in my head, as I go along.

Tell, rather than write, because I have nothing to write with and writing is in any case forbidden. But if it's a story, even in my head, I must be telling it to someone. You don't tell a story only to yourself. There's always someone else.

Even when there is no one.

A story is like a letter. *Dear You*, I'll say. Just *you*, without a name. Attaching a name attaches *you* to the world of fact, which is riskier, more hazardous: who knows what the chances are out there, of survival, yours? I will say *you*, *you*, like an old love song. *You* can mean more than one.

You can mean thousands.

I'm not in any immediate danger, I'll say to you.

I'll pretend you can hear me.

But it's no good, because I know you can't.

* * *

It strikes me that, although I know he's a Commander, I don't know what he's a Commander of. What does he control, what is his field, as they used to say? They don't have specific titles.

"Oh," I say, trying to sound as if I understand.

"You might say I'm a sort of scientist," he says. "Within limits, of course. "

After that he doesn't say anything for a while, and neither do I. We are out-waiting each other.

I'm the one to break first. "Well, maybe you could tell me something I've been wondering about."

He shows interest. "What might that be?"

I'm heading into danger, but I can't stop myself. "It's a phrase I remember from somewhere." Best not to say where. "I think it's in Latin, and I thought maybe . . ." I know he has a Latin dictionary. He has dictionaries of several kinds, on the top shelf to the left of the fireplace.

"Tell me," he says. Distanced, but more alert, or am I imagining it?

"*Nolite te bastardes carborundorum*," I say.

"What?" he says.

I haven't pronounced it properly. I don't know how. "I could spell it," I say. "Write it down."

He hesitates at this novel idea. Possibly he doesn't remember I can. I've never held a pen or a pencil, in this room, not even to add up the scores. Women can't add, he once said, jokingly. When I asked him what he meant, he said, For them, one and one and one and one don't make four.

What do they make? I said, expecting five or three.

Just one and one and one and one, he said.

But now he says, "All right," and thrusts his roller-tip pen across the desk at me almost defiantly, as if taking a dare. I look around for something to write on and he hands me the score pad, a desktop notepad with a little smile-button face printed at the top of the page. They still make those things.

I print the phrase carefully, copying it down from inside my head, from inside my closet. *Nolite te bastardes carborundorum.* Here, in this context, it's neither prayer nor command, but a sad graffiti, scrawled once, abandoned. The pen between my fingers is sensuous, alive almost, I can feel its power, the power of the words it contains. Pen Is Envy, Aunt Lydia would say, quoting another Center motto, warning us away from such objects. And they were right, it is envy. Just holding it is envy. I envy the Commander his pen. It's one more thing I would like to steal.

The Commander takes the smile-button page from me and looks at it. Then he begins to laugh, and is he blushing? "That's not real Latin," he says. "That's just a joke."

"A joke?" I say, bewildered now. It can't be only a joke. Have I risked this, made a grab at knowledge, for a mere joke? "What sort of a joke?"

"You know how schoolboys are," he says. His laughter is nostalgic, I see now, the laughter of indulgence towards his former self. He gets up, crosses to the bookshelves, takes down a book from his trove; not the dictionary though. It's an old book, a textbook it looks like, dog-eared and inky. Before showing it to me he thumbs through it, contemplative, reminiscent; then, "Here," he says, laying it open on the desk in front of me.

What I see first is a picture: the Venus de Milo, in a black-and-white photo, with a mustache and a black brassiere and armpit hair drawn clumsily on her. On the opposite page is the Coliseum in Rome, labeled in English, and below, a conjugation: *sum es est, sumus estis sunt.* "There," he says, pointing, and in the margin I see it, written in the same ink as the hair on the Venus. *Nolite te bastardes carborundorum.*

"It's sort of hard to explain why it's funny unless you know Latin," he says. "We used to write all kinds of things like that. I don't know where we got them, from older boys perhaps." Forgetful of me and of himself, he's turning the pages. "Look at this," he says. The picture is called *The Sabine Women,* and in the margin is scrawled: *pim pis pit, pimus pistis pants.* "There was another one," he says. "*Cim, cis, cit . . .*" He stops, returning to the present, embarrassed. Again he smiles; this time you could call it a grin. I imagine freckles on him, a cowlick. Right now I almost like him.

"But what did it mean?" I say.

"Which?" he says. "Oh. It meant, 'Don't let the bastards grind you down.' I guess we thought we were pretty smart, back then."

I force a smile, but it's all before me now. I can see why she wrote that, on the wall of the cupboard, but I also see that she must have learned it here, in this room. Where else? She was never a schoolboy. With him, during some previous period of boyhood reminiscence, of confidences exchanged. I have not been the first then. To enter his silence, play children's word games with him.

"What happened to her?" I say.

He hardly misses a beat. "Did you know her somehow?"

"Somehow," I say.

"She hanged herself," he says; thoughtfully, not sadly. "That's why we had the light fixture removed. In your room." He pauses. "Serena found out," he says, as if this explains it. And it does.

If your dog dies, get another.

"What with?" I say.

He doesn't want to give me any ideas. "Does it matter?" he says. Torn bedsheet, I figure. I've considered the possibilities.

"I suppose it was Cora who found her," I say. That's why she screamed.

"Yes," he says. "Poor girl." He means Cora.

"Maybe I shouldn't come here anymore," I say.

"I thought you were enjoying it," he says lightly, watching me, however, with intent bright eyes. If I didn't know better I would think it was fear. "I wish you would."

"You want my life to be bearable to me," I say. It comes out not as a question but as a flat statement; flat and without dimension. If my life is bearable, maybe what they're doing is all right after all.

"Yes," he says. "I do. I would prefer it."

"Well then," I say. Things have changed. I have something on him, now. What I have on him is the possibility of my own death. What I have on him is his guilt. At last.

"What would you like?" he says, still with that lightness, as if it's a money transaction merely, and a minor one at that: candy, cigarettes.

"Besides hand lotion, you mean," I say.

"Besides hand lotion," he agrees.

"I would like . . ." I say. "I would like to know." It sounds indecisive, stupid even, I say it without thinking.

"Know what?" he says.

"Whatever there is to know," I say; but that's too flippant. "What's going on."

Ayn Rand

from THE FOUNTAINHEAD

Ayn Rand, who immigrated to the United States in 1926 from the Soviet Union and dedicated her writerly life to attacking the Soviet model of collectivism and extolling the virtues of individual freedom, creativity, and selfishness. In The Fountainhead, *her 1943 blockbuster, Howard Roark, an architect and the novel's protagonist, is on trial for blowing up a building, one that he designed but that was being built at odds with his vision. In this excerpt, Roark, representing himself, addresses the court and community in his own defense and, through the theater of a trial, exonerates himself and speaks to the essential truths of human existence.*

A tree branch hung in the open window. The leaves moved against the sky, implying sun and summer and an inexhaustible earth to be used. Dominique thought of the world as background. Wynand thought of two hands bending a tree branch to explain the meaning of life. The leaves dropped, touching the spires of New York's skyline far across the river. The skyscrapers stood like shafts of sunlight, washed white by distance and summer. A crowd filled the county courtroom, witnessing the trial of Howard Roark.

Roark sat at the defense table. He listened calmly.

Dominique sat in the third row of spectators. Looking at her, people felt as if they had seen a smile. She did not smile. She looked at the leaves in the window.

Gail Wynand sat at the back of the courtroom. He had come in, alone, when the room was full. He had not noticed the stares and the flashbulbs exploding around him. He had stood in the aisle for a moment, surveying the

The Estate of Ayn Rand has given permission reluctantly to the inclusion of the following excerpts. The Executor regards these excerpts as out-of-context highlights which, though provocative, do not convey the logic or depth of Ayn Rand's view.

place as if there were no reason why he should not survey it. He wore a gray summer suit and a panama hat with a drooping brim turned up at one side. His glance went over Dominique as over the rest of the courtroom. When he sat down, he looked at Roark. From the moment of Wynand's entrance Roark's eyes kept returning to him. Whenever Roark looked at him, Wynand turned away.

"The motive which the state proposes to prove," the prosecutor was making his opening address to the jury, "is beyond the realm of normal human emotions. To the majority of us it will appear monstrous and inconceivable."

* * *

"Even as the dynamite which swept a building away, his motive blasted all sense of humanity out of this man's soul. We are dealing, gentlemen of the jury, with the most vicious explosive on earth—the egotist!"

On the chairs, on the window sills, in the aisles, pressed against the walls, the human mass was blended like a monolith, except for the pale ovals of faces. The faces stood out, separate, lonely, no two alike. Behind each, there were the years of a life lived or half over, effort, hope and an attempt, honest or dishonest, but an attempt. It had left on all a single mark in common: on lips smiling with malice, on lips loose with renunciation, on lips tight with uncertain dignity—on all—the mark of suffering.

". . . In this day and age, when the world is torn by gigantic problems, seeking an answer to questions that hold the survival of man in the balance—this man attached to such a vague intangible, such an unessential as his artistic opinions sufficient importance to let it become his sole passion and the motivation of a crime against society."

The people had come to witness a sensational case, to see celebrities, to get material for conversation, to be seen, to kill time. They would return to unwanted jobs, unloved families, unchosen friends, to drawing rooms, evening clothes, cocktail glasses and movies, to unadmitted pain, murdered hope, desire left unreached, left hanging silently over a path on which no step was taken, to days of effort not to think, not to say, to forget and give in and give up. But each of them had known some unforgotten moment—a morning when nothing had happened, a piece of music heard suddenly and never heard in the same way again, a stranger's face seen in a bus—a moment when each had known a different sense of living. And each remembered other moments, on a sleepless night, on an afternoon of steady rain, in a church, in an empty street at sunset, when each had wondered why there was so much suffering and ugliness in the world. They had not tried to find the answer and they had gone on living as if no answer were necessary. But each had known a moment when, in lonely, naked honesty, he had felt the need of an answer.

". . . a ruthless, arrogant egotist who wished to have his own way at any price . . ."

Twelve men sat in the jury box. They listened, their faces attentive and emotionless. People had whispered that it was a tough-looking jury. There were two executives of industrial concerns, two engineers, a mathematician, a truck driver, a brick-layer, an electrician, a gardener and three factory workers. The impaneling of the jury had taken some time. Roark had challenged many talesmen. He had picked these twelve. The prosecutor had agreed, telling himself that this was what happened when an amateur undertook to handle his own defense; a lawyer would have chosen the gentlest types, those most likely to respond to an appeal for mercy; Roark had chosen the hardest faces.

". . . Had it been some plutocrat's mansion, but a *housing project*, gentlemen of the jury, a housing project!"

The judge sat erect on the tall bench. He had gray hair and the stern face of an army officer.

". . . a man trained to serve society, a builder who became a destroyer . . ."

The voice went on, practiced and confident. The faces filling the room listened with the response they granted to a good week-day dinner: satisfying and to be forgotten within an hour. They agreed with every sentence; they had heard it before, they had always heard it, this was what the world lived by; it was self-evident—like a puddle before one's feet.

* * *

Roark took the oath. He stood by the steps of the witness stand. The audience looked at him. They felt he had no chance. They could drop the nameless resentment, the sense of insecurity which he aroused in most people. And so, for the first time, they could see him as he was: a man totally innocent of fear.

The fear of which they thought was not the normal kind, not a response to a terrible danger, but the chronic, unconfessed fear in which they all lived. They remembered the misery of the moments when, in loneliness, a man thinks of the bright words he could have said, but had not found, and hates those who robbed him of his courage. The misery of knowing how strong and able one is in one's own mind, the radiant picture never to be made real. Dreams? Self-delusion? Or a murdered reality, unborn, killed by that corroding emotion without name—fear—need—dependence—hatred?

Roark stood before them as each man stands in the innocence of his own mind. But Roark stood like that before a hostile crowd—and they knew suddenly that no hatred was possible to him. For the flash of an instant, they grasped the manner of his consciousness. Each asked himself: do I need anyone's approval?—does it matter?—am I tied? And for that instant, each man was free—free enough to feel benevolence for every other man in the room.

It was only a moment; the moment of silence when Roark was about to speak.

"Thousands of years ago, the first man discovered how to make fire. He was probably burned at the stake he had taught his brothers to light. He was considered an evildoer who had dealt with a demon mankind dreaded. But thereafter men had fire to keep them warm, to cook their food, to light their caves. He had left them a gift they had not conceived and he had lifted darkness off the earth. Centuries later, the first man invented the wheel. He was probably torn on the rack he had taught his brothers to build. He was considered a transgressor who ventured into forbidden territory. But thereafter, men could travel past any horizon. He had left them a gift they had not conceived and he had opened the roads of the world.

"That man, the unsubmissive and first, stands in the opening chapter of every legend mankind has recorded about its beginning. Prometheus was chained to a rock and torn by vultures—because he had stolen the fire of the gods. Adam was condemned to suffer—because he had eaten the fruit of the tree of knowledge. Whatever the legend, somewhere in the shadows of its memory mankind knew that its glory began with one and that that one paid for his courage.

"Throughout the centuries there were men who took first steps down new roads armed with nothing but their own vision. Their goals differed, but they all had this in common: that the step was first, the road new, the vision unborrowed, and the response they received—hatred. The great creators—the thinkers, the artists, the scientists, the inventors—stood alone against the men of their time. Every great new thought was opposed. Every great new invention was denounced. The first motor was considered foolish. The airplane was considered impossible. The power loom was considered vicious. Anesthesia was considered sinful. But the men of unborrowed vision went ahead. They fought, they suffered and they paid. But they won."

* * *

"Men have been taught that it is a virtue to agree with others. But the creator is the man who disagrees. Men have been taught that it is a virtue to swim with the current. But the creator is the man who goes against the current. Men have been taught that it is a virtue to stand together. But the creator is the man who stands alone.

"Men have been taught that the ego is the synonym of evil, and selflessness the ideal of virtue. But the creator is the egotist in the absolute sense, and the selfless man is the one who does not think, feel, judge, or act. These are functions of the self."

* * *

"The only good which men can do to one another and the only statement of their proper relationship is—Hands off!

"Now observe the results of a society built on the principle of individualism. This, our country. The noblest country in the history of men. The country of greatest achievement, greatest prosperity, greatest freedom. This country was not based on selfless service, sacrifice, renunciation or any precept of altruism. It was based on a man's right to the pursuit of happiness. His own happiness. Not anyone else's. A private, personal, selfish motive. Look at the results. Look into your own conscience.

"It is an ancient conflict. Men have come close to the truth, but it was destroyed each time and one civilization fell after another. Civilization is the progress toward a society of privacy. The savage's whole existence is public, ruled by the laws of his tribe. Civilization is the process of setting man free from men."

* * *

"Now you know why I dynamited Cortlandt.

"I designed Cortlandt. I gave it to you. I destroyed it.

"I destroyed it because I did not choose to let it exist. It was a double monster. In form and in implication. I had to blast both. The form was mutilated by two second-handers who assumed the right to improve upon that which they had not made and could not equal. They were permitted to do it by the general implication that the altruistic purpose of the building superseded all rights and that I had no claim to stand against it."

* * *

Roark stood, his legs apart, his arms straight at his sides, his head lifted—as he stood in an unfinished building. Later, when he was seated again at the defense table, many men in the room felt as if they still saw him standing; one moment's picture that would not be replaced.

The picture remained in their minds through the long legal discussions that followed. They heard the judge state to the prosecutor that the defendant had, in effect, changed his plea: he had admitted his act, but had not pleaded guilty of the crime; an issue of temporary legal insanity was raised; it was up to the jury to decide whether the defendant knew the nature and quality of his act, or, if he did, whether he knew that the act was wrong. The prosecutor raised no objection; there was an odd silence in the room; he felt certain that he had won his case already. He made his closing address. No one remembered what he said. The judge gave his instructions to the jury. The jury rose and left the courtroom.

* * *

Those who had been on their feet remained standing, frozen, until the judge returned to the bench. The jury filed into the courtroom.

"The prisoner will rise and face the jury," said the clerk of the court.

Howard Roark stepped forward and stood facing the jury. At the back of the room, Gail Wynand got up and stood also.

"Mr. Foreman, have you reached a verdict?"

"We have."

"What is your verdict?"

"Not guilty."

The first movement of Roark's head was not to look at the city in the window, at the judge or at Dominique. He looked at Wynand.

Wynand turned sharply and walked out. He was the first man to leave the courtroom.

PART IV

The Law Made Low

The law is capable of righting the worst forms of injustice, but it is equally adept at being the very source of that injustice—aggravating the crime; inflaming the grievance. There are those who have committed no crimes and yet are punished as if they had, or who have committed crimes but have been punished too harshly and undeservingly. The result has left them permanently damaged and beyond the scope of rehabilitation. And there are victims who find themselves traumatized—indeed, further victimized—by the law. In the worst cases, the legal system's blindness to backstory and disregard of emotional complexity renders it incapable of true wisdom and fair judgments.

Michel Foucault

from DISCIPLINE AND PUNISH: THE BIRTH OF THE PRISON

The late twentieth-century French postmodernist, structuralist philosopher Michel Foucault devoted some of his later writings to the question of prisons, punishment, and discipline. He concluded that there have been two types of prisons: those that were instruments of monarchies, focused on public executions and torture; and those that are more modern in origin, run by professionals, such as psychologists, interested in discipline and punishment. In this excerpt from his 1975 book, Discipline and Punish: The Birth of the Prison, *Foucault explains how the evolution of prisons has moved from torture and inquisition to investigation and observation.*

The eighteenth century invented the techniques of discipline and the examination, rather as the Middle Ages invented the judicial investigation. But it did so by quite different means. The investigation procedure, an old fiscal and administrative technique, had developed above all with the reorganization of the Church and the increase of the princely states in the twelfth and thirteenth centuries. At this time it permeated to a very large degree the jurisprudence first of the ecclesiastical courts, then of the lay courts. The investigation as an authoritarian search for a truth observed or attested was thus opposed to the old procedures of the oath, the ordeal, the judicial duel, the judgment of God or even of the transaction between private individuals. The investigation was the sovereign power arrogating to itself the right to establish the truth by a number of regulated techniques. Now, although the investigation has since then been an integral part of western justice (even up to our own day), one must not forget either its political origin, its link with the birth of the states and of monarchical sovereignty, or its later extension and its role in the formation of knowledge. In fact, the investigation has been the no doubt crude, but fundamental element in the constitution of the empirical sciences; it has been the juridico-political matrix of this experimental knowledge, which, as we know, was very rapidly released at the end of the Middle Ages. It is perhaps true to say that, in Greece, mathematics were born from techniques of measurement; the sciences of nature, in any case, were born, to some extent, at the end of the Middle Ages, from the practices of investigation. The great empirical knowledge that covered the things of the world and transcribed them into the ordering of an indefinite discourse that observes, describes and establishes the "facts" (at a time when the western world was beginning the economic and political conquest of this same world) had its operating model no doubt in the Inquisition—that immense invention that our recent mildness has placed in the dark recesses of our memory. But what this politico-juridical, administrative and criminal, religious and lay, investigation was to the sciences of nature, disciplinary analysis has been to the sciences of man. These sciences, which have so delighted our "humanity" for over a century, have their technical matrix in the petty, malicious minutiae of the disciplines and their investigations. These investigations are perhaps to psychology, psychiatry, pedagogy, criminology, and so many other strange sciences, what the terrible power of investigation was to the calm knowledge of the animals, the plants or the earth. Another power, another knowledge. On the threshold of the classical age, Bacon, lawyer and statesman, tried to develop a methodology of investigation for the empirical sciences. What Great Observer will produce the methodology of examination for the human sciences? Unless, of course, such a thing is not possible. For, although it is true that, in becoming a technique for the empirical sciences, the investigation has detached itself from the inquisitorial procedure, in which it was historically rooted, the examination has remained extremely close to the disciplinary power that shaped it. It has always been and still is an intrinsic element of the disciplines. Of course it seems to have undergone a speculative purification by integrating itself with such sciences as psychology and psychiatry. And, in effect, its appearance in the form of tests, interviews, interrogations and consultations is apparently in order to rectify the mechanisms of discipline: educational psychology is supposed to correct the rigours of the school, just as the medical or psychiatric interview is supposed to rectify the effects of the discipline of work. But we must not be misled; these techniques merely refer individuals from one disciplinary authority to another, and they reproduce, in a concentrated or formalized form, the schema of power-knowledge proper to each discipline (on this subject, cf. Tort). The great investigation that gave rise to the sciences of nature has become detached from its politico-juridical model; the examination, on the other hand, is still caught up in disciplinary technology.

In the Middle Ages, the procedure of investigation gradually superseded the old accusatory justice, by a process initiated from above; the disciplinary technique, on the other hand, insidiously and as if from below, has invaded a penal justice that is still, in principle, inquisitorial. All the great movements of extension that characterize modern penality—the problematization of the criminal behind his crime, the concern with a punishment that is a correction, a therapy, a normalization, the division of the act of judgment between various authorities that are supposed to measure, assess, diagnose, cure, transform individuals—all this betrays the penetration of the disciplinary examination into the judicial inquisition.

What is now imposed on penal justice as its point of application, its "useful" object, will no longer be the body of the guilty man set up against the body of the king; nor will it be the juridical subject of an ideal contract; it will be the disciplinary individual. The extreme point of penal justice under the Ancien Régime was the infinite segmentation of the body of the regicide: a manifestation of the strongest power over the body of the greatest criminal, whose total destruction made the crime explode into its truth. The ideal point of penality today would be an indefinite discipline: an interrogation without end, an investigation that would be extended without limit to a meticulous and ever more analytical observation, a judgment that would at the same time be the constitution of a file that was never closed, the calculated leniency of a penalty that would be interlaced with the ruthless curiosity of an examination, a procedure that would be at the same time the permanent measure of a gap in relation to an inaccessible norm and the asymptotic movement that strives to meet in infinity. The public execution was the logical culmination of a procedure governed by the Inquisition. The practice of placing individuals under "observation" is a natural extension of a justice imbued with disciplinary methods and examination procedures. Is it surprising that the cellular prison, with its regular chronologies, forced labour, its authorities of surveillance and registration, its experts in normality, who continue and multiply the functions of the judge, should have become the modern instrument of penality? Is it surprising that prisons resemble factories, schools, barracks, hospitals, which all resemble prisons?

Victor Hugo

from LES MISÉRABLES

Victor Hugo's Les Misérables *(1862) is now better known as a Broadway musical than as a nineteenth-century masterpiece of a French novel with much to say about judgment, punishment, and redemption. Set during the aftermath of the French Revolution,* Les Misérables *tells the story of Jean Valjean, the protagonist, sentenced to nineteen years in prison for stealing a loaf of bread. Later he forfeits his parole and is hunted and haunted by police inspector Javert, who has become a symbol of legal excess and zealotry. In this excerpt, the novel examines the combined assault of society and law in having treated Jean Valjean so cruelly and unfairly, and the moral and psychological consequences he suffered from experiencing the full weight of this injustice.*

Let us try to say it.

It is necessary that society should look at these things, because it is itself which creates them.

He was, as we have said, an ignorant man, but he was not a fool. The light of nature was ignited in him. Unhappiness, which also possesses a clearness of vision of its own, augmented the small amount of daylight which existed in this mind. Beneath the cudgel, beneath the chain, in the cell, in hardship, beneath the burning sun of the galleys, upon the plank bed of the convict, he withdrew into his own consciousness and meditated.

He constituted himself the tribunal.

He began by putting himself on trial.

He recognized the fact that he was not an innocent man unjustly punished. He admitted that he had committed an extreme and blameworthy act; that that loaf of bread would probably not have been refused to him had he asked for it; that, in any case, it would have been better to wait until he could get it through compassion or through work; that it is not an unanswerable argument to say,

"Can one wait when one is hungry?" That, in the first place, it is very rare for any one to die of hunger, literally; and next, that, fortunately or unfortunately, man is so constituted that he can suffer long and much, both morally and physically, without dying; that it is therefore necessary to have patience; that that would even have been better for those poor little children; that it had been an act of madness for him, a miserable, unfortunate wretch, to take society at large violently by the collar, and to imagine that one can escape from misery through theft; that that is in any case a poor door through which to escape from misery through which infamy enters; in short, that he was in the wrong.

Then he asked himself—

Whether he had been the only one in fault in his fatal history. Whether it was not a serious thing, that he, a laborer, out of work, that he, an industrious man, should have lacked bread. And whether, the fault once committed and confessed, the chastisement had not been ferocious and disproportioned. Whether there had not been more abuse on the part of the law, in respect to the penalty, than there had been on the part of the culprit in respect to his fault. Whether there had not been an excess of weights in one balance of the scale, in the one which contains expiation. Whether the over-weight of the penalty was not equivalent to the annihilation of the crime, and did not result in reversing the situation, of replacing the fault of the delinquent by the fault of the repression, of converting the guilty man into the victim, and the debtor into the creditor, and of ranging the law definitely on the side of the man who had violated it.

Whether this penalty, complicated by successive aggravations for attempts at escape, had not ended in becoming a sort of outrage perpetrated by the stronger upon the feebler, a crime of society against the individual, a crime which was being committed afresh every day, a crime which had lasted nineteen years.

He asked himself whether human society could have the right to force its members to suffer equally in one case for its own unreasonable lack of foresight, and in the other case for its pitiless foresight; and to seize a poor man forever between a defect and an excess, a default of work and an excess of punishment.

Whether it was not outrageous for society to treat thus precisely those of its members who were the least well endowed in the division of goods made by chance, and consequently the most deserving of consideration.

These questions put and answered, he judged society and condemned it.

He condemned it to his hatred.

He made it responsible for the fate which he was suffering, and he said to himself that it might be that one day he should not hesitate to call it to account. He declared to himself that there was no equilibrium between the harm which he had caused and the harm which was being done to him; he finally arrived at the conclusion that his punishment was not, in truth, unjust, but that it most assuredly was iniquitous.

Anger may be both foolish and absurd; one can be irritated wrongfully; one is exasperated only when there is some show of right on one's side at bottom. Jean Valjean felt himself exasperated.

And besides, human society had done him nothing but harm; he had never seen anything of it save that angry face which it calls Justice, and which it shows to those whom it strikes. Men had only touched him to bruise him. Every contact with them had been a blow. Never, since his infancy, since the days of his mother, of his sister, had he ever encountered a friendly word and a kindly glance. From suffering to suffering, he had gradually arrived at the conviction that life is a war; and that in this war he was the conquered. He had no other weapon than his hate. He resolved to whet it in the galleys and to bear it away with him when he departed.

* * *

Certainly,—and we make no attempt to dissimulate the fact,—the observing physiologist would have beheld an irremediable misery; he would, perchance, have pitied this sick man, of the law's making; but he would not have even essayed any treatment; he would have turned aside his gaze from the caverns of which he would have caught a glimpse within this soul, and, like Dante at the portals of hell, he would have effaced from this existence the word which the finger of God has, nevertheless, inscribed upon the brow of every man,—hope.

Was this state of his soul, which we have attempted to analyze, as perfectly clear to Jean Valjean as we have tried to render it for those who read us? Did Jean Valjean distinctly perceive, after their formation, and had he seen distinctly during the process of their formation, all the elements of which his moral misery was composed? Had this rough and unlettered man gathered a perfectly clear perception of the succession of ideas through which he had, by degrees, mounted and descended to the lugubrious aspects which had, for so many years, formed the inner horizon of his spirit? Was he conscious of all that passed within him, and of all that was working there? That is something which we do not presume to state; it is something which we do not even believe. There was too much ignorance in Jean Valjean, even after his misfortune, to prevent much vagueness from still lingering there. At times he did not rightly know himself what he felt. Jean Valjean was in the shadows; he suffered in the shadows; he hated in the shadows; one might have said that he hated in advance of himself. He dwelt habitually in this shadow, feeling his way like a blind man and a dreamer. Only, at intervals, there suddenly came to him, from without and from within, an access of wrath, a surcharge of suffering, a livid and rapid flash which illuminated his whole soul, and caused to appear abruptly all around him, in front, behind, amid the gleams of a frightful light, the hideous precipices and the somber perspective of his destiny.

The flash passed, the night closed in again; and where was he? He no longer knew. The peculiarity of pains of this nature, in which that which is pitiless— that is to say, that which is brutalizing—predominates, is to transform a man, little by little, by a sort of stupid transfiguration, into a wild beast; sometimes into a ferocious beast.

* * *

He spoke but little. He laughed not at all. An excessive emotion was required to wring from him, once or twice a year, that lugubrious laugh of the convict, which is like the echo of the laugh of a demon. To all appearance, he seemed to be occupied in the constant contemplation of something terrible.

He was absorbed, in fact.

Athwart the unhealthy perceptions of an incomplete nature and a crushed intelligence, he was confusedly conscious that some monstrous thing was resting on him. In that obscure and wan shadow within which he crawled, each time that he turned his neck and essayed to raise his glance, he perceived with terror, mingled with rage, a sort of frightful accumulation of things, collecting and mounting above him, beyond the range of his vision,—laws, prejudices, men, and deeds,—whose outlines escaped him, whose mass terrified him, and which was nothing else than that prodigious pyramid which we call civilization. He distinguished, here and there in that swarming and formless mass, now near him, now afar off and on inaccessible table-lands, some group, some detail, vividly illuminated; here the galley-sergeant and his cudgel; there the gendarme and his sword; yonder the mitered archbishop; away at the top, like a sort of sun, the Emperor, crowned and dazzling. It seemed to him that these distant splendors, far from dissipating his night, rendered it more funereal and more black. All this—laws, prejudices, deeds, men, things—went and came above him, over his head, in accordance with the complicated and mysterious movement which God imparts to civilization, walking over him and crushing him with I know not what peacefulness in its cruelty and inexorability in its indifference. Souls which have fallen to the bottom of all possible misfortune, unhappy men lost in the lowest of those limbos at which no one any longer looks, the reproved of the law, feel the whole weight of this human society, so formidable for him who is without, so frightful for him who is beneath, resting upon their heads.

* * *

To sum up, in conclusion, that which can be summed up and translated into positive results in all that we have just pointed out, we will confine ourselves to the statement that, in the course of nineteen years, Jean Valjean, the inoffensive tree-pruner of Faverolles, the formidable convict of Toulon, had become capable, thanks to the manner in which the galleys had moulded him, of two sorts of evil action: firstly, of evil action which was rapid, unpremeditated, dashing, entirely instinctive, in the nature of reprisals for the evil which he had undergone; secondly, of evil action which was serious, grave, consciously argued out and premeditated, with the false ideas which such a misfortune can furnish. His deliberate deeds passed through three successive phases, which natures of a certain stamp can alone traverse,—reasoning, will, perseverance. He had for moving causes his habitual wrath, bitterness of soul, a profound sense of indignities suffered, the reaction even against the good, the innocent, and the just, if there are any such. The point of departure, like the point of arrival, for all his thoughts, was hatred of human law; that hatred which, if it be not arrested in its development by some providential incident, becomes, within a given time, the hatred of society, then the hatred of the human race, then the hatred of creation, and which manifests itself by a vague, incessant, and brutal desire to do harm to some living being, no matter whom. It will be perceived that it was not without reason that Jean Valjean's passport described him as a very dangerous man.

From year to year this soul had dried away slowly, but with fatal sureness. When the heart is dry, the eye is dry. On his departure from the galleys it had been nineteen years since he had shed a tear.

Bob Dylan and Jacques Levy

from "HURRICANE"

Troubadour Bob Dylan wrote "Hurricane" in 1976 as a way to call attention to the case of Rubin "Hurricane" Carter, an African American boxer who was wrongly convicted, along with another black man, of murdering three white people inside a bar in Paterson, New Jersey, in 1967. Believing that Carter was innocent after meeting with him and reading his autobiography, and that the case was emblematic of the kinds of racially biased miscarriages of justice common to the era, Dylan played two benefit concerts, one in New York and the other in Houston, to raise money for Carter's legal defense. The song and the concerts brought renewed publicity to Carter's imprisonment and, in 1976, he received a new trial, where he was convicted yet again. Carter's conviction was not overturned until 1984.

Pistol shots ring out in the barroom night
Enter Patty Valentine from the upper hall.
She sees the bartender in a pool of blood,
Cries out, "My God, they killed them all!"
Here comes the story of the Hurricane,
The man the authorities came to blame
For somethin' that he never done,
Put him in a prison cell, but one time he could-a been
The champion of the world.

Three bodies lyin' there does Patty see
And another man named Bello, movin' around mysteriously.
"I didn't do it," he says, and he throws up his hands
"I was only robbin' the register, I hope you understand."

I saw them leaving," he says, and he stops
"One of us had better call up the cops,"
And so Patty calls the cops
And they arrive on the scene with their red lights flashin'
In the hot New Jersey night.

Meanwhile, far away in another part of town
Rubin Carter and a couple of friends are drivin' around.
Number one contender for the middleweight crown
Had no idea what kinda shit was about to go down
When a cop pulled him over to the side of the road
Just like the time before and the time before that.
In Paterson that's just the way things go.
If you're black you might as well not show up on the street
'Less you wanna draw the heat.

Alfred Bello had a partner and he had a rap for the cops,
Him and Arthur Dexter Bradley were just out prowlin' around
He said, "I saw two men runnin' out, they looked like middleweights
They jumped into a white car with out-of-state plates."
And Miss Patty Valentine just nodded her head.
Cop said, "Wait a minute, boys, this one's not dead"
So they took him to the infirmary
And though this man could hardly see
They told him that he could identify the guilty men.

Four in the mornin' and they haul Rubin in,
Take him to the hospital and they bring him upstairs.
The wounded man looks up through his one dyin' eye
Says, "Wha'd you bring him in here for? He ain't the guy!"
Yes, here's the story of the Hurricane,
The man the authorities came to blame
For somethin' that he never done.
Put in a prison cell, but one time he could-a been
The champion of the world.

But then they took him to the jailhouse
Where they try to turn a man into a mouse.

All of Rubin's cards were marked in advance
The trial was a pig-circus, he never had a chance.
The judge made Rubin's witnesses drunkards from the slums
To the white folks who watched he was a revolutionary bum
And to the black folks he was just a crazy nigger.
No one doubted that he pulled the trigger.
And though they could not produce the gun,
The D.A. said he was the one who did the deed
And the all-white jury agreed.

Rubin Carter was falsely tried.
The crime was murder "one," guess who testified?
Bello and Bradley and they both baldly lied
And the newspapers, they all went along for the ride.
How can the life of such a man
Be in the palm of some fool's hand?
To see him obviously framed
Couldn't help but make me feel ashamed to live in a land
Where justice is a game.

Now all the criminals in their coats and their ties
Are free to drink martinis and watch the sun rise
While Rubin sits like Buddha in a ten-foot cell
An innocent man in a living hell.
That's the story of the Hurricane,
But it won't be over till they clear his name
And give him back the time he's done.
Put him in a prison cell, but one time he could-a been
The champion of the world.

Johnny Cash

"FOLSOM PRISON BLUES"

*"Folsom Prison Blues," one of country music legend Johnny Cash's most beloved
song, was recorded in 1956, and then again in 1968 in the renowned live concert
performance from Folsom Prison that was re-created in the 2005 feature film*
Walk the Line. *Cash wrote many songs about prison life and the lives of those who
have violated the law and are forced to pay the consequences of their crimes with
the loss of their liberty.*

I hear the train a comin'
It's rollin' 'round the bend,
And I ain't seen the sunshine,
Since, I don't know when,
I'm stuck in Folsom Prison,
And time keeps draggin' on,
But that train keeps a-rollin',
On down to San Antone.

When I was just a baby,
My Mama told me, "Son,
Always be a good boy,
Don't ever play with guns,"
But I shot a man in Reno,
Just to watch him die,
When I hear that whistle blowin',
I hang my head and cry.

I bet there's rich folks eatin',
In a fancy dining car,

They're probably drinkin' coffee,
And smokin' big cigars,
But I know I had it comin',
I know I can't be free,
But those people keep a-movin',
And that's what tortures me.

Well, if they freed me from this prison,
If that railroad train was mine,
I bet I'd move out over a little,
Farther down the line,
Far from Folsom Prison,
That's where I want to stay,
And I'd let that lonesome whistle,
Blow my Blues away.

Albert Camus

from THE STRANGER

The Stranger *(1942), by French novelist and existentialist Albert Camus, tells the story of Meursault, who soon after attending the funeral of his mother is involved in a murder in which he shoots an Arab man five times on an Algerian beach. Yet the trial seems to be focused more on Meursault's conduct at his mother's funeral and during the days thereafter than on the factual events that led to the Arab's death. In this excerpt, as witnesses are being called to testify, Meursault narrates, in typically detached, neutral tones, his own observations about the trial, in which he is being portrayed as a depraved human being for not having properly mourned and honored his mother.*

But I can honestly say that the time from summer to summer went very quickly. And I knew as soon as the weather turned hot that something new was in store for me. My case was set down for the last session of the Court of Assizes, and that session was due to end some time in June. The trial opened with the sun glaring outside. My lawyer had assured me that it wouldn't last more than two or three days. "Besides," he had added, "the court will be pressed for time. Yours isn't the most important case of the session. Right after you, there's a parricide coming up."

They came for me at seven-thirty in the morning and I was driven to the courthouse in the prison van. The two policemen took me into a small room that smelled of darkness. We waited, seated near a door through which we could hear voices, shouts, chairs being dragged across the floor, and a lot of commotion which made me think of those neighborhood fêtes when the hall is cleared for dancing after the concert. The policemen told me we had to wait for the judges and one of them offered me a cigarette, which I turned down. Shortly after that he asked me if I had the "jitters." I said no—and that, in a way, I was even interested in seeing a trial. I'd never had the chance before. "Yeah," said the other policeman, "but it gets a little boring after a while."

A short time later a small bell rang in the room. Then they took my handcuffs off. They opened the door and led me into the dock. The room was packed. Despite the blinds, the sun filtered through in places and the air was already stifling. They hadn't opened the windows. I sat down with the policemen standing on either side of me. It was then that I noticed a row of faces in front of me. They were all looking at me: I realized that they were the jury. But I can't say what distinguished one from another. I had just one impression: I was sitting across from a row of seats on a streetcar and all these anonymous passengers were looking over the new arrival to see if they could find something funny about him. I knew it was a silly idea since it wasn't anything funny they were after but a crime. There isn't much difference, though—in any case that was the idea that came to me.

* * *

My lawyer arrived, in his gown, surrounded by lots of colleagues. He walked over to the reporters and shook some hands. They joked and laughed and looked completely at ease, until the moment when the bell in the court rang. Everyone went back to his place. My lawyer walked over to me, shook my hand, and advised me to respond briefly to the questions that would be put to me, not to volunteer anything, and to leave the rest to him. To my left I heard the sound of a chair being pulled out and I saw a tall, thin man dressed in red and wearing a pince-nez who was carefully folding his robe as he sat down. That was the prosecutor. A bailiff said, "All rise." At the same time two large fans started to whir. Three judges, two in black, the third in red, entered with files in hand and walked briskly to the rostrum which dominated the room. The man in the red gown sat on the chair in the middle, set his cap down in front of him, wiped his bald little head with a handkerchief, and announced that the court was now in session.

* * *

I wiped away the sweat covering my face, and I had barely become aware of where I was and what I was doing when I heard the director of the home being called. He was asked whether Maman ever complained about me, and he said yes but that some of it was just a way the residents all had of complaining about their relatives. The judge had him clarify whether she used to reproach me for having put her in the home, and the director again said yes. But this time he didn't add anything else. To another question he replied that he had been surprised by my calm the day of the funeral. He was asked what he meant by "calm." The director then looked down at the tips of his shoes and said that I hadn't wanted to see Maman, that I hadn't cried once, and that I had left right after the funeral without paying my last respects at her grave. And one other thing had surprised him: one of the men who worked for the undertaker had told him I didn't know how old Maman was. There was a brief silence, and then the judge asked him if he was sure I was the man he had just been speaking of. The director didn't understand the question, so the judge told him, "It's a formality." He then asked the prosecutor if he had any questions to put to the witness, and the prosecutor exclaimed, "Oh no, that is quite sufficient!" with such glee and with such a triumphant look in my direction that for the first time in years I had this stupid urge to cry, because I could feel how much all these people hated me.   ·

After asking the jury and my lawyer if they had any questions, the judge called the caretaker. The same ritual was repeated for him as for all the others. As he took the stand the caretaker glanced at me and then looked away. He answered the questions put to him. He said I hadn't wanted to see Maman, that I had smoked and slept some, and that I had had some coffee. It was then I felt a stirring go through the room and for the first time I realized that I was guilty. The caretaker was asked to repeat the part about the coffee and the cigarette. The prosecutor looked at me with an ironic gleam in his eye. At that point my lawyer asked the caretaker if it wasn't true that he had smoked a cigarette with me. But the prosecutor objected vehemently to this question. "Who is on trial here and what kind of tactics are these, trying to taint the witnesses for the prosecution in an effort to detract from testimony that remains nonetheless overwhelming!" In spite of all that, the judge directed the caretaker to answer the question. The old man looked embarrassed and said, "I know I was wrong to do it. But I couldn't refuse the cigarette when monsieur offered it to me." Lastly, I was asked if I had anything to add. "Nothing," I said, "except that the witness is right. It's true, I did offer him a cigarette." The caretaker gave me a surprised and somehow grateful look. He hesitated and then he said that he was the one who offered me the coffee. My lawyer was exultant and stated loudly that the jury would take note of the fact. But the prosecutor shouted over our heads and said, "Indeed, the gentlemen of the jury will take note of the fact. And they will conclude that a stranger may offer a cup of coffee, but that beside the body of the one who brought him into the world, a son should have refused it." The caretaker went back to his bench.

When Thomas Pérez's turn came, a bailiff had to hold him up and help him get to the witness stand. Pérez said it was really my mother he had known and that he had seen me only once, on the day of the funeral. He was asked how I had acted that day and he replied, "You understand, I was too sad. So I didn't see anything. My sadness made it impossible to see anything. Because for me it was a very great sadness. And I even fainted. So I wasn't able to see monsieur." The prosecutor asked him if he had at least seen me cry. Perez answered no. The prosecutor in turn said, "The gentlemen of the jury will take note." But my lawyer got angry. He asked Pérez in what seemed to be an exaggerated tone of voice if he had seen me *not* cry. Pérez said, "No." The spectators laughed. And my lawyer, rolling up one of his sleeves, said with finality, "Here we have a perfect reflection of this entire trial: everything is true and nothing is true!" The prosecutor had a blank expression on his face, and with a pencil he was poking holes in the title page of his case file.

* * *

Marie entered. She had put on a hat and she was still beautiful. But I liked her better with her hair loose. From where I was sitting, I could just make out the slight fullness of her breasts, and I recognized the little pout of her lower lip. She seemed very nervous. Right away she was asked how long she had known me. She said since the time she worked in our office. The judge wanted to know what her relation to me was. She said she was my friend. To another question she answered yes, it was true that she was supposed to marry me. Flipping through a file, the prosecutor asked her bluntly when our "liaison" had begun. She indicated the date. The prosecutor remarked indifferently that if he was not mistaken, that was the day after Maman died. Then in a slightly ironic tone he said that he didn't mean to dwell on such a delicate matter, and that he fully appreciated Marie's misgivings, but (and here his tone grew firmer) that he was duty bound to go beyond propriety. So he asked Marie to describe briefly that day when I had first known her. Marie didn't want to, but at the prosecutor's insistence, she went over our swim, the movies, and going back to my place. The prosecutor said that after Marie had given her statements to the examining magistrate, he had consulted the movie listings for that day. He added that Marie herself would tell the court what film was showing. In an almost expressionless voice she did in fact tell the court that it was a Fernandel film. By the time she had finished there was complete silence in the courtroom. The prosecutor then rose and, very gravely and with what struck me as real emotion in his voice, his finger pointing at me, said slowly and distinctly, "Gentlemen of the jury, the day after his mother's death, this man was out swimming, starting up a dubious liaison, and going to the movies, a comedy, for laughs. I have nothing further to say." He sat down in the still-silent courtroom. But all of a sudden Marie began to sob, saying it wasn't like that, there was more to it, and that she was being made to say the opposite of what she was thinking, that she knew me and I hadn't done anything wrong. But at a signal from the judge, the bailiff ushered her out and the trial proceeded.

* * *

[M]y lawyer had lost his patience, and, raising his hands so high that his sleeves fell, revealing the creases of a starched shirt, he shouted, "Come now, is my client on trial for burying his mother or for killing a man?" The spectators laughed. But the prosecutor rose to his feet again, adjusted his robe, and declared that only someone with the naiveté of his esteemed colleague could fail to appreciate that between these two sets of facts there existed a profound, fundamental, and tragic relationship. "Indeed," he loudly exclaimed, "I accuse this man of burying his mother with crime in his heart!" This pronouncement seemed to have a strong effect on the people in the courtroom. My lawyer shrugged his shoulders and wiped the sweat from his brow. But he looked shaken himself, and I realized that things weren't going well for me.

Herman Melville

from BILLY BUDD, SAILOR

Herman Melville, nineteenth-century American author of Moby-Dick, *was also the author of a classic novella dealing with a criminal trial conducted under martial law.* Billy Budd, Sailor *(1891), features a false accusation of mutiny that leads to a murder and then the trial and execution of an otherwise innocent man. In this excerpt, Captain Vere, the ship's captain, explains why Billy Budd should be treated harshly even though the officers on the ship believe that Billy Budd did not commit a capital crime. The excerpt demonstrates that sometimes justice is guided not by what's right or legal but by outside political forces, such as, in this case, the fear of mutinies on the high seas.*

Who in the rainbow can draw the line where the violet tint ends and the orange tint begins? Distinctly we see the difference of the colors, but where exactly does the one first blindingly enter into the other? So with sanity and insanity. In pronounced cases there is no question about them. But in some supposed cases, in various degrees supposedly less pronounced, to draw the exact line of demarcation few will undertake, though for a fee becoming considerate some professional experts will. There is nothing nameable but that some men will, or undertake to, do it for pay.

Whether Captain Vere, as the surgeon professionally and privately surmised, was really the sudden victim of any degree of aberration, every one must determine for himself by such light as this narrative may afford.

That the unhappy event which has been narrated could not have happened at a worse juncture was but too true. For it was close on the heel of the suppressed insurrections, an aftertime very critical to naval authority, demanding from every English sea commander two qualities not readily interfusable—prudence and rigor. Moreover, there was something crucial in the case.

In the jugglery of circumstances preceding and attending the event on board the *Bellipotent*, and in the light of that martial code whereby it was formally to be judged, innocence and guilt personified in Claggart and Budd in effect changed places. In a legal view the apparent victim of the tragedy was he who had sought to victimize a man blameless; and the indisputable deed of the latter, navally regarded, constituted the most heinous of military crimes. Yet more. The essential right and wrong involved in the matter, the clearer that might be, so much the worse for the responsibility of a loyal sea commander, inasmuch as he was not authorized to determine the matter on that primitive basis.

Small wonder then the *Bellipotent's* captain, though in general a man of rapid decision, felt that circumspectness not less than promptitude was necessary. Until he could decide upon his course, and in each detail; and not only so, but until the concluding measure was upon the point of being enacted, he deemed it advisable, in view of all the circumstance, to guard as much as possible against publicity.

* * *

Feeling that unless quick action was taken on it, the deed of the foretopman, so soon as it should be known on the gun decks, would tend to awaken any slumbering embers of the Nore among the crew, a sense of the urgency of the case overruled in Captain Vere every other consideration. But though a conscientious disciplinarian, he was no lover of authority for mere authority's sake. Very far was he from embracing opportunities for monopolizing to himself the perils of moral responsibility, none at least that could properly be referred to an official superior or shared with him by his official equals or even subordinates. So thinking, he was glad it would not be at variance with usage to turn the matter over to a summary court of his own officers, reserving to himself, as the one on whom the ultimate accountability would rest, the right of maintaining a supervision of it, or formally or informally interposing at need. Accordingly a drumhead court was summarily convened, he electing the individuals composing it: the first lieutenant, the captain of marines, and the sailing master.

* * *

The court was held in the same cabin where the unfortunate affair had taken place. This cabin, the commander's, embraced the entire area under the poop deck. Aft, and on either side, was a small stateroom, the one now temporarily a jail and the other a dead-house, and a yet smaller compartment, leaving a space between expanding forward into a goodly oblong of length coinciding with the ship's beam. A skylight of moderate dimension was overhead, and at each end of the oblong space were two sashed porthole windows easily convertible back into embrasures for short carronades.

All being quickly in readiness, Billy Budd was arraigned, Captain Vere necessarily appearing as the sole witness in the case, and as such temporarily sinking his rank, though singularly maintaining it in a matter apparently trivial, namely, that he testified from the ship's weather side, with that object having caused the court to sit on the lee side. Concisely he narrated all that had led up to the catastrophe, omitting nothing in Claggart's accusation and deposing as to the manner in which the prisoner had received it. At this testimony the three officers glanced with no little surprise at Billy Budd, the last man they would have suspected either of the mutinous design alleged by Claggart or the undeniable deed he himself had done. The first lieutenant, taking judicial primacy and turning toward the prisoner, said, "Captain Vere has spoken. Is it or is it not as Captain Vere says?"

In response came syllables not so much impeded in the utterance as might have been anticipated. They were these: "Captain Vere tells the truth. It is just as Captain Vere says, but it is not as the master-at-arms said. I have eaten the King's bread and I am true to the King."

"I believe you, my man," said the witness, his voice indicating a suppressed emotion not otherwise betrayed.

"God will bless you for that, your honor!" not without stammering said Billy, and all but broke down. But immediately he was recalled to self-control by another question, to which with the same emotional difficulty of utterance he said, "No, there was no malice between us. I never bore malice against the master-at-arms. I am sorry that he is dead. I did not mean to kill him. Could I have used my tongue I would not have struck him. But he foully lied to my face and in presence of my captain, and I had to say something, and I could only say it with a blow, God help me!"

In the impulsive aboveboard manner of the frank one the court saw confirmed all that was implied in words that just previously had perplexed them, coming as they did from the testifier to the tragedy and promptly following Billy's impassioned disclaimer of mutinous intent—Captain Vere's words, "I believe you, my man."

* * *

"One question more," said the officer of marines, now first speaking and with a troubled earnestness. "You tell us that what the master-at-arms said against you was a lie. Now why should he have so lied, so maliciously lied, since you declare there was no malice between you?"

At that question, unintentionally touching on a spiritual sphere wholly obscure to Billy's thoughts, he was nonplussed, evincing a confusion indeed that some observers, such as can readily be imagined, would have construed into involuntary evidence of hidden guilt. Nevertheless, he strove some way to answer, but all at once relinquished the vain endeavor, at the same time turning an appealing glance towards Captain Vere as deeming him his best helper and friend. Captain Vere, who had been seated for a time, rose to his feet, addressing the interrogator. "The question you put to him comes naturally enough. But how can he rightly answer it?—or anybody else, unless indeed it be he who lies within there," designating the compartment where lay the corpse. "But the prone one there will not rise to our summons. In effect, though, as it seems to me, the point you make is hardly material. Quite aside from any conceivable motive actuating the master-at-arms, and irrespective of the provocation to the blow, a martial court must needs in the present case confine its attention to the blow's consequence, which consequence justly is to be deemed not otherwise than as the striker's deed."

This utterance, the full significance of which it was not at all likely that Billy took in, nevertheless caused him to turn a wistful interrogative look toward the speaker, a look in its dumb expressiveness not unlike that which a dog of generous breed might turn upon his master, seeking in his face some elucidation of a previous gesture ambiguous to the canine intelligence. Nor was the same utterance without marked effect upon the three officers, more especially the soldier. Couched in it seemed to them a meaning unanticipated, involving a prejudgment on the speaker's part. It served to augment a mental disturbance previously evident enough.

The soldier once more spoke, in a tone of suggestive dubiety, addressing at once his associates and Captain Vere: "Nobody is present—none of the ship's company, I mean—who might shed lateral light, if any is to be had, upon what remains mysterious in this matter."

"That is thoughtfully put," said Captain Vere; "I see your drift. Ay, there is a mystery; but, to use a scriptural phrase, it is a 'mystery of iniquity,' a matter for psychologic theologians to discuss. But what has a military court to do with it? Not to add that for us any possible investigation of it is cut off by the lasting tongue-tie of—him—in yonder," again designating the mortuary stateroom. "The prisoner's deed—with that alone we have to do."

To this, and particularly the closing reiteration, the marine soldier, knowing not how aptly to reply, sadly abstained from saying aught. The first lieutenant, who at the outset had not unnaturally assumed primacy in the court, now overrulingly instructed by a glance from Captain Vere, a glance more effective than words, resumed that primacy. Turning to the prisoner, "Budd," he said, and scarce in equable tones, "Budd, if you have aught further to say for yourself, say it now."

Upon this the young sailor turned another quick glance toward Captain Vere; then, as taking a hint from that aspect, a hint confirming his own instinct that silence was now best, replied to the lieutenant, "I have said all, sir."

* * *

Presently he came to a stand before the three. After scanning their faces he stood less as mustering his thoughts for expression than as one only deliberating how best to put them to well-meaning men not intellectually mature, men with whom it was necessary to demonstrate certain principles that were axioms to himself. Similar impatience as to talking is perhaps one reason that deters some minds from addressing any popular assemblies.

When speak he did, something, both in the substance of what he said and his manner of saying it, showed the influence of unshared studies modifying and tempering the practical training of an active career. This, along with his phraseology, now and then was suggestive of the grounds whereon rested that imputation of a certain pedantry socially alleged against him by certain naval men of wholly practical cast, captains who nevertheless would frankly concede that His Majesty's navy mustered no more efficient officer of their grade than Starry Vere.

What he said was to this effect: "Hitherto I have been but the witness, little more; and I should hardly think now to take another tone, that of your coadjutor for the time, did I not perceive in you—at the crisis too—a troubled hesitancy, proceeding, I doubt not, from the clash of military duty with moral scruple—scruple vitalized by compassion. For the compassion, how can I otherwise than share it? But, mindful of paramount obligations, I strive against scruples that may tend to enervate decision. Not, gentlemen, that I hide from

myself that the case is an exceptional one. Speculatively regarded, it well might
be referred to a jury of casuists. But for us here, acting not as casuists or moral-
ists, it is a case practical, and under martial law practically to be dealt with.

"But your scruples: do they move as in a dusk? Challenge them. Make them
advance and declare themselves. Come now; do they import something like
this: If, mindless of palliating circumstances, we are bound to regard the death
of the master-at-arms as the prisoner's deed, then does that deed constitute a
capital crime whereof the penalty is a mortal one. But in natural justice is
nothing but the prisoner's overt act to be considered? How can we adjudge to
summary and shameful death a fellow creature innocent before God, and
whom we feel to be so?—Does that state it aright? You sign sad assent. Well, I
too feel that, the full force of that. It is Nature. But do these buttons that we
wear attest that our allegiance is to Nature? No, to the King. Though the
ocean, which is inviolate Nature primeval, though this be the element where
we move and have our being as sailors, yet as the King's officers lies our duty
in a sphere correspondingly natural? So little is that true, that in receiving our
commissions we in the most important regards ceased to be natural free
agents. When war is declared are we the commissioned fighters previously
consulted? We fight at command. If our judgments approve the war, that is
but coincidence. So in other particulars. So now. For suppose condemnation
to follow these present proceedings. Would it be so much we ourselves that
would condemn as it would be martial law operating through us? For that law
and the rigor of it, we are not responsible. Our avowed responsibility is in this:
That however pitilessly that law may operate, we nevertheless adhere to it and
administer it.

"But the exceptional in the matter moves the hearts within you. Even so too
is mine moved. But let not warm hearts betray heads that should be cool.
Ashore in a criminal case will an upright judge allow himself off the bench to
be waylaid by some tender kinswoman of the accused seeking to touch him
with her tearful plea? Well the heart here denotes the feminine in man is as
that piteous woman, and hard though it be, she must here be ruled out."

He paused, earnestly studying them for a moment; then resumed.

"But something in your aspect seems to urge that it is not solely the heart
that moves in you, but also the conscience, the private conscience. But tell me
whether or not, occupying the position we do, private conscience should not

yield to that imperial one formulated in the code under which alone we offi-
cially proceed?"

Here the three men moved in their seats, less convinced than agitated by
the course of an argument troubling but the more the spontaneous conflict
within.

Perceiving which, the speaker paused for a moment; then abruptly chang-
ing his tone, went on.

"To steady us a bit, let us recur to the facts.—In war-time at sea a man-of-
war's man strikes his superior in grade, and the blow kills. Apart from its effect, the blow itself is, according to the Articles of War, a capital crime.
Furthermore—"

"Ay, Sir," emotionally broke in the officer of marines, "in one sense it was.
But surely Budd purposed neither mutiny nor homicide."

"Surely not, my good man. And before a court less arbitrary and more merciful than a martial one, that plea would largely extenuate. At the Last Assizes
it shall acquit. But how here? We proceed under the law of the Mutiny Act. In
feature no child can resemble his father more than that Act resembles in spirit
the thing from which it derives—War. In His Majesty's service—in this ship
indeed—there are Englishmen forced to fight for the King against their will.
Against their conscience, for aught we know. Though as their fellow-creatures
some of us may appreciate their position, yet as navy officers, what reck we of
it? Still less recks the enemy. Our impressed men he would fain cut down in
the same swath with our volunteers. As regards the enemy's naval conscripts,
some of whom may even share our own abhorrence of the regicidal French Di-
rectory, it is the same on our side. War looks but to the frontage, the appearance. And the Mutiny Act, War's child, takes after the father. Budd's intent or
non-intent is nothing to the purpose.

"But while, put to it by these anxieties in you which I can not but respect, I
only repeat myself—while thus strangely we prolong proceedings that should
be summary—the enemy may be sighted and an engagement result. We must
do; and one of two things must we do—condemn or let go."

"Can we not convict and yet mitigate the penalty?" asked the sailing master, here speaking, and falteringly, for the first.

"Gentlemen, were that clearly lawful for us under the circumstances, consider the consequences of such clemency. The people" (meaning the ship's

company) "have native sense; most of them are familiar with our naval usage and tradition; and how would they take it? Even could you explain to them—which our official position forbids—they, long molded by arbitrary discipline, have not that kind of intelligent responsiveness that might qualify them to comprehend and discriminate. No, to the people the foretopman's deed, however it be worded in the announcement, will be plain homicide committed in a flagrant act of mutiny. What penalty for that should follow, they know. But it does not follow. *Why?* they will ruminate. You know what sailors are. Will they not revert to the recent outbreak at the Nore? Ay. They know the well-founded alarm—the panic it struck throughout England. Your clement sentence they would account pusillanimous. They would think that we flinch, that we are afraid of them—afraid of practicing a lawful rigor singularly demanded at this juncture lest it should provoke new troubles. What shame to us such a conjecture on their part, and how deadly to discipline. You see then, whither, prompted by duty and the law, I steadfastly drive. But I beseech you, my friends, do not take me amiss. I feel as you do for this unfortunate boy. But did he know our hearts, I take him to be of that generous nature that he would feel even for us on whom in this military necessity so heavy a compulsion is laid."

* * *

Not unlikely they were brought to something more or less akin to that harassed frame of mind which in the year 1842 actuated the Commander of the U.S. brig-of-war *Somers* to resolve, under the so-called Articles of War, Articles modeled upon the English Mutiny Act, to resolve upon the execution at sea of a midshipman and two sailors as mutineers designing the seizure of the brig. Which resolution was carried out though in a time of peace and within not many days' of home. An act vindicated by a naval court of inquiry subsequently convened ashore. History, and here cited without comment. True, the circumstances on board the *Somers* were different from those on board the *Bellipotent*. But the urgency felt, well-warranted or otherwise, was much the same.

Says a writer whom few know, "Forty years after a battle it is easy for a noncombatant to reason about how it ought to have been fought. It is another thing personally and under fire to direct the fighting while involved in the obscuring smoke of it. Much so with respect to other emergencies involving considerations both practical and moral, and when it is imperative promptly to act. The greater the fog the more it imperils the steamer, and speed is put on though at the hazard of running somebody down. Little ween the snug card-players in the cabin of the responsibilities of the sleepless man on the bridge."

In brief, Billy Budd was formally convicted and sentenced to be hung at the yardarm in the early morning watch, it being now night. Otherwise, as is customary in such cases, the sentence would forthwith have been carried out. In wartime on the field or in the fleet, a mortal punishment decreed by a drumhead court—on the field sometimes decreed by but a nod from the general—follows without delay on the heel of conviction without appeal.

E.L. Doctorow

from THE BOOK OF DANIEL

In this excerpt from E.L. Doctorow's The Book of Daniel *(1971), a fictional treatment of the Rosenberg trial and its aftermath, the Isaacson (i.e., Rosenberg) children ask questions about the fate of their parents, who are on trial for espionage and face the death penalty. The children, who have not seen their parents throughout this ordeal, are not the subject of these proceedings, but the excerpt shows that the long arm of the law affects not only the parties to the action but their families, too.*

"Where is Mommy?" Susan said.

Ascher sighed. "In jail. She's in jail."

"What is jail?"

"Jail is a place people stay instead of home. Like a hotel. Like a school. They are other places to stay instead of home."

"Jail is worse," Daniel said to Susan. "You can't come home if you want to."

"All right," Ascher said. "All right."

"Will they put me in jail?" Susan said.

"No, don't worry."

"Is my mommy coming home?"

"Daniel, I cannot go on explaining these things to her."

"Is my mommy dead?"

Ascher stood up and raised his arms in exasperation. "Please, little girl! Enough. Your mommy is not dead!" The gesture startled Susan. She burst into tears. Daniel went to her and put his arm around her. "She misses our mother and father," Daniel explained over his shoulder.

"What is wrong, what is the matter?" Aunt Frieda called from upstairs.

"Nothing," Ascher yelled. "Nothing is the matter. Now children," he said lowering his voice, "there are things to be done. Shhh, don't cry, Susan. Your aunt is packing up your clothes. I want you to help her so she'll know what to take. Any of your toys and things like that, you will have to show her what is important to you. And you both look—unkempt. Can't you wash yourselves a little bit? Can't you make yourselves clean?"

"I'll wash her," Daniel said. "And there are things like our toothbrushes. We'll have to take those."

"That's right."

Daniel patted Susan till she was no longer crying. Her body shook with sobs that were like hiccups. He said to Ascher: "Why can't we go see them? The guards can search me and they can search her and they'll see that we don't have guns or anything like that."

"Well, it is not a matter of guards, Daniel. Your mother and father both feel that it would upset you to see them in the jail."

"Why?"

"Because when the time came to leave they wouldn't be able to leave with you. And you and especially your sister might not understand and be upset."

"Maybe they would be upset too," Daniel reflected.

"That's right. And so it would be worse than not seeing you at all."

"Well, how will they know where we are?" Daniel said.

"They asked me to ask your aunt if you could stay with her. I will report to them that you are with her."

"Do they know the address?"

"They know it."

"If we write to them from there will they get the letter?"

"I have arranged it so they will."

"I got the letter they sent," Daniel said. "When you see them tell them to write more often."

"But you see I told you, Daniel, they are allowed to write just one letter a week. So you can get no more than one letter a week. They also have to write each other."

"You mean they aren't in the same place?"

"Your father is in one jail and your mother is in another jail which is for women. They haven't seen each other since your father was arrested."

* * *

"You mean they are by themselves?"

"Yes."

"They're alone?"

"Yes."

"Are they unhappy?"

"They are not too happy."

"Are they frightened?"

"No, they are not frightened. They are innocent so they have nothing to be frightened of. They know they will be released after their trial. We shall prove that they are not guilty. And then you will all be together again. You hear that, Susele? Your mommy and daddy will return to you and hug you and kiss you and you will all be living together again. So you must be a good girl and do what your brother tells you. So go now both of you and help your aunt."

Theodore Dreiser

from AN AMERICAN TRAGEDY

Theodore Dreiser's classic 1925 novel, An American Tragedy, *has been adapted into a feature film and an opera, and even Woody Allen's film* Match Point *may have been influenced by it. Set in upstate New York in the early part of the twentieth century, and loosely based on a true story, the book is told in Dreiser's naturalistic, sometimes melodramatic style. It features the murder trial of Clyde Griffiths, accused of drowning his pregnant girlfriend, Roberta Alden. The defense argued that Alden died in a boating accident, but the circumstantial evidence did not make Griffiths sympathetic to the jury. In this excerpt, the long trial is over and Clyde awaits the verdict and contemplates the forces against him and the fact of his life being placed in the hands of twelve strangers.*

Many men were far more cruel in their love life than this young boy had ever dreamed of being, and of course they were not necessarily hung for that. And in passing technically on whether this boy had actually committed the crime charged, it was incumbent upon this jury to see that no generous impulse relating to what this poor girl might have suffered in her love-relations with this youth be permitted to sway them to the belief or decision that for that this youth had committed the crime specifically stated in the indictment. Who among both sexes were not cruel at times in their love life, the one to the other?

And then a long and detailed indictment of the purely circumstantial nature of the evidence—no single person having seen or heard anything of the alleged crime itself, whereas Clyde himself had explained most clearly how he came to find himself in the peculiar situation in which he did find himself. And after that, a brushing aside of the incident of the folder, as well as Clyde's not remembering the price of the boat at Big Bittern, his stopping to bury the tripod and his being so near Roberta and not aiding her, as either being mere

accidents of chance, or memory, or, in the case of his failing to go to her rescue, of his being dazed, confused, frightened—"hesitating fatally but not
criminally at the one time in his life when he should not have hesitated"—a
really strong if Jesuitical plea, which was not without its merits and its weight.

And then Mason, blazing with his conviction that Clyde was a murderer of
the coldest and blackest type, and spending an entire day in riddling the "spi-
der's tissue of lies and unsupported statements" with which the defense was
hoping to divert the minds of the jury from the unbroken and unbreakable
chain of amply substantiated evidence wherewith the prosecution had proved
this "bearded man" to be the "red-handed murderer" that he was. And with
hours spent in retracing the statements' of the various witnesses. And other
hours in denouncing Clyde, or re-telling the bitter miseries of Roberta so
much so that the jury, as well as the audience, was once more on the verge of
tears. And with Clyde deciding in his own mind as he sat between Belknap
and Jephson, that no jury such as this was likely to acquit him in the face of
evidence so artfully and movingly recapitulated.

And then Oberwaltzer from his high seat finally instructing the jury:
"Gentlemen—all evidence is, in a strict sense, more or less circumstantial,
whether consisting of facts which permit the inference of guilt or whether
given by an eyewitness. The testimony of an eyewitness is, of course, based
upon circumstances.

"If any of the material facts of the case are at variance with the probability
of guilt, it will be the duty of you gentlemen to give the defendant the benefit
of the doubt raised.

"And it must be remembered that evidence is not to be discredited or de-
cried because it is circumstantial. It may often be more reliable evidence than
direct evidence.

"Much has been said here concerning motive and its importance in this
case, but you are to remember that proof of motive is by no means indispensable or essential to conviction. While a motive may be shown as a *circumstance* to aid in *fixing* a crime, yet the people are not required to prove a
motive.

"If the jury finds that Roberta Alden accidentally or involuntarily fell out of
the boat and that the defendant made no attempt to rescue her, that does not
make the defendant guilty and the jury must find the defendant 'not guilty.'
On the other hand, if the jury finds that the defendant in any way, intention-

ally, there and then brought about or contributed to that fatal accident, either by a blow or otherwise, it must find the defendant guilty.

"While I do not say that you must agree upon your verdict, I would suggest that you ought not, any of you, place your minds in a position which will not yield if after careful deliberation you find you are wrong."

So, Justice Oberwaltzer—solemnly and didactically from his high seat to the jury.

And then, that point having been reached, the jury rising and filing from the room at five in the afternoon. And Clyde immediately thereafter being removed to his cell before the audience proper was allowed to leave the building. There was constant fear on the part of the sheriff that he might be attacked. And after that five long hours in which he waited, walking to and fro, to and fro, in his cell, or pretending to read or rest, the while Kraut and Sissel, tipped by various representatives of the press for information as to how Clyde "took it" at this time, slyly and silently remained as near as possible to watch.

And in the meantime Justice Oberwaltzer and Mason and Belknap and Jephson, with their attendants and friends, in various rooms of the Bridgeburg Central Hotel, dining and then waiting impatiently, with the aid of a few drinks, for the jury to agree, and wishing and hoping that the verdict would be reached soon, whatever it might be.

And in the meantime the twelve men-farmers, clerks and storekeepers, re-canvassing for their own mental satisfaction the fine points made by Mason and Belknap and Jephson. Yet out of the whole twelve but one man—Samuel Upham, a druggist—(politically opposed to Mason and taken with the personality of Jephson)—sympathizing with Belknap and Jephson. And so pretending that he had doubts as to the completeness of Mason's proof until at last after five ballots were taken he was threatened with exposure and the public rage and obloquy which was sure to follow in case the jury was hung. "We'll fix you. You won't get by with this without the public knowing exactly where you stand." Whereupon, having a satisfactory drug business in North Mansfield, he at once decided that it was best to pocket this opposition to Mason and agree.

* * *

The trial from start to finish had been unfair. Prejudice and bias had governed its every step. Such bullying and browbeating and innuendo as Mason had indulged in before the jury would never pass as fair or adequate in any higher court. And a new trial—on appeal—would certainly be granted—

although by whom such an appeal was to be conducted he was not now prepared to discuss.

And now, recalling that, Clyde saying to himself that it did not so much
matter perhaps, after all. It could not, really—or could it? Yet think what these
words meant in case he could not get a new trial! Death! That is what it would
mean if this were final—and perhaps it was final. And then to sit in that chair
he had seen in his mind's eye for so long—these many days and nights when
he could not force his mind to drive it away. Here it was again before him—
that dreadful, ghastly chair—only closer and larger than ever before—there in
the very center of the space between himself and Justice Oberwaltzer. He
could see it plainly now—squarish, heavy-armed, heavy-backed, some straps
at the top and sides. God! Supposing no one would hale him now! Even the
Griffiths might not be willing to pay out any more money! Think of that! The
Court of Appeals to which Jephson and Belknap had referred might not be
willing to help him either. And then these words would be final. They would!
They would! God! His jaws moved slightly, then set—because at the moment
he became conscious that they were moving. Besides, at that moment Belknap
was rising and asking for an individual poll of the jury, while Jephson leaned
over and whispered: "Don't worry about it. It isn't final. We'll get a reversal as
sure as anything." Yet as each of the jurors was saying: "Yes"—Clyde was listening to them, not to Jephson. Why should each one say that with so much
emphasis? Was there not one who felt that he might not have done as Mason
had said—struck her intentionally? Was there not one who even half-believed
in that change of heart which Belknap and Jephson had insisted that he had
experienced? He looked at them all—little and big. They were like a blackish-
brown group of wooden toys with creamish-brown or old ivory faces and
hands. Then he thought of his mother. She would hear of this now, for here
were all these newspaper writers and artists and photographers assembled to
hear this. And what would the Griffiths—his uncle and Gilbert—think now?
And Sondra! Sondra! Not a word from her. And through all this he had been
openly testifying, as Belknap and Jephson had agreed that he must do—to the
compelling and directing power of his passion for her—the real reason for all
this! But not a word. And she would not send him any word now, of course—
she who had been going to marry him and give him everything!

But in the meantime the crowd about him silent although—or perhaps because—intensely satisfied. The little devil hadn't "gotten by." He hadn't fooled the twelve sane men of this county with all that bunk about a change of heart. What rot! While Jephson sat and stared, and Belknap, his strong face written all over with contempt and defiance, making his motions. And Mason and Burleigh and Newcomb and Redmond, thinly repressing their intense satisfaction behind masks preternaturally severe, the while Belknap continued with a request that the sentence be put off until the following Friday—a week hence, when he could more conveniently attend, but with Justice Oberwaltzer replying that he thought not—unless some good reason could be shown. But on the morrow, if counsel desired, he would listen to an argument. If it were satisfactory he would delay sentence—otherwise, pronounce it the following Monday.

Yet, even so, Clyde was not concerned with this argument at the moment. He was thinking of his mother and what she would think—feel. He had been writing her so regularly, insisting always that he was innocent and that she must not believe all, or even a part, of what she read in the newspapers. He was going to be acquitted sure. He was going to go on the stand and testify for himself. But now . . . now . . . oh, he needed her now—so much. Quite every one, as it seemed now, had forsaken him. He was terribly, terribly alone. And he must send her some word quickly. He must. He must. And then asking Jephson for a piece of paper and a pencil, he wrote: "Mrs. Asa Griffiths, care of Star of Hope Mission, Denver, Colorado. Dear mother—I am convicted—Clyde." And then handing that to Jephson, he asked him, nervously and weakly, if he would see that it was sent right away. "Right away, son, sure," replied Jephson, touched by his looks, and waving to a press boy who was near gave it to him together with the money.

And then, while this was going on, all the public exits being locked until Clyde, accompanied by Sissel and Kraut, had been ushered through the familiar side entrance through which he had hoped to escape. And while all the press and the public and the still-remaining jury gazing, for even yet they had not seen enough of Clyde but must stare into his face to see how he was taking it. And because of the local feeling against him, Justice Oberwaltzer, at Slack's request, holding court unadjourned until word was brought that Clyde was once more locked in his cell, whereupon the doors were re-opened. And then the crowd surging out but only to wait at the courtroom door in order to glimpse, as he passed out, Mason, who now, of all the figures in this case, was the true hero—the nemesis of Clyde—the avenger of Roberta. But he not appearing at first but instead Jephson and Belknap together, and not so much depressed as solemn, defiant—Jephson, in particular, looking unconquerably contemptuous. Then some one calling: "Well, you didn't get him off just the same," and Jephson replying, with a shrug of his shoulders, "Not yet, but this county isn't all of the law either." Then Mason, immediately afterward—a heavy, baggy overcoat thrown over his shoulder, his worn soft hat pulled low over his eyes—and followed by Burleigh, Heit, Newcomb and others as a royal train—while he walked in the manner of one entirely oblivious of the meaning or compliment of this waiting throng. For was he not now a victor and an elected judge! And as instantly being set upon by a circling, huzzahing mass— the while a score of those nearest sought to seize him by the hand or place a grateful pat upon his arm or shoulder. "Hurray for Orville!" "Good for you, Judge!" (his new or fast-approaching title). "By God! Orville Mason, for you deserve the thanks of this county!" "Hy-oh! Heigh! Heigh!" "Three cheers for Orville Mason!" And with that the crowd bursting into three resounding huzzahs—which Clyde in his cell could clearly hear and at the same time sense the meaning of.

They were cheering Mason for convicting him. In that large crowd out there there was not one who did not believe him totally and completely guilty. Roberta—her letters—her determination to make him marry her—her giant fear of exposure—had dragged him down to this. To conviction. To death, maybe. Away from all he had longed for—away from all he had dreamed he might possess. And Sondra! Sondra! Not a word! Not a word! And so now, fearing that Kraut or Sissel or some one might be watching (ready to report even now his every gesture), and not willing to show after all how totally collapsed and despondent he really was, he sat down and taking up a magazine pretended to read, the while he looked far, far beyond it to other scenes—his mother—his brother and sisters—the Griffiths—all he had known. But finding these unsubstantiated mind visions a little too much, he finally got up and throwing off his clothes climbed into his iron cot.

"Convicted! Convicted!" And that meant that he must die! God! But how blessed to be able to conceal his face upon a pillow and not let any one see— however accurately they might guess!

Alice Sebold

from LUCKY

Before she received wide acclaim as the author of the novel The Lovely Bones, *Alice Sebold wrote a powerful memoir of her experience as a Syracuse freshman of being attacked and raped on the last night of school. The police advised her that she had been lucky, since the last student attacked at the same location was murdered and dismembered.* Lucky, *published in 1999, recounts, among other things, her encounter with the criminal justice system and the dehumanizing way in which victims of sexual assault are so often treated and mistreated. When this happens, the law ends up actually inflaming the original injury. In this excerpt, Sebold endures the cross-examination of two defense attorneys.*

Both defense attorneys who represented Madison over the course of the year shared certain traits. They were shortish, balding, and had something fetid going on on their upper lips. Whether it was an unkempt mustache as in Meggesto's case, or grainy beads of sweat, it was an ugliness I focused on as each one cross-examined me.

I felt if I was going to win, I had to hate the attorneys representing him. They may have been earning a paycheck, or randomly assigned to the case, had children they loved or a terminally ill mother to take care of. I didn't care. They were there to destroy me. I was there to fight back.

"Is it Miss See-bold—is that the way it is pronounced?"

"Yes."

"Miss Sebold, you said you were at 321 Westcott Street on the night of the incident?"

"Umm-hmm."

The tone of his voice was condemning, as if I had been a bad little girl and told a lie.

"How long had you been there on this evening?"

"From approximately eight to midnight."

"Did you have anything to drink while there?"

"I had nothing at all to drink."

"Did you have anything to smoke while you were there?"

"Nothing at all to smoke."

"Did you have any cigarettes?"

"No."

"You didn't smoke that evening?"

"No."

"You had nothing to drink that evening?"

"No."

That tack not having worked, he moved on to his next.

"How long have you worn glasses?"

"Since I was in the third grade."

"Do you know what your vision is without glasses?"

"I am nearsighted and can see very well close up. I don't know exactly, but it isn't that bad. I can see road signs and such."

"Do you have a driver's license?"

"Yes, I do."

"Do you need your license?"

"Yes, I do."

"You maintain your driver's license?"

"Yes."

I didn't know what he was doing. It made sense to me that he might ask if my license required me to wear corrective lenses. But he didn't. Was I a better or worse person with a license? Was I firmly an adult and not a child, making it less a crime to rape me? I never figured out his reasoning.

* * *

"Did you think you needed your glasses on this evening in October?"

He meant May, but no one corrected him.

"It was night, yes."

"Do you see poorer at night?"

"No, I don't."

"Was there any special reason you brought your glasses?"

"No."

"Is it a fair statement to say you wear your glasses when you leave the dorm all the time?"

"No."

"Was there any special reason you wore your glasses that evening?"

"Probably because they were a week old and I liked them. They were new."

He jumped on this: "New prescription or just new design of frame?"

"Just new design of frame."

"Prescription the same?"

"Yes."

* * *

Could he know that he was making his point and losing it simultaneously? That my prescription had been updated six months before the rape. I didn't know what he was doing but I was going to follow him at every turn. He wanted to back me into a maze I couldn't get out of. I was determined. I felt I had what Gallagher had—mettle. I could feel it in my veins.

"Umm-hmm," I said.

"And I believe you say that, at some point during this struggle, your glasses were knocked from you, is that correct?"

"Yes."

"It was a dark area, is that correct?"

"Yes."

"How dark would you say it was?"

"Not that dark. It was light enough so I could see physical features—face, plus the fact that his face was very close to mine and since I am nearsighted and not farsighted, my vision is good up close."

He turned to the side and looked up a moment. For a second, adrenaline pumping in my veins, I watched the court. Everyone was still. This was business as usual to them. Another prelim on another rape case. Ho hum.

"I believe you said at some point this individual kissed you?" He was good, sweaty lip, bad mustache, and all. He went, with a keen, deft precision, right to my heart. The kissing hurts still. The fact that it was only under my rapist's orders that I kissed back often seems not to matter. The intimacy of it stings. Since then I've always thought that under rape in the dictionary it should tell the truth. It is not just forcible intercourse; rape means to inhabit and destroy everything.

"Yes," I said.

"When you say, 'kissed you,' do you mean on the mouth?"

"Yes."

"Were you both standing?"

"Yes."

"In relation to your height, how tall was the individual?"

He chose the kiss to lead me to the rapist's height. "Approximately the same height or an inch above," I said.

"How tall are you, Miss Sebold?"

"Five, five and a half."

"You would say this individual was probably the same height or maybe an inch taller?"

"Umm-hmm."

"When you were standing there, looking at him, he looked to be about the same height, is that correct?"

"Umm-hmm."

"Just about that?"

"Yes."

His tone, since questioning my vision, had changed. There was now not even a trace of respect in it. Seeing that he had not yet gotten the best of me, he had switched into a sort of hateful overdrive. I felt threatened by him. Even though, by all measures, I was safe in that courtroom and surrounded by professionals, I was afraid.

"I believe you testified that the description you gave on that night indicated he was of a muscular build?"

"Yes."

"Short and had short black hair?"

"Yes."

"Do you remember telling the police, when you made your voluntary affidavit, you thought he was about one hundred and fifty pounds?"

"Yes."

"Is that your best estimate as to the weight of this individual?"

"I am really not very good with weight," I said. "I don't know the ratio of muscle or fat in someone's body."

"You do recall telling him it was one hundred and fifty pounds?"

"The police officers gave me an estimation of what they might weigh, a man, and I said, yes, that looked approximately correct."

"Are you saying you were influenced by what the police officer told you?"

"No, he was just giving me an example to follow. It seemed approximately close."

"Based on what the police officer gave you and your physical observation, is your testimony on May eighth your best estimate of the weight of this individual is one hundred and fifty pounds?"

"Yes."

"Have you heard anything that would change your mind at this point?"

"No."

His energy zoomed. He looked just like a boy who is savoring the last bite of cake. Mr. Meggesto had gotten something back after losing on vision, but I didn't know what.

I was tired now. I was doing my best, but I felt my energy drain. I had to get it back.

"I believe you say you were struck in the face a number of times?"

"Yes."

"And that you were bleeding?"

"Yes."

"And your glasses had been knocked from you?"

In hindsight I wish I had the wherewithal to say, "None of this made me blind."

"Yes," I said.

* * *

I felt hushed by him now. The gloves were off.

"Can you tell me briefly what you were wearing on the night of October fifth?"

Mr. Ryan stood and corrected the date. "May eighth."

"On May eighth," Mr. Meggesto rephrased, "tell me what you were wearing."

"Calvin Klein jeans, blue work shirt, heavy beige cable-knit cardigan sweater, moccasins, and underwear." I hated this question. Knew, even on that stand, what it was all about.

"Was that cardigan sweater one that pulled on or buttoned up the front?"

"Buttons up the front."

"You didn't have to take it over your head to get it off? Is that correct?"

"Right."

I was seething. I had gotten my energy back because what my clothes had to do with why or how I was raped seemed obvious: nothing.

"I believe you testified this individual attempted to disrobe you and, failing that, ordered you to do so?"

"Right, I had a belt on. He couldn't work the belt correctly from the opposite side of me. He said, 'You do it,' so I did."

"This was the belt holding up your Calvin Klein jeans?"

He emphasized "Calvin Klein" with a sneer I was unprepared for. It had come to this.

"Yes."

"He was facing you?"

"Yes."

"Your testimony was he wasn't able to work the clasp, whatever the gimmick was, that closed that belt?"

"Umm-hmm."

"You did it on his orders?"

"Yes."

Now it was his turn to take a point. He questioned me on the rapist's knife. I had seen it only in the photos of the crime scene and in my mind's eye. I admitted to Meggesto that, though the rapist had threatened me and made gestures to retrieve it from his back pocket, because of the struggle on my part, I had never seen it.

"Is it a fair statement to say you were very frightened by all this?" Meggesto asked, moving on.

"Yes."

"When did you first become frightened?"

"As soon as I heard footsteps behind me."

"Did your pulse beat increase?"

"I imagine some, yes," I said. I didn't understand why he was asking me this.

"Do you recall?"

"No, I don't recall if my pulse beat increased."

"Do you recall becoming scared and breathing short and fast?"

"I recall becoming scared, and whatever physical things come from that, I probably had them, but I wasn't hyperventilating or anything like that."

"Do you remember anything else other than being scared?"

"Mental state?" I thought I'd say it since that's what I thought he was driving at.

"No," he said, "I mean physically. Do you remember how your body acted when you were frightened? Did you tremble, increase in pulse rate, have any change in breathing?"

"No, I don't remember any specific changes except for the fact that I was screaming. I did keep telling the rapist that I was going to vomit, because my mother gave me articles that said if you say you are going to vomit, they won't rape you."

"That was a ruse to use on this individual and might scare him off?"

"Yes."

* * *

"When did you see him after May of 1981?"

I told him of the incident on October 5. I detailed the time, location, and my sighting, at the same time, of the redheaded policeman who had turned out to be Officer Clapper. I told him I had called the police and had come back to the Public Safety Building to give a description of the rapist.

"You gave a description of whom?" he asked.

Mr. Ryan objected. "I think we have gone outside the scope of direct examination," he said. "Anything further would be for a Wade Hearing."

I had no idea what that was. The three men, Mr. Ryan, Mr. Meggesto, and Judge Anderson, debated what had been stipulated prior to the preliminary. They reached an agreement. Mr. Meggesto could continue concerning the arrest of the individual. But the judge warned that he was "going into it"—the issue of identification. The judge's last words recorded in the transcript are "Come on." Even now I hear the fatigue in them. His major motivation, I feel certain, was to wrap it up and get to lunch.

Frantic, because I had not understood the decision or even, frankly, what the hell they had been talking about, I tried to focus back on Mr. Meggesto. Whatever was said, it gave him permission to attack again.

"After you crossed the street and went to Huntington Hall, did you ever see this individual again?"

"No."

"Were you shown any photographs?"

"No." At the time I didn't know that there was no photo lineup in my case because a mug shot of Gregory Madison did not exist.

"Ever taken to a lineup?"

"No."

"You came there and made an identification at the police station?"

"Yes."

"That is after you called your mother?"

"Yes."

"And after that you were informed someone was arrested?"

"I wasn't informed that night. I was informed, I think it was this Thursday morning, by Officer Lorenz."

"So, you didn't know of your own knowledge whether or not the individual that you saw on October fifth was the individual that was arrested?"

"There was no way I could know that unless the police who arrested him—"

"The question is, yes or no, do you know whether or not the individual—"

This time when he cut me off, it made me mad.

"As they described the man, it was the man they arrested—"

"Question is, do you know?"

"I haven't seen him since he was arrested."

"You didn't see him."

"The man I described on the eighth of May and the individual on October fifth is the man that raped me."

"That is your testimony, you believe the man you saw on October fifth—"

"*I know* the man I saw on October fifth is the man that raped me."

"The man you say is the man who raped you is the same man you saw on October fifth?"

"Right."

"But you don't know whether that man was arrested?"

"Well, I didn't arrest him, how would I know?"

"That is my question—you don't know?"

"All right, I don't know, then." What else could I say? He had proven, very dramatically, that I was not a member of the Syracuse Police Department.

Mr. Meggesto turned to the judge. "I don't think I have anything further," he said.

But he wasn't done. I stayed in the witness stand while the judge listened, and then debated, the point of identification with him. It turned out that Ryan's purpose had been to have Madison in the court, that by Madison's having waived his right to appear, all Ryan now had to prove was that a rape had taken place on May eighth and that I had identified a man I believed to be my assailant. There was confusion. Ryan believed that in Madison waiving his right to appear Meggesto had forfeited the question of identification. That was not Meggesto's understanding.

"Held for action of the grand jury," the judge said finally. He was tired. I concluded from the movements of Ryan and Meggesto—they were closing up their briefcases—that I was done.

PART V

The Law Laborious

The busywork that comprises the business of law can often leave clients enraged, attorneys soullessly depleted, and law students hopelessly confused—all desperate to raise their hands in surrender by reciting, along with Bartleby, the scrivener: "We prefer not to." When this happens, the high ideals of justice are transformed—in the minds of innocent bystanders and the casualties of the law alike—into absurd tragedies, taking place in the bleakest of houses, producing surreal outcomes, all reflected through the prism of a cracked looking glass rather than a purer vision of justice sensibly and reliably guaranteed.

Charles Dickens

from BLEAK HOUSE

Charles Dickens was no lover of lawyers, and his 1852–53 novel, Bleak House, *was his biggest broadside against the legal profession. The never-ending, soul-destroying case of Jarndyce and Jarndyce was the laughingstock of his fictional tale and has now become a metaphor for a legal system that produces no relief, just misery and ruin. In the first excerpt, the reader is treated to the metaphorical fog that surrounds Lincoln's Inn, the Temple Bar, and the High Court of Chancery—the pillars of London's legal establishment; in the second selection, the reader experiences the sense of defeat and deflation that coincides with the case's end.*

Fog everywhere. Fog up the river, where it flows among green aits and meadows; fog down the river, where it rolls defiled among the tiers of shipping and the waterside pollutions of a great (and dirty) city. Fog on the Essex marshes, fog on the Kentish heights. Fog creeping into the cabooses of collier-brigs; fog lying out on the yards and hovering in the rigging of great ships; fog drooping on the gunwales of barges and small boats. Fog in the eyes and throats of ancient Greenwich pensioners, wheezing by the firesides of their wards; fog in the stem and bowl of the afternoon pipe of the wrathful skipper, down in his close cabin; fog cruelly pinching the toes and fingers of his shivering little 'prentice boy on deck. Chance people on the bridges peeping over the parapets into a nether sky of fog, with fog all round them, as if they were up in a balloon and hanging in the misty clouds.

Gas looming through the fog in divers places in the streets, much as the sun may, from the spongey fields, be seen to loom by husbandman and ploughboy. Most of the shops lighted two hours before their time—as the gas seems to know, for it has a haggard and unwilling look.

The raw afternoon is rawest, and the dense fog is densest, and the muddy streets are muddiest near that leaden-headed old ·obstruction, appropriate ornament for the threshold of a leaden-headed old corporation, Temple Bar. And hard by Temple Bar, in Lincoln's Inn Hall, at the very heart of the fog, sits the Lord High Chancellor in his High Court of Chancery.

Never can there come fog too thick, never can there come mud and mire too deep, to assort with the groping and floundering condition which this High Court of Chancery, most pestilent of hoary sinners, holds this day in the sight of heaven and earth.

On such an afternoon, if ever, the Lord High Chancellor ought to be sitting here—as here he is—with a foggy glory round his head, softly fenced in, with crimson cloth and curtains, addressed by a large advocate with great whiskers, a little voice, and an interminable brief, and outwardly directing his contemplation to the lantern in the roof, where he can see nothing but fog. On such an afternoon some score of members of the High Court of Chancery bar ought to be—as here they are—mistily engaged in one of the ten thousand stages of an endless cause, tripping one another up on slippery precedents, groping knee-deep in technicalities, running their goat-hair and horsehair warded heads against walls of words and making a pretense of equity with serious faces, as players might. On such an afternoon the various solicitors in the cause, some two or three of whom have inherited it from their fathers, who made a fortune by it, ought to be—as are they not?—ranged in a line, in a long matted well (but you might look in vain for the truth at the bottom of it) between the registrar's red table and the silk gowns, with bills, cross-bills, answers, rejoinders, injunctions, affidavits, issues, references to masters, masters' reports, mountains of costly nonsense, piled before them. Well may the court be dim, with wasting candles here and there; well may the fog hang heavy in it, as if it would never get out; well may the stained-glass windows lose their colour and admit no light of day into the place; well may the uninitiated from the streets, who peep in through the glass panes in the door, be deterred from entrance by its owlish aspect and by the drawl, languidly echoing to the roof from the padded dais where the Lord High Chancellor looks into the lantern that has no light in it and where the attendant wigs are all stuck in a fog-bank! This is the Court of Chancery, which has its decaying houses and its blighted lands in every shire, which has its worn-out lunatic in every madhouse and its dead in every churchyard, which has its ruined suitor with his slipshod heels and threadbare dress borrowing and begging through the round of every man's acquaintance, which gives to monied might the means abundantly of wearying out the right, which so exhausts finances, patience, courage, hope, so overthrows the brain and breaks the heart, that there is not an honourable man among its practitioners who would not give—who does not often give—the warning, "Suffer any wrong that can be done you rather than come here!"

* * *

Jarndyce and Jarndyce drones on. This scarecrow of a suit has, in course of time, become so complicated that no man alive knows what it means. The parties to it understand it least, but it has been observed that no two Chancery lawyers can talk about it for five minutes without coming to a total disagreement as to all the premises. Innumerable children have been born into the cause; innumerable young people have married into it; innumerable old people have died out of it. Scores of persons have deliriously found themselves made parties in Jarndyce and Jarndyce without knowing how or why; whole families have inherited legendary hatreds with the suit. The little plaintiff or defendant who was promised a new rocking-horse when Jarndyce and Jarndyce should be settled has grown up, possessed himself of a real horse, and trotted away into the other world. Fair wards of court have faded into mothers and grandmothers; a long procession of Chancellors has come in and gone out; the legion of bills in the suit have been transformed into mere bills of mortality; there are not three Jarndyces left upon the earth perhaps since old Tom Jarndyce in despair blew his brains out at a coffee-house in Chancery Lane; but Jarndyce and Jarndyce still drags its dreary length before the court, perennially hopeless.

Jarndyce and Jarndyce has passed into a joke. That is the only good that has ever come of it. It has been death to many, but it is a joke in the profession. Every master in Chancery has had a reference out of it. Every Chancellor was "in it," for somebody or other, when he was counsel at the bar. Good things have been said about it by blue-nosed, bulbous-shoed old benchers in select port-wine committee after dinner in hall. Articled clerks have been in the habit of fleshing their legal wit upon it. The last Lord Chancellor handled it neatly, when, correcting Mr. Blowers, the eminent silk gown who said that such a thing might happen when the sky rained potatoes, he observed, "or when we get through Jarndyce and Jarndyce, Mr. Blowers"—a pleasantry that particularly tickled the maces, bags, and purses.

How many people out of the suit Jarndyce and Jarndyce has stretched forth its unwholesome hand to spoil and corrupt would be a very wide question.

From the master upon whose impaling files reams of dusty warrants in Jarndyce and Jarndyce have grimly writhed into many shapes, down to the copying-clerk in the Six Clerks' Office who has copied his tens of thousands of Chancery folio-pages under that eternal heading, no man's nature has been made better by it. In trickery, evasion, procrastination, spoliation, botheration, under false pretences of all sorts, there are influences that can never come to good. The very solicitors' boys who have kept the wretched suitors at bay, by protesting time out of mind that Mr. Chizzle, Mizzle, or otherwise was particularly engaged and had appointments until dinner, may have got an extra moral twist and shuffle into themselves out of Jarndyce and Jarndyce. The receiver in the cause has acquired a goodly sum of money by it but has acquired too a distrust of his own mother and a contempt for his own kind. Chizzle, Mizzle, and otherwise have lapsed into a habit of vaguely promising themselves that they will look into that outstanding little matter and see what can be done for Drizzle—who was not well used—when Jarndyce and Jarndyce shall be got out of the office. Shirking and sharking in all their many varieties have been sown broadcast by the ill-fated cause; and even those who have contemplated its history from the outermost circle of such evil have been insensibly tempted into a loose way of letting bad things alone to take their own bad course, and a loose belief that if the world go wrong it was in some off hand manner never meant to go right.

Thus, in the midst of the mud and at the heart of the fog, sits the Lord High Chancellor in his High Court of Chancery.

* * *

This made us some quarter of an hour late, and when we came to Westminster Hall we found that the day's business was begun. Worse than that, we found such an unusual crowd in the Court of Chancery that it was full to the door, and we could neither see nor hear what was passing within. It appeared to be something droll, for occasionally there was a laugh and a cry of "Silence!" It appeared to be something interesting, for every one was pushing and striving to get nearer. It appeared to be something that made the professional gentlemen very merry, for there were several young counsellors in wigs and whiskers on the outside of the crowd, and when one of them told the others about it, they put their hands in their pockets, and quite doubled themselves up with laughter, and went stamping about the pavement of the Hall.

We asked a gentleman by us if he knew what cause was on. He told us Jarndyce and Jarndyce. We asked him if he knew what was doing in it. He said really, no he did not, nobody ever did, but as well as he could make out, it was over. Over for the day? we asked him. No, he said, over for good.

Over for good!

When we heard this unaccountable answer, we looked at one another quite lost in amazement. Could it be possible that the will had set things right at last and that Richard and Ada were going to be rich? It seemed too good to be true. Alas it was!

Our suspense was short, for a break-up soon took place in the crowd, and the people came streaming out looking flushed and hot and bringing a quantity of bad air with them. Still they were all exceedingly amused and were more like people coming out from a farce or a juggler than from a court of justice. We stood aside, watching for any countenance we knew, and presently great bundles of paper began to be carried out—bundles in bags, bundles too large to be got into any bags, immense masses of papers of all shapes and no shapes, which the bearers staggered under, and threw down for the time being, anyhow, on the Hall pavement, while they went back to bring out more. Even these clerks were laughing. We glanced at the papers, and seeing Jarndyce and Jarndyce everywhere, asked an official-looking person who was standing in the midst of them whether the cause was over. Yes, he said, it was all up with it at last, and burst out laughing too.

At this juncture we perceived Mr. Kenge coming out of court with an affable dignity upon him, listening to Mr. Vholes, who was deferential and carried his own bag. Mr. Vholes was the first to see us. "Here is Miss Summerson, sir," he said. "And Mr. Woodcourt."

"Oh, indeed! Yes. Truly!" said Mr. Kenge, raising his hat to me with polished politeness. "How do you do? Glad to see you. Mr. Jarndyce is not here?"

No. He never came there, I reminded him.

"Really," returned Mr. Kenge, "it is as well that he is *not* here today, for his—shall I say, in my good friend's absence, his indomitable singularity of opinion?—might have been strengthened, perhaps; not reasonably, but might have been strengthened."

"Pray what has been done to-day?" asked Allan.

"I beg your pardon?" said Mr. Kenge with excessive urbanity.

"What has been done to-day?"

"What has been done," repeated Mr. Kenge. "Quite so. Yes. Why, not much has been done; not much. We have been checked—brought up suddenly, I would say—upon the—shall I term it threshold?"

"Is this will considered a genuine document, sir?" said Allan. "Will you tell us that?"

"Most certainly, if I could," said Mr. Kenge; "but we have not gone into that, we have not gone into that."

"We have not gone into that," repeated Mr. Vholes as if his low inward voice were an echo.

"You are to reflect, Mr. Woodcourt," observed Mr. Kenge, using his silver trowel persuasively and smoothingly, "that this has been a great cause, that this has been a protracted cause, that this has been a complex cause. Jarndyce and Jarndyce has been termed, not inaptly, a monument of Chancery practice."

"And patience has sat upon it a long time," said Allan.

"Very well indeed, sir," returned Mr. Kenge with a certain condescending laugh he had. "Very well! You are further to reflect, Mr. Woodcourt," becoming dignified almost to severity, "that on the numerous difficulties, contingencies, masterly fictions, and forms of procedure in this great cause, there has been expended study, ability, eloquence, knowledge, intellect, Mr. Woodcourt, high intellect. For many years, the—a—I would say the flower of the bar, and the—a—I would presume to add, the matured autumnal fruits of the woolsack—have been lavished upon Jarndyce and Jarndyce. If the public have the benefit, and if the country have the adornment, of this great grasp, it must be paid for in money or money's worth, sir."

"Mr. Kenge," said Allan, appearing enlightened all in a moment. "Excuse me, our time presses. Do I understand that the whole estate is found to have been absorbed in costs?"

"Hem! I believe so," returned Mr. Kenge. "Mr. Vholes, what do *you* say?"

"I believe so," said Mr. Vholes.

"And that thus the suit lapses and melts away?"

"Probably," returned Mr. Kenge. "Mr. Vholes?"

"Probably," said Mr. Vholes.

"My dearest life," whispered Allan, "this will break Richard's heart!"

There was such a shock of apprehension in his face, and he knew Richard so perfectly, and I too had seen so much of his gradual decay, that what my dear girl had said to me in the fullness of her foreboding love sounded like a knell in my ears.

"In case you should be wanting Mr. C., sir," said Mr. Vholes, coming after us, "you'll find him in court. I left him there resting himself a little. Good day, sir; good day, Miss Summerson." As he gave me that slowly devouring look of his, while twisting up the strings of his bag before he hastened with it after Mr. Kenge, the benignant shadow of whose conversational presence he seemed afraid to leave, he gave one gasp as if he had swallowed the last morsel of his client, and his black buttoned-up unwholesome figure glided away to the low door at the end of the Hall.

Herman Melville

from "BARTLEBY, THE SCRIVENER"

When Herman Melville fictionalized the legal profession on dry ground, specifi-
cally, a Wall Street law firm in the mid-nineteenth century, rather than on the high
seas, he was equally unsympathetic to the life of lawyers. "Bartleby, the Scrivener,"
written in 1853, looks at one such cog in the machinery of justice and the damag-
ing consequences of the bureaucracy of law, which weakens the spirit and deadens
the soul and leaves at least one fictional law clerk gasping for human choice.

I am a rather elderly man. The nature of my avocations, for the last thirty
years, has brought me into more than ordinary contact with what would seem
an interesting and somewhat singular set of men, of whom, as yet, nothing,
that I know of, has ever been written—I mean, the law-copyists or scriveners.
I have known very many of them, professionally and privately, and if I pleased,
could relate divers histories, at which good-natured gentlemen might smile,
and sentimental souls might weep. But I waive the biographies of all other
scriveners, for a few passages in the life of Bartleby, who was a scrivener, the
strangest I ever saw, or heard of. While, of other law-copyists, I might write
the complete life, of Bartleby nothing of that sort can be done. I believe that
no materials exist, for a full and satisfactory biography of this man. It is an ir-
reparable loss to literature. Bartleby was one of those beings of whom nothing
is ascertainable, except from the original sources, and, in his case, those are
very small. What my own astonished eyes saw of Bartleby, *that* is all I know of
him, except, indeed, one vague report which will appear in the sequel.

Ere introducing the scrivener, as he first appeared to me, it is fit I make
some mention of myself, my *employés*, my business, my chambers, and general
surroundings; because some such description is indispensable to an adequate
understanding of the chief character about to be presented. Imprimis: I am a
man who, from his youth upwards, has been filled with a profound conviction

that the easiest way of life is the best. Hence, though I belong to a profession proverbially energetic and nervous, even to turbulence, at times, yet nothing of that sort have I ever suffered to invade my peace. I am one of those unambitious lawyers who never addresses a jury, or in any way draws down public applause; but in the cool tranquility of a snug retreat, do a snug business among rich men's bonds, and mortgages, and title-deeds. All who know me, consider me an eminently *safe* man. The late John Jacob Astor, a personage little given to poetic enthusiasm, had no hesitation in pronouncing my first grand point to be prudence; my next, method. I do not speak it in vanity, but simply record the fact, that I was not unemployed in my profession by the late John Jacob Astor; a name which, I admit, I love to repeat; for it hath a rounded and orbicular sound to it, and rings like unto bullion. I will freely add, that I was not insensible to the late John Jacob Astor's good opinion.

Some time prior to the period at which this little history begins, my avocations had been largely increased. The good old office, now extinct in the State of New York, of a Master in Chancery, had been conferred upon me. It was not a very arduous office, but very pleasantly remunerative. I seldom lose my temper; much more seldom indulge in dangerous indignation at wrongs and outrages; but, I must be permitted to be rash here, and declare, that I consider the sudden and violent abrogation of the office of Master of Chancery, by the new Constitution, as a—premature act; inasmuch as I had counted upon a life-lease of the profits, whereas I only received those of a few short years. But this is by the way.

My chambers were up stairs at No. —— Wall-street. At one end they looked upon the white wall of the interior of a spacious sky-light shaft, penetrating the building from top to bottom.

This view might have been considered rather tame than otherwise, deficient in what landscape painters call "life." But, if so, the view from the other end of my chambers offered, at least, a contrast, if nothing more. In that direction, my windows commanded an unobstructed view of a lofty brick wall, black by age and everlasting shade; which wall required no spy-glass to bring out its lurking beauties, but, for the benefit of all near-sighted spectators, was pushed up to within ten feet of my window panes. Owing to the great height of the surrounding buildings, and my chambers being on the second floor, the interval between this wall and mine not a little resembled a huge square cistern.

* * *

In answer to my advertisement, a motionless young man one morning, stood upon my office threshold, the door being open, for it was summer. I can see that figure now—pallidly neat, pitiably respectable, incurably forlorn! It was Bartleby.

After a few words touching his qualifications, I engaged him, glad to have among my corps of copyists a man of so singularly sedate an aspect, which I thought might operate beneficially upon the flighty temper of Turkey, and the fiery one of Nippers.

I should have stated before that ground glass folding-doors divided my premises into two parts, one of which was occupied by my scriveners, the other by myself. According to my humor, I threw open these doors, or closed them. I resolved to assign Bartleby a corner by the folding-doors, but on my side of them, so as to have this quiet man within easy call, in case any trifling thing was to be done. I placed his desk close up to a small side window in that part of the room, a window which originally had afforded a lateral view of certain grimy back-yards and bricks, but which, owing to subsequent erections, commanded at present no view at all, though it gave some light. Within three feet of the panes was a wall, and the light came down from far above, between two lofty buildings, as from a very small opening in a dome. Still further to a satisfactory arrangement, I procured a high green folding screen, which might entirely isolate Bartleby from my sight, though not remove him from my voice. And thus, in a manner, privacy and society were conjoined.

At first, Bartleby did an extraordinary quantity of writing. As if long famishing for something to copy, he seemed to gorge himself on my documents. There was no pause for digestion. He ran a day and night line, copying by sunlight and by candle-light. I should have been quite delighted with his application, had he been cheerfully industrious. But he wrote on silently, palely, mechanically.

It is, of course, an indispensable part of a scrivener's business to verify the accuracy of his copy, word by word. Where there are two or more scriveners in an office, they assist each other in this examination, one reading from the copy, the other holding the original. It is a very dull, wearisome, and lethargic affair. I can readily imagine that, to some sanguine temperaments, it would be altogether intolerable. For example, I cannot credit that the mettlesome poet, Byron, would have contentedly sat down with Bartleby to examine a law document of, say five hundred pages, closely written in a crimpy hand.

Now and then, in the haste of business, it had been my habit to assist in comparing some brief document myself, calling Turkey or Nippers for this purpose. One object I had, in placing Bartleby so handy to me behind the screen, was, to avail myself of his services on such trivial occasions. It was on the third day, I think, of his being with me, and before any necessity had arisen for having his own writing examined, that, being much hurried to complete a small affair I had in hand, I abruptly called to Bartleby. In my haste and natural expectancy of instant compliance, I sat with my head bent over the original on my desk, and my right hand sideways, and somewhat nervously extended with the copy, so that, immediately upon emerging from his retreat, Bartleby might snatch it and proceed to business without the least delay.

In this very attitude did I sit when I called to him, rapidly stating what it was I wanted him to do—namely, to examine a small paper with me. Imagine my surprise, nay, my consternation, when, without moving from his privacy, Bartleby, in a singularly mild, firm voice, replied, "I would prefer not to."

I sat awhile in perfect silence, rallying my stunned faculties. Immediately it occurred to me that my ears had deceived me, or Bartleby had entirely misunderstood my meaning. I repeated my request in the clearest tone I could assume; but in quite as clear a one came the previous reply, "I would prefer not to."

"Prefer not to," echoed I, rising in high excitement, and crossing the room with a stride. "What do you mean? Are you moon-struck? I want you to help me compare this sheet here—take it," and I thrust it towards him.

"I would prefer not to," said he.

I looked at him steadfastly. His face was leanly composed; his gray eye dimly calm. Not a wrinkle of agitation rippled him. Had there been the least uneasiness, anger, impatience or impertinence in his manner; in other words, had there been any thing ordinarily human about him, doubtless I should have violently dismissed him from the premises. But as it was, I should have as soon thought of turning my pale plaster-of-paris bust of Cicero out of doors. I stood gazing at him awhile, as he went on with his own writing, and then re-seated myself at my desk. This is very strange, thought I. What had one best do? But my business hurried me: I concluded to forget the matter for the present, reserving it for my future leisure. So calling Nippers from the other room, the paper was speedily examined.

A few days after this, Bartleby concluded four lengthy documents, being quadruplicates of a week's testimony taken before me in my High Court of Chancery. It became necessary to examine them. It was an important suit, and great accuracy was imperative. Having all things arranged, I called Turkey, Nippers, and Ginger Nut, from the next room, meaning to place the four copies in the hands of my four clerks, while I should read from the original. Accordingly, Turkey, Nippers, and Ginger Nut had taken their seats in a row, each with his document in his hand, when I called to Bartleby to join this interesting group.

"Bartleby! quick, I am waiting."

I heard a slow scrape of his chair legs on the uncarpeted floor, and soon he appeared standing at the entrance of his hermitage.

"What is wanted?" said he, mildly.

"The copies, the copies," said I hurriedly. "We are going to examine them. There"—and I held towards him the fourth quadruplicate.

"I would prefer not to," he said, and gently disappeared behind the screen.

For a few moments I was turned into a pillar of salt, standing at the head of my seated column of clerks. Recovering myself, I advanced towards the screen, and demanded the reason for such extraordinary conduct.

"*Why* do you refuse?"

"I would prefer not to."

With any other man I should have flown outright into a dreadful passion, scorned all further words, and thrust him ignominiously from my presence. But there was something about Bartleby that not only strangely disarmed me, but, in a wonderful manner, touched and disconcerted me. I began to reason with him.

"These are your own copies we are about to examine. It is labor saving to you, because one examination will answer for your four papers. It is common usage. Every copyist is bound to help examine his copy. Is it not so? Will you not speak? Answer!"

"I prefer not to," he replied in a flutelike tone. It seemed to me that, while I had been addressing him, he carefully revolved every statement that I made; fully comprehended the meaning; could not gainsay the irresistible conclusion; but, at the same time, some paramount consideration prevailed with him to reply as he did.

"You are decided, then, not to comply with my request—a request made according to common usage and common sense?"

He briefly gave me to understand, that on that point my judgment was sound. Yes: his decision was irreversible.

* * *

What I saw that morning persuaded me that the scrivener was the victim of innate and incurable disorder. I might give alms to his body; but his body did not pain him; it was his soul that suffered, and his soul I could not reach.

David E. Kelley

from THE PRACTICE

David E. Kelley, the creator and chief writer for such diverse television legal dramas as Boston Legal, Ally McBeal, Picket Fences, *and the Emmy-winning* The Practice, *is a former attorney who left the legal profession to write television scripts for* LA Law. *The rest is television history. Every David E. Kelley show, and every script, is fused with ethical and moral questions about the legal system, from the attorney-client privilege to the way in which lawyers treat one another as partners, colleagues, and adversaries. In this 2004 excerpt from* The Practice, *Alan Shore, played by James Spader, delivers an intellectually and emotionally honest summation to the jury in a case in which he was forced to sue his former partners for failing to compensate him appropriately after he was discharged from the firm.*

ALAN SHORE'S SUMMATION

When this firm hired me, they knowingly engaged the services of an embezzler. They let me go about my evil sinister business and make them rich. And *then* they tossed me. (*a beat*) I had an uncle, he'd bring dessert to every family get-together, and everyone would fawn, saying "you're so thoughtful, you're so generous." He admitted to me he wasn't generous at all. He was hungry. And his logic was if he brought a pie, he'd get a slice. (*then*) I brought the pie, ladies and gentlemen. They didn't give me my slice. (*a beat*) And as for all my despicable, unethical, immoral, treacherous, sleazy conduct—they called me everything but a terrorist, didn't they . . . —this business is not an ethical arena. (*then*) Our legal system is adversarial by nature where it is often the very *function* of a lawyer's job to prevent the truth from ever coming out, we get *paid* to suppress and squash and conceal evidence, this is the system that freed O.J., it is taught to every first-year law student, don't ever, *ever* equate legal ethics with morality, they're almost *always* mutually exclusive. It's an ugly world where underhandedness is sometimes *celebrated*, I didn't enter Eugene Young's church, it was a law firm, a *criminal* law firm, the dirtiest kind, where lawyers get up in court, as Mr. Young has many times, and knowingly falsely accuse innocent people of murder, *why*, for the noble cause of getting the real killer off. Eugene Young has put guilty people back on the street to *kill again* sometimes, he's in the business of freeing serial rapists, but hey, I brought the firm down by pretending to be an airline executive, I guess I just don't get it. (*a beat*) He goes behind my back, tells my client I'm unstable for the purpose of *stealing* that client, this somehow falls *within* the bounds of integrity, I guess I just don't get it. (*quietly*) There's a couple of things Eugene Young just can't seem to get. First . . . I'm just an unscrupulous guy trying to get by in an unscrupulous profession. And second . . . I respect him profoundly. There's perhaps nobody I respect more. (*to Eugene*) In the eight or so months I've known you . . . I've found you to be utterly beyond reproach. Which is why I'm so surprised he would take all that money I brought in and then fire me . . . just to avoid giving me my slice.

Scott Turow

from ONE L

Long before Scott Turow became a world-famous writer of wise and witty legal thrillers, he was a first-year law student at Harvard Law School taking notes not just for class but also for an exposé that would eventually become required reading for all future law students, as well as anyone interested in how lawyers are trained to become lawyers. One L, published in 1977, is a critical and penetrating look at the competitive, dizzying experience of surviving the first year of a lawyer's legal education—with a cast of interesting characters, both students and professors—and the author's own honest reflections and self-awareness about his initiation into the law. In these two excerpts, Turow examines the way in which law school transforms the minds and souls of law students, and what reforms might be introduced to humanize the experience.

When we started jurisdiction in Procedure, Nicky Morris made what seemed an important comment.

"About now," he said, "law school begins to become more than just learning a language. You also have to start learning rules and you'll find pretty quickly that there's quite a premium placed on mastering the rules and knowing how to apply them.

"But in learning rules, don't feel as if you've got to forsake a sense of moral scrutiny. The law in almost all its phases is a reflection of competing value systems. Don't get your heads turned around to the point that you feel because you're learning a rule, you've necessarily taken on the values that produced the rule in the first place."

The remark struck a number of people, and as we left class for lunch, I talked about what Nicky had said with Gina Spitz. Gina came on as the last of the tough cookies. She'd just graduated from Barnard and she was full of the bristle

of New York City. She was big, feisty, outspoken, and glitteringly bright. But
what Nicky had said had touched her in a way that left her sounding plaintive.

"They're turning me into someone else," she said referring to our professors. "They're making me different."

I told her that was called education and she told me, quite rightly, that I was
being flip.

"It's someone I don't *want* to be," she said. "Don't you get the feeling all the
time that you're being indoctrinated?"

I was not sure that I did, but as Gina and I sat at lunch, I began to realize
that for her and many other people in the section, there was a crisis going on,
one which had not yet affected me as acutely.

On one hand the problem was as simple as the way Nicky had put it. Students felt they were being forced to identify with rules and social notions that
they didn't really agree with. In Contracts, for instance, it had already become
clear that Perini was an ardent free-market exponent, someone who believed
that the national economy should function without any government regula-
tion. Perini quickly succeeded in showing us that many of the common-law
contract rules reflected free-market assumptions. When he threw the floor
open for comment about whether those free-market rules were desirable or
not, Perini's fearsomeness made it hard to contest him.

But there was a subtler difficulty in our education, one which went to the
basis of legal thinking itself and which became especially apparent in class. We
were learning more than a process of analysis or a set of rules. In our discussions with the professors, as they questioned us and picked at what we said, we
were also being tacitly instructed in the strategies of legal argument, in putting
what had been analyzed back together in a way that would make our contentions persuasive to a court. We all quickly saw that that kind of argument
was supposed to be reasoned, consistent, progressive in its logic. Nothing was
taken for granted; nothing was proven just because it was strongly felt. All of
our teachers tried to impress upon us that you do not sway a judge with emotional declarations of faith. Nicky Morris often derided responses as "sentimental goo," and Perini on more than one occasion quickly dispatched
students who tried to argue by asserting supposedly irreducible principles.

Why, Perini asked one day, is the right to bargain and form contracts
granted to all adults, rather than a select group within the society?

Because that was fundamental, one student suggested, basic: All persons are created equal.

"Oh, *are* they?" Perini asked. "Did you create them, Mr. Vivian? Have you taken a survey?"

"I believe it," Vivian answered.

"Well, hooray," said Perini, "that proves a great deal. How do you *justify* that, Mr. Vivian?"

The demand that we examine and justify our opinions was not always easily fulfilled. Many of the deepest beliefs often seemed inarticulable in their foundations, or sometimes contradictory of other strongly felt principles. I found that frequently. I thought, for example, that wealth should be widely distributed, but there were many instances presented in class which involved taking from the poor, for whom I felt that property rights should be regarded as absolute.

Yet, with relative speed, we all seemed to gain skill in reconciling and justifying our positions. In the fourth week of school, Professor Mann promoted a class debate on various schemes for regulating prostitution, and I noticed the differences in style of argument from similar sessions we'd had earlier in the year. Students now spoke about crime statistics and patterns of violence in areas where prostitution occurred. They pointed to evidence, and avoided emotional appeals and arguments based on the depth and duration of their feelings.

But to Gina, the process which had brought that kind of change about was frightening and objectionable.

"I don't care if Bertram Mann doesn't want to know how I *feel* about prostitution," she said that day at lunch. "I *feel* a lot of things about prostitution and they have everything to do with the way I *think* about prostitution. I don't want to become the kind of person who tries to pretend that my feelings have nothing to do with my opinions. It's not *bad* to feel things."

Gina was not the only classmate making remarks like that. About the same time, from three or four others, people I respected, I heard similar comments, all to the effect that they were being limited, harmed, by the education, forced to substitute dry reason for emotion, to cultivate opinions which were "rational" but which had no roots in the experience, the life, they'd had before. They were being cut away from themselves.

Many of the people with these complaints were straight out of college. In thinking about it, I concluded that having survived the '60s, held a job, gotten married—having already lived on a number of principles—made me feel less vulnerable to a sense that what we learned in class would somehow corrupt some safer, central self. But there was no question that my friends' concern was genuine, and listening to them made me more self-conscious about the possible effects our education in the law was having on me.

At home, Annette told me that I had started to "lawyer" her when we quarreled, badgering and cross-examining her much as the professors did students in class. And it seemed to me there were other habits to be cautious of. It was a grimly literal, linear, step-by-step process of thought that we were learning. The kind of highly structured problem-solving method taught in each of Perini's classes, for instance—that business of sorting through details, then moving outward toward the broadest implications—was an immensely useful technical skill, but I feared it would calcify my approach to other subjects. And besides rigidity, there was a sort of mood to legal thinking which I found plainly unattractive.

"Legal thinking is nasty," I said to Gina at one point in our conversation, and I began to think later I'd hit on a substantial truth. Thinking like a lawyer involved being suspicious and distrustful. You reevaluated statements, inferred from silences, looked for loopholes and ambiguities. You did everything but take a statement at face value.

So on one hand you believed nothing. And on the other, for the sake of logical consistency, and to preserve long-established rules, you would accept the most ridiculous fictions—that a corporation was a person, that an apartment tenant was renting land and not a dwelling.

What all of that showed me was that the law as a way of looking at the world and my own more personal way of seeing things could not be thoroughly meshed; that at some point, somehow, I would have to *learn* those habits of mind without making them my own in the deepest sense. I had no idea quite how I'd go about that, but I knew that it was necessary.

"Every time we have one of these discussions in Criminal," Gina said, "I want to raise my hand and say: The most important thing is to be *compassionate*. But I know what kind of reaction I'd get from Mann—he'd tell me, That's nice, or just stare at the ceiling. I mean, am I wrong?"

I agreed that she was not, either in predicting Professor Mann's answer or in the opinion she'd expressed.

"It's a problem," I said, and I realized it was one that nobody yet had shown us how to solve.

* * *

"There will be change," Perini admitted. "Not even I can claim that the Harvard Law School is the greatest and most divine institution in existence."

Many of the directions for that change in the first-year curriculum are self-evident. At places more progressive than HLS there are already smaller classes, more opportunities for students to write and to make contact with the faculty, differing formats for evaluation of student performance, election to the Law Review without reference to grades. Harvard Law School itself is a far different place than it was in 1970, when my college friends entered. There was no such thing, then, as passing a professor's question in a first-year class; no teachers who, like Morris, tried to stress the broadest humanistic outlines of the law; no midyear exams. The case method, which once meant a reading diet of nothing but case reports, has given way in recent years to the addition of journal articles, of writings which make the learning of the law less a piece-by-piece puzzling through and more like the real lawyer's task: a comparison of new elements against a known context.

No doubt the changes will go on. Fresh from the front, I would add two observations about the specifics of legal education as I experienced them in my first year. That night in May, the faculty panel roundly agreed to the continuing vitality of the Socratic method. I would not differ directly, but the peculiar privilege which Socraticism grants a teacher to invade the security of every student in the room means that in the wrong hands it can become an instrument of terror. I never felt that my education gained by my being frightened, and I was often scared in class. Law faculties have too long excused, in the name of academic freedom, a failure to hold colleagues within basic limits of decency. They must formulate and enforce an etiquette of classroom behavior which insures that teachers cannot freely browbeat and exploit their students. To refuse leaves them in a subtle but persistent state of moral abdication. I know that it is hard to think of law students, headed for a life of privilege, as being among the downtrodden; and I also recognize that classroom terror has been a fixed aspect of legal education for at least a century. But the risk, the ultimate risk, of allowing students to make their first acquaintance with the law in such an atmosphere, in that state of hopeless fright, is that they will come away with a tacit but ineradicable impression that it is somehow characteristically "legal" to be heartless, to be brutal, and will carry that attitude with them into the execution of their professional tasks.

Those objections to heavy-handed Socraticism are, in a fashion, only a part of a larger concern with legal education of which I began to become conscious after my conversations with Gina last fall. The law is at war with ambiguity, with uncertainty. In the courtroom, the adversary system, plaintiff against defendant, guarantees that someone will always win, someone lose. No matter if justice is evenly with each side, no matter if the issues are dark and obscure, the rule of law will be declared. The law and the arbitrary certainty of some of its results are no doubt indispensable to the secure operation of a society where there is ceaseless conflict requiring resolution.

But a lot of those attitudes toward certainty seem to rub off on the law world at large. Many of the institutions of legal education show a similar seeking after sureness and definition, a desire to subdue the random element, to leave nothing to chance: the admissions process, where statistical formulas serve as the basis for decision; the law-school classroom, where all power and discretion are concentrated in the professor; the stratifications so clearly marked in the law-school population, with the best students segregated on the law review, and the faculty remote from all; and the notion of the meritocracy, the attempt to rank and to accord privilege by some absolute standard. All of these things amount in my mind to a fighting of the war against ambiguity and uncertainness in quarters where it is not called for, where the need which supports the custom of the courtroom is not present. Not even the law can abolish the fundamental unclearness of many human situations, but in the law schools there is precious little effort made to address the degree to which human choice is arbitrary. We are taught that there is always a reason, always a rationale, always an argument. Too much of what goes on around the law school and in the legal classroom seeks to tutor students in strategies for avoiding, for ignoring, for somehow subverting the unquantifiable, the inexact, the emotionally charged, those things which still pass in my mind under the label "human." In time, I came to take that quality in legal education as another of those forces which could make me less a person than I'd like to be, that foe I'd come here to meet.

Courses like Morris's and Zechman's which emphasized the uncertainties and contradictions inherent in the law are signs of what I consider progress. But students still see the operation of the law only in a secondhand and third-hand way, as it is revealed in carefully prepared case reports. Learning to think like a lawyer should involve more than the mastery of an important but abstract mental skill. Were I king of the universe—or dean of Harvard Law School—I would supplement case reading with use of other devices—film, drama, informal narrative, actual client contact like that provided in the upper-year clinical courses—seeking to cultivate sensitivity to the immediate human context in which the law so forcefully intervenes.

Reforms like that, like others which look to be on the horizon, seem to bode well for us all. A more humane and humanistic education in the law strikes me as far more fitting than a schooling characterized by terror and the suppression of feeling for those persons who, in time, will become this society's chief custodians of justice.

Lewis Carroll

from ALICE'S ADVENTURES IN WONDERLAND

Far more than a children's book, Lewis Carroll's Alice's Adventures in Wonderland *(1865) has long been considered an allegorical and satirical tale that speaks to many aspects of life and society—including the legal system. The book's zany trial scene reflects certain truths about the law as seen through a looking glass.*

The King and Queen of Hearts were seated on their throne when they arrived, with a great crowd assembled about them—all sorts of little birds and beasts, as well as the whole pack of cards: the Knave was standing before them, in chains, with a soldier on each side to guard him; and near the King was the White Rabbit, with a trumpet in one hand, and a scroll of parchment in the other. In the very middle of the court was a table, with a large dish of tarts upon it: they looked so good, that it made Alice quite hungry to look at them—"I wish they'd get the trial done," she thought, "and hand round the refreshments!" But there seemed to be no chance of this, so she began looking at everything about her, to pass away the time.

Alice had never been in a court of justice before, but she had read about them in books, and she was quite pleased to find that she knew the name of nearly everything there. "That's the judge," she said to herself, "because of his great wig."

The judge, by the way, was the King; and as he wore his crown over the wig, (look at the frontispiece if you want to see how he did it), he did not look at all comfortable, and it was certainly not becoming.

"And that's the jury-box," thought Alice, "and those twelve creatures," (she was obliged to say "creatures," you see, because some of them were animals, and some were birds), "I suppose they are the jurors." She said this last word two or three times over to herself, being rather proud of it: for she thought, and rightly too, that very few little girls of her age knew the meaning of it at all. However, "jury-men" would have done just as well.

The twelve jurors were all writing very busily on slates. "What are they do-ing?" Alice whispered to the Gryphon. "They can't have anything to put down yet, before the trial's begun."

"They're putting down their names," the Gryphon whispered in reply, "for fear they should forget them before the end of the trial."

"Stupid things!" Alice began in a loud, indignant voice, but she stopped hastily, for the White Rabbit cried out, "Silence in the court!" and the King put on his spectacles and looked anxiously round, to make out who was talking.

Alice could see, as well as if she were looking over their shoulders, that all the jurors were writing down "stupid things!" on their slates, and she could even make out that one of them didn't know how to spell "stupid," and that he had to ask his neighbour to tell him. "A nice muddle their slates'll be in be-fore the trial's over!" thought Alice.

One of the jurors had a pencil that squeaked. This of course, Alice could not stand, and she went round the court and got behind him, and very soon found an opportunity of taking it away. She did it so quickly that the poor lit-tle juror (it was Bill, the Lizard) could not make out at all what had become of it; so, after hunting all about for it, he was obliged to write with one finger for the rest of the day; and this was of very little use, as it left no mark on the slate.

"Herald, read the accusation!" said the King.

On this the White Rabbit blew three blasts on the trumpet, and then un-rolled the parchment scroll, and read as follows:—

> *The Queen of Hearts, she made some tarts,*
> *All on a summer day:*
> *The Knave of Hearts, he stole those tarts,*
> *And took them quite away!*

"Consider your verdict," the King said to the jury.

"Not yet, not yet!" the Rabbit hastily interrupted. "There's a great deal to come before that!"

"Call the first witness," said the King; and the White Rabbit blew three blasts on the trumpet, and called out, "First witness!"

The first witness was the Hatter. He came in with a teacup in one hand and a piece of bread-and-butter in the other. "I beg pardon, your Majesty," he began, "for bringing these in: but I hadn't quite finished my tea when I was sent for."

"You ought to have finished," said the King. "When did you begin?"

The Hatter looked at the March Hare, who had followed him into the court, arm-in-arm with the Dormouse. "Fourteenth of March, I think it was," he said.

"Fifteenth," said the March Hare.

"Sixteenth," added the Dormouse.

"Write that down," the King said to the jury, and the jury eagerly wrote down all three dates on their slates, and then added them up, and reduced the answer to shillings and pence.

"Take off your hat," the King said to the Hatter.

"It isn't mine," said the Hatter.

"Stolen!" the King exclaimed, turning to the jury, who instantly made a memorandum of the fact.

"I keep them to sell," the Hatter added as an explanation; "I've none of my own. I'm a hatter."

Here the Queen put on her spectacles, and began staring at the Hatter, who turned pale and fidgeted.

"Give your evidence," said the King; "and don't be nervous, or I'll have you executed on the spot."

This did not seem to encourage the witness at all: he kept shifting from one foot to the other, looking uneasily at the Queen, and in his confusion he bit a large piece out of his teacup instead of the bread-and-butter.

Just at this moment Alice felt a very curious sensation, which puzzled her a good deal until she made out what it was: she was beginning to grow larger again, and she thought at first she would get up and leave the court; but on second thoughts she decided to remain where she was as long as there was room for her.

"I wish you wouldn't squeeze so," said the Dormouse, who was sitting next to her. "I can hardly breathe."

"I can't help it," said Alice very meekly: "I'm growing."

"You've no right to grow here," said the Dormouse.

"Don't talk nonsense," said Alice more boldly: "you know you're grow-ing too."

"Yes, but I grow at a reasonable pace," said the Dormouse: "not in that ridiculous fashion." And he got up very sulkily and crossed over to the other side of the court.

All this time the Queen had never left off staring at the Hatter, and, just as the Dormouse crossed the court, she said to one of the officers of the court, "Bring me the list of the singers in the last concert!" on which the wretched Hatter trembled so, that he shook both his shoes off.

"Give your evidence," the King repeated angrily, "or I'll have you executed, whether you're nervous or not."

"I'm a poor man, your Majesty," the Hatter began, in a trembling voice, "—and I hadn't begun my tea—not above a week or so—and what with the bread-and-butter getting so thin—and the twinkling of the tea—"

"The twinkling of the what?" said the King.

"It began with the tea," the Hatter replied.

"Of course twinkling begins with a T!" said the King sharply. "Do you take me for a dunce? Go on!"

"I'm a poor man," the Hatter went on, "and most things twinkled after that—only the March Hare said—"

"I didn't!" the March Hare interrupted in a great hurry.

"You did!" said the Hatter.

"I deny it!" said the March Hare.

"He denies it," said the King; "leave out that part."

"Well, at any rate, the Dormouse said—" the Hatter went on, looking anxiously round to see if he would deny it too; but the Dormouse denied nothing, being fast asleep.

"After that," continued the Hatter, "I cut some more bread-and-butter—"

"But what did the Dormouse say?" one of the jury asked.

"That I can't remember," said the Hatter.

"You must remember," remarked the King, "or I'll have you executed."

The miserable Hatter dropped his teacup and bread-and-butter, and went down on one knee. "I'm a poor man, your Majesty," he began.

"You're a very poor speaker," said the King.

Here one of the guinea-pigs cheered, and was immediately suppressed by the officers of the court. (As that is rather a hard word, I will just explain to you how it was done. They had a large canvas bag, which tied up at the mouth with strings: into this they slipped the guinea-pig, head first, and then sat upon it.)

"I'm glad I've seen that done," thought Alice. "I've so often read in the newspapers, at the end of trials, 'There was some attempt at applause, which was immediately suppressed by the officers of the court,' and I never understood what it meant till now."

"If that's all you know about it, you may stand down," continued the King.

"I can't go no lower," said the Hatter: "I'm on the floor, as it is."

"Then you may sit down," the King replied.

Here the other guinea-pig cheered, and was suppressed.

"Come, that finished the guinea-pigs!" thought Alice. "Now we shall get on better."

"I'd rather finish my tea," said the Hatter, with an anxious look at the Queen, who was reading the list of singers.

"You may go," said the King, and the Hatter hurriedly left the court, without even waiting to put his shoes on.

"—and just take his head off outside," the Queen added to one of the officers: but the Hatter was out of sight before the officer could get to the door.

"Call the next witness!" said the King.

The next witness was the Duchess's cook. She carried the pepper-box in her hand, and Alice guessed who it was, even before she got into the court, by the way the people near the door began sneezing all at once.

"Give your evidence," said the King.

"Shan't," said the cook.

The King looked anxiously at the White Rabbit, who said in a low voice, "Your Majesty must cross-examine this witness."

"Well, if I must, I must," the King said, with a melancholy air, and, after folding his arms and frowning at the cook till his eyes were nearly out of sight, he said in a deep voice, "What are tarts made of?"

"Pepper, mostly," said the cook.

"Treacle," said a sleepy voice behind her.

"Collar that Dormouse," the Queen shrieked out. "Behead that Dormouse! Turn that Dormouse out of court! Suppress him! Pinch him! Off with his whiskers!"

For some minutes the whole court was in confusion, getting the Dormouse turned out, and, by the time they had settled down again, the cook had disappeared.

"Never mind!" said the King, with an air of great relief. "Call the next witness." And he added in an undertone to the Queen, "Really, my dear, you must cross-examine the next witness. It quite makes my forehead ache!"

Alice watched the White Rabbit as he fumbled over the list, feeling very curious to see what the next witness would be like, "—for they haven't got much evidence yet," she said to herself. Imagine her surprise, when the White Rabbit read out, at the top of his shrill little voice, the name "Alice!"

John Barth

from THE FLOATING OPERA

Postmodern American fiction writer John Barth's first novel, The Floating Opera *(1957), regarded as a nihilistic comedy about suicide, was also a hilarious will dispute that any trusts and estates lawyer would love. In the novel, a son attempts to receive his inheritance from a father who produced far too many wills, all of which were intended as much to disinherit as to bequeath. In this excerpt, narrated by Todd Andrews, the suicidal and cynical lawyer, the reader soon realizes that this will contest is more like a contest of will.*

That will-o'-the-wisp, the law: where shall I begin to speak of it? Is the law the legal rules, or their interpretations by judges, or by juries? Is it the precedent or the present fact? The norm or the practice? I think I'm not interested in what the law is.

Surely, though, I am curious about things that the law can be made to do, but this disinterestedly, without involvement. A child encounters a toy tractor, winds it up, and sets it climbing over a book. The tractor climbs well. The child puts another book here, so, and angles the first. The tractor surmounts them, with difficulty. The child opens the pages of the first book, leans the second obliquely against it, and places his shoe behind the two. The tractor tries, strains, spins, whirrs, and falls like a turtle on its back, treads racing uselessly. The child moves on to his crayons and picture puzzles, no expression on his face. I don't know what you mean, sir, when you speak of justice.

* * *

All right. I have no general opinions about the law, or about justice, and if I sometimes set little obstacles, books and slants, in the path of the courts, it is because I'm curious, merely, to see what will happen. On those occasions when the engine of the law falls impotently sprawling, I make a mental note of it, and without a change of expression, go on to my boat or my Inquiry.

Winning or losing litigations is of no concern to me, and I think I've never made a secret of that fact to my clients.

They come to me, as they come before the law, because they think they have a case. The law and I are uncommitted.

One more thing, before I explain the contest over Harrison Mack Senior's will: if you have followed this chapter so far, you might sensibly ask, "Doesn't your attitude—which is, after all, irresponsible—allow for the defeat, even the punishment, of the innocent, and at times the victory of the guilty? And does this not concern you?" It does indeed allow for the persecution of innocence— though perhaps not so frequently as you might imagine. And this persecution concerns me, in the sense that it holds my attention, but not especially in the sense that it bothers me. Under certain circumstances, to be explained later, I am not averse to pillorying the innocent, to throwing my stone, with the crowd, at some poor martyr. Irresponsibility, yes: I affirm, I insist upon my basic and ultimate irresponsibility. Yes indeed.

It did not deeply concern me, as I said before, whether Harrison received his inheritance or not, though I stood to profit by some fifty thousand dollars or more if he did. In any world but ours, the case of the Mack estate would be fantastic; even in ours, it received considerable publicity from the Maryland press.

* * *

Now of the several characteristics of Harrison *père*, three were important to the case: he was in the habit of using his wealth as a club to keep his kin in line; he was, apparently, addicted to the drawing up of wills; and, especially in his last years, he was obsessively jealous of the products of his mind and body, and permitted none to be destroyed.

* * *

All these falls from and reinstatements to grace, of course, required emendations of Father Mack's will, and a number of extrafamiliar circumstances also demanded frequent revision of his bequests. His country club admits someone he doesn't like: the club must be disinherited. A pickle-truck driver runs down a state policeman checking on overloaded vehicles: the driver must be defended in court and provided for explicitly in the will. After the old man's death, when his safe was opened, a total of seventeen complete and distinct testamentary instruments was found, chronologically arranged, each beginning with a revocation of the preceding one. He hadn't been able to throw any of his soul-children into the fire.

Now this situation, though certainly unusual, would in itself have presented no particular problem of administration, because the law provides that where there are several wills, the last shall be considered representative of the testator's real intentions, other things being equal. And each of these wills explicitly revoked the preceding one. But alas, with Mr. Mack all other things weren't equal. Not only did his physical well-being deteriorate in his last years, through arthritis to leukemia to the grave; his sanity deteriorated also, gradually, along the continuum from relative normalcy through marked eccentricity to jibbering idiocy. In the first stages he merely inherited and disinherited his relatives and his society; in the second he no longer went to work, he required entertainment as well as care from his nurses, and he allowed nothing of his creation—including hair—and nail-clippings, urine, feces, and wills—to be thrown away; in the last stages he could scarcely move or talk, had no control whatever over his bodily functions, and recognized no one. To be sure, the stages were not dramatically marked, but blended into one another imperceptibly.

Of the seventeen wills (which represented by no means all the wills Mack had written, merely those written since he acquired his mania for preserving things), only the first two were composed during the time when the old man's sanity was pretty much indisputable; that is, prior to 1933. The first left about half the estate to Harrison Junior and the other half to Mother Mack, provided it could not be demonstrated to the court that she had drunk any sparkling burgundy since 1920. This one was dated 1924. The other, dated 1932, left about half the estate to Mrs. Mack unconditionally and the rest to Harrison, provided it could not be demonstrated to the court that during a five-year probationary period, 1932–37, Harrison had done, written, or said anything that could reasonably be construed as evidence of communist sympathies. This clause, incidentally, ran through most of the subsequent testaments as well.

Of the other fifteen documents, ten were composed in 1933 and 1934, years when the testator's sanity was open to debate. The last five, all written in the first three months of 1935, could be established without much difficulty, in court, as being the whims of a lunatic: one left everything to Johns Hopkins University on condition that the University's name be changed to Hoover College (the University politely declined); others bequeathed the whole shebang to the Atlantic Ocean or the A.F.L.

* * *

Froebel's arguments, essentially, were two: (1) That a man has not necessarily lost his business sense if he provides once for a complete reversal of bequests, of the sort seen in Will #6, assuming he is really dead set against sparkling burgundy; but then to reverse himself completely in the space of a few months indicates that something has snapped in his head, since there were no dramatic external changes to account for the new will. (2) That the bequest of the pickle jars appeared in no wills before #8, and in all the wills from #8 through #16, and that such a bequest is evidence tending to show that Mack no longer understood the nature of his estate.

"Not necessarily," I suggested. "Suppose he didn't love his wife?"

"Ah," Froebel replied quickly, "but he left the pickle jars to a different person each time, not to Mrs. Mack every time."

"But remember," I said, "he saved the mess because he liked it; the bequest of it, then, is an act of love. Would you call love insane?"

"Indeed not," Froebel answered. "But if he'd loved her, he'd have given her the property as well as the excrement."

"No indeed," I countered. "Remember that in one will he bequeathed all his money to the church because he disliked the church. Couldn't the bequest to my client be such an act, and the bequest to yours the real gift?"

"It could indeed," Froebel grinned. "Will you say that that's the case?"

"No, I shan't," I said. "I merely suggested the possibility."

"And in doing so," Froebel declared, "you suggest the possibility that Will Number Eight is as insane as Will Number Thirteen, the church will you mentioned. Anyone who bequeaths three millions of dollars as a punishment, I suggest, is out of perspective."

Oh, Bill Froebel was a lawyer. When it came to impromptu legal sophistry, he and I had no equals at the Maryland Bar.

* * *

"You told me there wasn't anything," I reminded Harrison, who had turned white.

"I swear there isn't!" he whispered back, but nevertheless he began perspiring and trembling a little. I sat back to see what Froebel had cooked up.

"What will you attempt to prove?" the Judge asked him.

"That as recently as last year, your honor, while his poor father was in the grave—perhaps speeded there (who knows?) by his son's regrettable irresponsibility—that just last year, your honor, this son, who is now so eager to take from his mother what is rightfully hers, was aiding and abetting actively, with large gifts of money, that doctrine against which his father's entire life was such an eloquent argument; confident, I doubt not, that he could conceal his surreptitious Bolshevism until such time as he was in a position to devote the whole of the Mack estate toward overthrowing the way of life that made its accumulation possible!"

Froebel was a past master of the detached noun clause: judge and spectators were stirred.

"For heaven's sake!" Harrison whispered. "You don't think he means my Spanish donations!"

"If you were silly enough to make any, then I daresay he does," I replied, appalled anew at Harrison's innocence.

And indeed, the "Spanish donations" were precisely what Froebel had in mind. He offered in evidence photostated checks, four of them, for one thousand dollars each, made out to an American subscription agency representing the Spanish Loyalist government. They were dated March 10, May 19, September 2, and October 7, and all were signed Harrison A. Mack, Jr.

Judge Lasker examined the photostats and frowned. "Did you write these checks?" he asked Harrison, passing the pictures to him.

"Of course!" Harrison yelled. "What the hell's that—"

"Order!" suggested the Judge. "Aren't you aware that the Loyalist movement is run by the Communist Party? Directed from the Kremlin?"

"Aw, come on!" Harrison pleaded, until I poked him and he sat down.

"May I point out," Froebel continued blandly, "that not only is a gift to the Loyalists in essence a gift to Moscow, but this particular subscription agency is a Party organization under FBI surveillance. A man may donate to the Loyalists through honest, if vague, liberalism, I daresay; but one doesn't send checks to this subscription outfit unless one is sympathetic with the Comintern. Young Mr. Mack, like too many of our idle aristocrats, is, I fear, a blue blood with a Red heart."

I believe it was this final metaphor that won Froebel the judgment. I saw the newspaper people virtually doff their hats in tribute, and scribble the immortal words for the next editions of their papers. Even the Judge smiled benignly upon the trope: I could see that it struck him square in the prejudices, and found a welcome there.

There was some further discussion, but no one listened closely; everyone was repeating to himself, with a self-satisfied smile, that too many young aristocrats are blue bloods with Red hearts. Blue bloods with Red hearts! How could mere justice cope with poetry? Men, I think, are ever attracted to the bon mot rather than the mot juste, and judges, no less than other men, are often moved by considerations more aesthetic than judicial. Even I was not a little impressed, and regretted only that we had no jury to be overwhelmed by such a purple plum from the groves of advocacy. A blue blood with a Red heart! How brandish reasonableness against music? Should I hope to tip the scales with puny logic, when Froebel had Parnassus in his pan? In vain might I warn Judge Lasker that, through the press, all America was watching, and Europe as well, for his decision.

* * *

"Do you give up?" I asked him. "Or shall I appeal?"

He clutched at the hope. "Can we appeal?"

"Sure," I said. "Don't you see how unlogical Lasker's reasoning is?"

"Unlogical! It was so logical it overwhelmed me!"

"Not at all. He said the subscription agency was Sympathetic to communism. You give money to the agency; therefore you're Sympathetic to communism. It's like saying that if you give money to a Salvation Army girl who happens to be a vegetarian you're sympathetic to vegetarians. The communists support the Loyalists; you support the Loyalists; therefore you're a communist."

Harrison was tremendously relieved, but so weak he could scarcely stand. He laughed shortly.

"Well! That puts us back in the race, doesn't it? Ha, I'd thought there for a while—Christ, Toddy, you've saved my ass again! Damned judge! We've got it now, boy!"

I shook my head, and he went white again.

"What the hell's wrong?"

"I'll appeal," I said, "but we'll lose again, I guess."

"How's that? Lose again!" He laughed, and sucked in his breath.

"Forget about the logic," I said. "Nobody really cares about the logic. They make up their minds by their prejudices about Spain. I think you'd have lost here even without Froebel's metaphor. I'd have to talk Lasker into liberalism to win the case."

I went on to explain that of the seven judges of the Court of Appeals who would review the decision, three were Republicans with a pronounced anti-liberal bias, two were fairly liberal Democrats, one was a reactionary "Southern Democrat," more anti-liberal than the Republicans, and the seventh, an unenthusiastic Democrat, was relatively unbiased.

"I know them all," I said. "Abrams, Moore, and Stevens, the Republicans, will vote against you. Forrester, the Southern Democrat, would vote for you if it were a party issue, but it's not; he'll go along with the Republicans. Stedman and Barnes, the liberals, will go along with you, and I think Haddaway will too, because he likes me and because he dislikes Lasker's bad logic."

"But hell, that's four to three!" Harrison cried. "That means I lose!"

"As I said."

"How about the Maryland Supreme Court?"

"That's too much to predict," I said. "I don't know that they've declared themselves on Spain, and I don't know them personally. But they've affirmed almost every important verdict of the Court of Appeals in three years."

Harrison was crushed. "It's unjust!"

I smiled. "You know how these things are."

PART VI

The Lawyer as Lout

Noble professions are not immune to the occasional ignoble practitioner. While there are lawyerly heroes, for sure, who deserve our trust, the literature of law is much keener on depicting lawyers as unfeeling scoundrels, sinister in their possession of our secrets, endlessly stalling for their own self-gain, more apt to exploit human misery than to plead for the relief of our pain.

Carl Sandburg

"THE LAWYERS KNOW TOO MUCH"

American poet Carl Sandburg's "The Lawyers Know Too Much," written in 1922, is one of his better-known poems. Every lawyer should keep a copy of these caution-ary words on his or her desk.

The lawyers, Bob, know too much.
They are chums of the books of old John Marshall.
They know it all, what a dead hand wrote,
A stiff dead hand and its knuckles crumbling,
The bones of the fingers a thin white ash.
The lawyers know
a dead man's thought too well.

In the heels of the higgling lawyers, Bob,
Too many slippery ifs and buts and howevers,
Too much hereinbefore provided whereas,
Too many doors to go in and out of.

When the lawyers are through
What is there left, Bob?
Can a mouse nibble at it
And find enough to fasten a tooth in?

Why is there always a secret singing
When a lawyer cashes in?
Why does a hearse horse snicker
Hauling a lawyer away?

The work of a bricklayer goes to the blue.
The knack of a mason outlasts a moon.
The hands of a plasterer hold a room together.
The land of a farmer wishes him back again.
Singers of songs and dreamers of plays
Build a house no wind blows over.
The lawyers—tell me why a hearse horse snickers
hauling a lawyer's bones.

Henrik Ibsen

from A DOLL'S HOUSE

Norwegian playwright Henrik Ibsen's most highly regarded play, A Doll's House, written in 1879, is a late-nineteenth-century portrait of a woman forced to confront the rules of a male-dominated society, with laws and marital bonds that presume her submission to her husband and the will of the patriarchy. In this excerpt, Nora, a doll in her own home, faces a harsh lesson about the formality and senselessness of legal rules and the character of those who so heartlessly enforce them.

KROGSTAD: (*coming a step nearer*) Listen to me, Mrs. Helmer. Either you have a very bad memory or you know very little of business. I shall be obliged to remind you of a few details.

NORA: What do you mean?

KROGSTAD: When your husband was ill, you came to me to borrow two hundred and fifty pounds.

NORA: I didn't know anyone else to go to.

KROGSTAD: I promised to get you that amount—

NORA: Yes, and you did so.

KROGSTAD: I promised to get you that amount, on certain conditions. Your mind was so taken up with your husband's illness, and you were so anxious to get the money for your journey, that you seem to have paid no attention to the conditions of our bargain. Therefore it will not be amiss if I remind you of them. Now, I promised to get the money on the security of a bond which I drew up.

NORA: Yes, and which I signed.

KROGSTAD: Good. But below your signature there were a few lines constituting your father a surety for the money; those lines your father should have signed.

NORA: Should? He did sign them.

KROGSTAD: I had left the date blank; that is to say, your father should himself have inserted the date on which he signed the paper. Do you remember that?

NORA: Yes, I think I remember—

KROGSTAD: Then I gave you the bond to send by post to your father. Is that not so?

NORA: Yes.

KROGSTAD: And you naturally did so at once, because five or six days afterwards you brought me the bond with your father's signature. And then I gave you the money.

NORA: Well, haven't I been paying it off regularly?

KROGSTAD: Fairly so, yes. But—to come back to the matter in hand—that must have been a very trying time for you, Mrs. Helmer?

NORA: It was, indeed.

KROGSTAD: Your father was very ill, wasn't he?

NORA: He was very near his end.

KROGSTAD: And died soon afterwards?

NORA: Yes.

KROGSTAD: Tell me, Mrs. Helmer, can you by any chance remember what day your father died?—on what day of the month, I mean.

NORA: Papa died on the 29th of September.

KROGSTAD: That is correct; I have ascertained it for myself. And, as that is so, there is a discrepancy (*taking a paper from his pocket*) which I cannot account for.

NORA: What discrepancy? I don't know—

KROGSTAD: The discrepancy consists, Mrs. Helmer, in the fact that your father signed this bond three days after his death.

NORA: What do you mean? I don't understand—

KROGSTAD: Your father died on the 29th of September. But, look here; your father has dated his signature the 2nd of October. It is a discrepancy, isn't it? (NORA *is silent.*) Can you explain it to me? (NORA *is still silent.*) It is a remarkable thing, too, that the words "2nd of October," as well as the year, are not written in your father's handwriting but in one that I think I know. Well, of course it can be explained; your father may have forgotten to date his signature, and someone else may have dated it haphazard before they knew of his death. There is no harm in that. It all depends on the signature of the name;

and that is genuine, I suppose, Mrs. Helmer? It was your father himself who signed his name here?

NORA: (*after a short pause, throws her head up and looks defiantly at him*) No, it was not. It was I that wrote papa's name.

KROGSTAD: Are you aware that is a dangerous confession?

NORA: In what way? You shall have your money soon.

KROGSTAD: Let me ask you a question; why did you not send the paper to your father?

NORA: It was impossible; papa was so ill. If I had asked him for his signature, I should have had to tell him what the money was to be used for; and when he was so ill himself I couldn't tell him that my husband's life was in danger—it was impossible.

KROGSTAD: It would have been better for you if you had given up your trip abroad.

NORA: No, that was impossible. That trip was to save my husband's life; I couldn't give that up.

KROGSTAD: But did it never occur to you that you were committing a fraud on me?

NORA: I couldn't take that into account; I didn't trouble myself about you at all. I couldn't bear you, because you put so many heartless difficulties in my way, although you knew what a dangerous condition my husband was in.

KROGSTAD: Mrs. Helmer, you evidently do not realize clearly what it is that you have been guilty of. But I can assure you that my one false step, which lost me all my reputation, was nothing more or nothing worse than what you have done.

NORA: You? Do you ask me to believe that you were brave enough to run a risk to save your wife's life?

KROGSTAD: The law cares nothing about motives.

NORA: Then it must be a very foolish law.

KROGSTAD: Foolish or not, it is the law by which you will be judged, if I produce this paper in court.

NORA: I don't believe it. Is a daughter not to be allowed to spare her dying father anxiety and care? Is a wife not to be allowed to save her husband's life? I don't know much about law; but I am certain that there must be laws permitting such things as that. Have you no knowledge of such laws—you who are a lawyer? You must be a very poor lawyer, Mr. Krogstad.

KROGSTAD: Maybe. But matters of business—such business as you and I have had together—do you think I don't understand that? Very well. Do as you please. But let me tell you this—if I lose my position a second time, you shall lose yours with me. (*He bows, and goes out through the hall.*)

NORA: (*appears buried in thought for a short time, then tosses her head*) Nonsense! Trying to frighten me like that!—I am not so silly as he thinks. (*Begins to busy herself putting the children's things in order.*) And yet—? No, it's impossible! I did it for love's sake.

* * *

NORA: What are all those papers?

HELMER: Bank business.

NORA: Already?

HELMER: I have got authority from the retiring manager to undertake the necessary changes in the staff and in the rearrangement of the work; and I must make use of the Christmas week for that, so as to have everything in order for the new year.

NORA: Then that was why this poor Krogstad—

HELMER: Hm!

* * *

NORA: That is nice of you. (*Goes to the Christmas Tree. A short pause.*) How pretty the red flowers look—. But, tell me, was it really something very bad that this Krogstad was guilty of?

HELMER: He forged someone's name. Have you any idea what that means?

NORA: Isn't it possible that he was driven to do it by necessity?

HELMER: Yes; or, as in so many cases, by imprudence. I am not so heartless as to condemn a man altogether because of a single false step of that kind.

NORA: No, you wouldn't, would you, Torvald?

HELMER: Many a man has been able to retrieve his character, if he has openly confessed his fault and taken his punishment.

NORA: Punishment—?

HELMER: But Krogstad did nothing of that sort; he got himself out of it by a cunning trick, and that is why he has gone under altogether.

NORA: But do you think it would—?

HELMER: Just think how a guilty man like that has to lie and play the hypocrite with every one, how he has to wear a mask in the presence of those near and

dear to him, even before his own wife and children. And about the children—
that is the most terrible part of it all, Nora.

NORA: How?

HELMER: Because such an atmosphere of lies infects and poisons the whole life
of a home. Each breath the children take in such a house is full of the germs
of evil.

NORA: (*coming nearer him*) Are you sure of that?

HELMER: My dear, I have often seen it in the course of my life as a lawyer. Almost everyone who has gone to the bad early in life has had a deceitful mother.

NORA: Why do you only say—mother?

HELMER: It seems most commonly to be the mother's influence, though naturally a bad father's would have the same result. Every lawyer is familiar with
the fact. This Krogstad, now, has been persistently poisoning his own children
with lies and dissimulation; that is why I say he has lost all moral character.
(*Holds out his hands to her.*) That is why my sweet little Nora must promise me
not to plead his cause. Give me your hand on it. Come, come, what is this?
Give me your hand. There now, that's settled. I assure you it would be quite
impossible for me to work with him; I literally feel physically ill when I am in
the company of such people.

Robert Frost

from "THE SELF-SEEKER"

American poet Robert Frost, recipient of four Pulitzer Prizes, entered the legal literary arena in 1914 with his poem "The Self-seeker," which addresses the way Americans seek justice and monetary damages through the law, assisted by lawyers who are often more interested in catching their train than in relieving our pain.

"Willis, I didn't want you here to-day:
The lawyer's coming for the company.
I'm going to sell my soul, or, rather, feet.
Five hundred dollars for the pair, you know."

"With you the feet have nearly been the soul;
And if you're going to sell them to the devil,
I want to see you do it. When's he coming?"

"I half suspect you knew, and came on purpose
To try to help me drive a better bargain."

"Well, if it's true! Yours are no common feet.
The lawyer don't know what it is he's buying:
So many miles you might have walked you won't walk.
You haven't run your forty orchids down.
What does he think?—How are the blessed feet?
The doctor's sure you're going to walk again?"

"He thinks I'll hobble. It's both legs and feet."

"They must be terrible—I mean to look at."

"I haven't dared to look at them uncovered.
Through the bed blankets I remind myself
Of a starfish laid out with rigid points."

"The wonder is it hadn't been your head."

"It's hard to tell you how I managed it.
When I saw the shaft had me by the coat,
I didn't try too long to pull away,
Or fumble for my knife to cut away,
I just embraced the shaft and rode it out—
Till Weiss shut off the water in the wheel-pit.
That's how I think I didn't lose my head.
But my legs got their knocks against the ceiling."

"Awful. Why didn't they throw off the belt
Instead of going clear down in the wheel-pit?"

"They say some time was wasted on the belt—
Old streak of leather—doesn't love me much
Because I make him spit fire at my knuckles,
The way Ben Franklin used to make the kite-string.
That must be it. Some days he won't stay on.
That day a woman couldn't coax him off.
He's on his rounds now with his tail in his mouth
Snatched right and left across the silver pulleys.
Everything goes the same without me there.
You can hear the small buzz saws whine, the big saw
Caterwaul to the hills around the village
As they both bite the wood. It's all our music.
One ought as a good villager to like it.
No doubt it has a sort of prosperous sound,
And it's our life."

"Yes, when it's not our death."

"You make that sound as if it wasn't so
With everything. What we live by we die by.
I wonder where my lawyer is. His train's in.
I want this over with; I'm hot and tired."

"You're getting ready to do something foolish."

* * *

"And I'm going to be worse instead of better.
You've got to tell me how far this is gone:
Have you agreed to any price?"

"Five hundred.
Five hundred—five—five! One, two, three, four, five.
You needn't look at me."

"I don't believe you."

"I told you, Willis, when you first came in.
Don't you be hard on me. I have to take
What I can get. You see they have the feet,
Which gives them the advantage in the trade.
I can't get back the feet in any case."

"But your flowers, man, you're selling out your flowers."

"Yes, that's one way to put it—all the flowers
Of every kind everywhere in this region
For the next forty summers—call it forty.
But I'm not selling those, I'm giving them,
They never earned me so much as one cent:
Money can't pay me for the loss of them.
No, the five hundred was the sum they named
To pay the doctor's bill and tide me over."

It's that or fight, and I don't want to fight—
I just want to get settled in my life,
Such as it's going to be, and know the worst,
Or best—it may not be so bad. The firm
Promise me all the shooks I want to nail."

* * *

There! there's the bell.

* * *

Willis brought up besides the Boston lawyer
A little barefoot girl who in the noise
Of heavy footsteps in the old frame house,
And baritone importance of the lawyer,
Stood for a while unnoticed with her hands
Shyly behind her.

"Well, and how is Mister—"
The lawyer was already in his satchel
As if for papers that might bear the name
He hadn't at command. "You must excuse me,
I dropped in at the mill and was detained."

"Looking round, I suppose," said Willis.

"Yes,
Well, yes."

"Hear anything that might prove useful?"

The Broken One saw Anne. "Why, here is Anne.
What do you want, dear? Come, stand by the bed;
Tell me what is it?" Anne just wagged her dress
With both hands held behind her. "Guess," she said.

"Oh, guess which hand? My my! Once on a time
I knew a lovely way to tell for certain

By looking in the ears. But I forget it.
Er, let me see. I think I'll take the right.
That's sure to be right even if it's wrong.
Come, hold it out. Don't change.—A Ram's Horn orchid!
A Ram's Horn! What would I have got, I wonder,
If I had chosen left. Hold out the left.
Another Ram's Horn! Where did you find those,
Under what beech tree, on what woodchuck's knoll?"

Anne looked at the large lawyer at her side,
And thought she wouldn't venture on so much.

"Were there no others?"

"There were four or five.
I knew you wouldn't let me pick them all."

"I wouldn't—so I wouldn't. You're the girl!
You see Anne has her lesson learned by heart."

"I wanted there should be some there next year."

"Of course you did. You left the rest for seed,
And for the backwoods woodchuck. You're the girl!
A Ram's Horn orchid seedpod for a woodchuck
Sounds something like. Better than farmer's beans
To a discriminating appetite,
Though the Ram's Horn is seldom to be had
In bushel lots—doesn't come on the market.
But, Anne, I'm troubled; have you told me all?
You're hiding something. That's as bad as lying.
You ask this lawyer man. And it's not safe
With a lawyer at hand to find you out.
Nothing is hidden from some people, Anne.
You don't tell me that where you found a Ram's Horn
You didn't find a Yellow Lady's Slipper.

What did I tell you? What? I'd blush, I would.
Don't you defend yourself. If it was there,
Where is it now, the Yellow Lady's Slipper?"

"Well, wait—it's common—it's too common."

"Common?
The Purple Lady's Slipper's commoner."

"I didn't bring a Purple Lady's Slipper
To You—to you I mean—they're both too common."

The lawyer gave a laugh among his papers
As if with some idea that she had scored.
                    * * *
The lawyer wore a watch the case of which
Was cunningly devised to make a noise
Like a small pistol when he snapped it shut
At such a time as this. He snapped it now.

"Well, Anne, go, dearie. Our affair will wait.
The lawyer man is thinking of his train.
He wants to give me lots and lots of money
Before he goes, because I hurt myself,
And it may take him I don't know how long.
                    * * *
Now run.—Get out your documents! You see
I have to keep on the good side of Anne.
I'm a great boy to think of number one.
And you can't blame me in the place I'm in.
Who will take care of my necessities
Unless I do?"

"A pretty interlude,"
The lawyer said. "I'm sorry, but my train—
Luckily terms are all agreed upon.

You only have to sign your name. Right—there."

"You, Will, stop making faces. Come round here
Where you can't make them. What is it you want?
I'll put you out with Anne. Be good or go."

"You don't mean you will sign that thing unread?"

"Make yourself useful then, and read it for me.
Isn't it something I have seen before?"

"You'll find it is. Let your friend look at it."

"Yes, but all that takes time, and I'm as much
In haste to get it over with as you.
But read it, read it. That's right, draw the curtain:
Half the time I don't know what's troubling me.—
What do you say, Will? Don't you be a fool,
You! crumpling folkses legal documents.
Out with it if you've any real objection."

"Five hundred dollars!"

"What would you think right?"

"A thousand wouldn't be a cent too much;
You know it, Mr. Lawyer. The sin is
Accepting anything before he knows
Whether he's ever going to walk again.
It smells to me like a dishonest trick."

"I think—I think—from what I heard to-day—
And saw myself—he would be ill-advised—"

"What did you hear, for instance?" Willis said.

"Now the place where the accident occurred—"

The Broken One was twisted in his bed.
"This is between you two apparently.
Where I come in is what I want to know.
You stand up to it like a pair of cocks.
Go outdoors if you want to fight. Spare me.
When you come back, I'll have the papers signed.
Will pencil do? Then, please, your fountain pen.
One of you hold my head up from the pillow."

Willis flung off the bed. "I wash my hands—
I'm no match—no, and don't pretend to be—"

The lawyer gravely capped his fountain pen.
"You're doing the wise thing: you won't regret it.
We're very sorry for you."

Willis sneered:
"Who's we?—some stockholders in Boston?
I'll go outdoors, by gad, and won't come back."

"Willis, bring Anne back with you when you come.
Yes. Thanks for caring. Don't mind Will: he's savage.
He thinks you ought to pay me for my flowers.
You don't know what I mean about the flowers.
Don't stop to try to now. You'll miss your train.
Good-bye." He flung his arms around his face.

Leo Tolstoy

from THE DEATH OF IVAN ILYCH

The author of War and Peace *and* Anna Karenina, *Russian novelist Leo Tolstoy also wrote* The Death of Ivan Ilych, *a novella about a lawyer turned high court judge whose accomplishments, values, and attitudes prove to be meaningless when he learns that he is dying. In this excerpt, Tolstoy describes a lawyer of stature but not one of moral virtue; the law as a profession is portrayed as comfortable but otherwise soulless.*

Ivan Ilych's life had been most simple and most ordinary and therefore most terrible.

He had been a member of the Court of Justice, and died at the age of forty-five. His father had been an official who after serving in various ministries and departments in Petersburg had made the sort of career which brings men to positions from which by reason of their long service they cannot be dismissed, though they are obviously unfit to hold any responsible position, and for whom therefore posts are specially created, which though fictitious carry salaries of from six to ten thousand rubles that are not fictitious, and in receipt of which they live on to a great age.

* * *

Having graduated from the School of Law and qualified for the tenth rank of the civil service, and having received money from his father for his equipment, Ivan Ilych ordered himself clothes at Scharmer's, the fashionable tailor, hung a medallion inscribed "respice finem" on his watch-chain, took leave of his professor and the prince who was patron of the school, had a farewell dinner with his comrades at Donon's first-class restaurant, and with his new and fashionable portmanteau, linen, clothes, shaving and other toilet appliances, and a traveling rug, all purchased at the best shops, he set off for one of the provinces where through his father's influence, he had been attached to the governor as an official for special service.

In the province Ivan Ilych soon arranged as easy and agreeable a position for himself as he had had at the School of Law. He performed his official task, made his career, and at the same time amused himself pleasantly and decorously. Occasionally he paid official visits to country districts where he behaved with dignity both to his superiors and inferiors, and performed the duties entrusted to him, which related chiefly to the sectarians, with an exactness and incorruptible honesty of which he could not but feel proud.

* * *

But now, as an examining magistrate, Ivan Ilych felt that everyone without exception, even the most important and self-satisfied, was in his power, and that he need only write a few words on a sheet of paper with a certain heading, and this or that important, self-satisfied person would be brought before him in the role of an accused person or a witness, and if he did not choose to allow him to sit down, would have to stand before him and answer his questions. Ivan Ilych never abused his power; he tried on the contrary to soften its expression, but the consciousness of it and the possibility of softening its effect, supplied the chief interest and attraction of his office. In his work itself, especially in his examinations, he very soon acquired a method of eliminating all considerations irrelevant to the legal aspect of the case, and reducing even the most complicated case to a form in which it would be presented on paper only in its externals, completely excluding his personal opinion of the matter, while above all observing every prescribed formality. The work was new and Ivan Ilych was one of the first men to apply the new Code of 1864.

On taking up the post of examining magistrate in a new town, he made new acquaintances and connections, placed himself on a new footing and assumed a somewhat different tone. He took up an attitude of rather dignified aloofness towards the provincial authorities, but picked out the best circle of legal gentlemen and wealthy gentry living in the town and assumed a tone of slight dissatisfaction with the government, of moderate liberalism, and of enlightened citizenship. At the same time, without at all altering the elegance of his toilet, he ceased shaving his chin and allowed his beard to grow as it pleased.

Charles Dickens

from BLEAK HOUSE

In this excerpt from Dickens's 1852–1853 masterpiece, Bleak House, *two types of lawyers are described: Tulkinghorn, a high-priced attorney who seems too comfortably interested in the secrets of his clients; and Vholes, a low-rent lawyer who represents little but the legal system's glacial inertia and false swagger.*

"But is the secret safe so far?" I asked. "Is it safe now, dearest mother?"

"No," replied my mother. "It has been very near discovery. It was saved by an accident. It may be lost by another accident—to-morrow, any day."

"Do you dread a particular person?"

"Hush! Do not tremble and cry so much for me. I am not worthy of these tears," said my mother, kissing my hands. "I dread one person very much."

"An enemy?"

"Not a friend. One who is too passionless to be either. He is Sir Leicester Dedlock's lawyer, mechanically faithful without attachment, and very jealous of the profit, privilege, and reputation of being master of the mysteries of great houses."

"Has he any suspicions?"

"Many."

"Not of you?" I said alarmed.

"Yes! He is always vigilant and always near me. I may keep him at a stand-still, but I can never shake him off."

"Has he so little pity or compunction?"

"He has none, and no anger. He is indifferent to everything but his calling. His calling is the acquisition of secrets and the holding possession of such power as they give him, with no sharer or opponent in it."

"Could you trust in him?"

"I shall never try. The dark road I have trodden for so many years will end where it will. I follow it alone to the end, whatever the end be. It may be near, it may be distant; while the road lasts, nothing turns me."

"Dear mother, are you so resolved?"

"I *am* resolved. I have long outbidden folly with folly, pride with pride, scorn with scorn, insolence with insolence, and have outlived many vanities with many more. I will outlive this danger, and outdie it, if I can. It has closed around me almost as awfully as if these woods of Chesney Wold had closed around the house, but my course through it is the same. I have but one; I can have but one."

* * *

The name of Mr. Vholes, preceded by the legend Ground-Floor, is inscribed upon a door-post in Symond's Inn, Chancery Lane—a little, pale, wall-eyed, woebegone inn like a large dust-binn of two compartments and a sifter. It looks as if Symond were a sparing man in his way and constructed his inn of old building materials which took kindly to the dry rot and to dirt and all things decaying and dismal, and perpetuated Symond's memory with congenial shabbiness. Quartered in this dingy hatchment commemorative of Symond are the legal bearings of Mr. Vholes.

Mr. Vholes's office, in disposition retiring and in situation retired, is squeezed up in a corner and blinks at a dead wall. Three feet of knotty-floored dark passage bring the client to Mr. Vholes's jet-black door, in an angle profoundly dark on the brightest midsummer morning and encumbered by a black bulk-head of cellarage staircase against which belated civilians generally strike their brows. Mr. Vholes's chambers are on so small a scale that one clerk can open the door without getting off his stool, while the other who elbows him at the same desk has equal facilities for poking the fire. A smell as of unwholesome sheep blending with the smell of must and dust is referable to the nightly (and often daily) consumption of mutton fat in candles and to the fretting of parchment forms and skins in greasy drawers. The atmosphere is otherwise stale and close. The place was last painted or whitewashed beyond the memory of man, and the two chimneys smoke, and there is a loose outer surface of soot everywhere, and the dull cracked windows in their heavy frames have but one piece of character in them, which is a determination to be always dirty and always shut unless coerced. This accounts for the phenomenon of the weaker of the two usually having a bundle of firewood thrust between its jaws in hot weather.

Mr. Vholes is a very respectable man. He has not a large business, but he is a very respectable man. He is allowed by the greater attorneys who have made good fortunes or are making them to be a most respectable man. He never misses a chance in his practice, which is a mark of respectability. He never takes any pleasure, which is another mark of respectability. He is reserved and serious, which is another mark of respectability. His digestion is impaired, which is highly respectable. And he is making hay of the grass which is flesh, for his three daughters. And his father is dependent on him in the Vale of Taunton.

The one great principle of the English law is to make business for itself. There is no other principle distinctly, certainly, and consistently maintained through all its narrow turnings. Viewed by this light it becomes a coherent scheme and not the monstrous maze the laity are apt to think it. Let them but once clearly perceive that its grand principle is to make business for itself at their expense, and surely they will cease to grumble.

* * *

The Chancellor is, within these ten minutes, "up" for the long vacation. Mr. Vholes, and his young client, and several blue bags hastily stuffed out of all regularity of form, as the larger sort of serpents are in their first gorged state, have returned to the official den. Mr. Vholes, quiet and unmoved, as a man of so much respectability ought to be, takes off his close black gloves as if he were skinning his hands, lifts off his tight hat as if he were scalping himself, and sits down at his desk. The client throws his hat and gloves upon the ground—tosses them anywhere, without looking after them or caring where they go; flings himself into a chair, half sighing and half groaning; rests his aching head upon his hand and looks the portrait of young despair.

"Again nothing done!" says Richard. "Nothing, nothing done!"

"Don't say nothing done, sir," returns the placid Vholes. "That is scarcely fair, sir, scarcely fair!"

"Why, what *is* done?" says Richard, turning gloomily upon him.

"That may not be the whole question," returns Vholes. "The question may branch off into what is doing, what is doing?"

"And what is doing?" asks the moody client.

Vholes, sitting with his arms on the desk, quietly bringing the tips of his five right fingers to meet the tips of his five left fingers, and quietly separating them again, and fixedly and slowly looking at his client, replies, "A good deal is doing, sir. We have put our shoulders to the wheel, Mr. Carstone, and the wheel is going round."

"Yes, with Ixion on it. How am I to get through the next four or five accursed months?" exclaims the young man, rising from his chair and walking about the room.

"Mr. C.," returns Vholes, following him close with his eyes wherever he goes, "your spirits are hasty, and I am sorry for it on your account. Excuse me if I recommend you not to chafe so much, not to be so impetuous, not to wear yourself out so. You should have more patience. You should sustain yourself better."

"I ought to imitate you, in fact, Mr. Vholes?" says Richard, sitting down again with an impatient laugh and beating the devil's tattoo with his boot on the patternless carpet.

"Sir," returns Vholes, always looking at the client as if he were making a lingering meal of him with his eyes as well as with his professional appetite. "Sir," returns Vholes with his inward manner of speech and his bloodless quietude, "I should not have had the presumption to propose myself as a model for your imitation or any man's. Let me but leave the good name to my three daughters, and that is enough for me; I am not a self-seeker. But since you mention me so pointedly, I will acknowledge that I should like to impart to you a little of my—come, sir, you are disposed to call it insensibility, and I am sure I have no objection—say insensibility—a little of my insensibility."

"Mr. Vholes," explains the client, somewhat abashed, "I had no intention to accuse you of insensibility."

"I think you had, sir, without knowing it," returns the equable Vholes. "Very naturally. It is my duty to attend to your interests with a cool head, and I can quite understand that to your excited feelings I may appear, at such times as the present, insensible. My daughters may know me better; my aged father may know me better. But they have known me much longer than you have, and the confiding eye of affection is not the distrustful eye of business. Not that I complain, sir, of the eye of business being distrustful; quite the contrary. In attending to your interests, I wish to have all possible checks upon me; it is right that I should have them; I court inquiry. But your interests demand that I should be cool and methodical, Mr. Carstone; and I cannot be otherwise— no, sir, not even to please you."

Mr. Vholes, after glancing at the official cat who is patiently watching a mouse's hole, fixes his charmed gaze again on his young client and proceeds in his buttoned-up, half-audible voice as if there were an unclean spirit in him that will neither come out nor speak out, "What are you to do, sir, you inquire, during the vacation. I should hope you gentlemen of the army may find many means of amusing yourselves if you give your minds to it. If you had asked me what *I* was to do during the vacation, I could have answered you more readily. I am to attend to your interests. I am to be found here, day by day, attending to your interests. That is my duty, Mr. C., and term-time or vacation makes no difference to me. If you wish to consult me as to your interests, you will find me here at all times alike. Other professional men go out of town. I don't. Not that I blame them for going; I merely say I don't go. This desk is your rock, sir!"

Mr. Vholes gives it a rap, and it sounds as hollow as a coffin. Not to Richard, though. There is encouragement in the sound to him. Perhaps Mr. Vholes knows there is.

"I am perfectly aware, Mr. Vholes," says Richard, more familiarly and good-humouredly, "that you are the most reliable fellow in the world and that to have to do with you is to have to do with a man of business who is not to be hoodwinked. But put yourself in my case, dragging on this dislocated life, sinking deeper and deeper into difficulty every day, continually hoping and continually disappointed, conscious of change upon change for the worse in myself, and of no change for the better in anything else, and you will find it a dark-looking case sometimes, as I do."

"You know," says Mr. Vholes, "that I never give hopes, sir. I told you from the first, Mr. C., that I never give hopes. Particularly in a case like this, where the greater part of the costs comes out of the estate, I should not be considerate of my good name if I gave hopes. It might seem as if costs were my object. Still, when you say there is no change for the better, I must, as a bare matter of fact, deny that."

"Aye?" returns Richard, brightening. "But how do you make it out?"

"Mr. Carstone, you are represented by—"

"You said just now—a rock."

"Yes, sir," says Mr. Vholes, gently shaking his head and rapping the hollow desk, with a sound as if ashes were falling on ashes, and dust on dust, "a rock. That's something. You are separately represented, and no longer hidden and lost in the interests of others. *That's* something. The suit does not sleep; we wake it up, we air it, we walk it about. *That's* something. It's not all Jarndyce, in fact as well as in name. *That's* something. Nobody has it all his own way now, sir. And *that's* something, surely."

Richard, his face flushing suddenly, strikes the desk with his clenched hand.

* * *

Vholes finally adds, by way of rider to this declaration of his principles, that as Mr. Carstone is about to rejoin his regiment, perhaps Mr. C. will favour him with an order on his agent for twenty pounds on account.

"For there have been many little consultations and attendances of late, sir," observes Vholes, turning over the leaves of his diary, "and these things mount up, and I don't profess to be a man of capital. When we first entered on our present relations I stated to you openly—it is a principle of mine that there never can be too much openness between solicitor and client—that I was not a man of capital and that if capital was your object you had better leave your papers in Kenge's office. No, Mr. C., you will find none of the advantages or disadvantages of capital here, sir. This," Vholes gives the desk one hollow blow again, "is your rock; it pretends to be nothing more."

The client, with his dejection insensibly relieved and his vague hopes rekindled, takes pen and ink and writes the draft, not without perplexed consideration and calculation of the date it may bear, implying scant effects in the agent's hands. All the while, Vholes, buttoned up in body and mind, looks at him attentively. All the while, Vholes's official cat watches the mouse's hole.

Lastly, the client, shaking hands, beseeches Mr. Vholes, for heaven's sake and earth's sake, to do his utmost to "pull him through" the Court of Chancery. Mr. Vholes, who never gives hopes, lays his palm upon the client's shoulder and answers with a smile, "Always here, sir. Personally, or by letter, you will always find me here, sir, with my shoulder to the wheel."

Russell Banks

from THE SWEET HEREAFTER

In his 1991 The Sweet Hereafter, *American novelist Russell Banks dissects the trauma and turmoil of a small depressed town forced to confront a school bus accident that kills fourteen of its children on their way to school. Can the legal system respond to so much collective and individual grief? Will compensatory damages make any of the parents feel better or relieve their pain? In this excerpt, Mitchell Stevens, a hard-bitten personal-injury attorney, drives into town to solicit clients for a negligence suit and begins his own journey of self-discovery and personal redemption.*

Angry? Yes, I'm angry; I'd be a lousy lawyer if I weren't. I suppose it's as if I've got this permanent boil on my butt and can't quite sit down. Which is not the same, you understand, as being hounded by greed; although I can see, of course, that it probably sometimes looked like greed to certain individuals who were not lawyers, when they saw a person like me driving all the way up there to the Canadian border, practically, saw me camping out in the middle of winter in a windy dingy little motel room for weeks at a time, bugging the hell out of decent people who were in the depths of despair and just wanted to be left alone. I can understand that.

But it wasn't greed that put me there; it's never been greed that sends me whirling out of orbit like that. It's anger. What the hell, I'm not ashamed of it. It's who I am. I'm not proud of it, either, but it makes me useful, at least. Which is more than you can say for greed.

That's what people don't get about negligence lawyers—good negligence lawyers, I mean, the kind who go after the sloppy fat cats with their corner offices and end up nailing their pelts to the wall. People immediately assume we're greedy, that it's money we're after, people call us ambulance-chasers and so on, like we're the proctologists of the profession, and, yes, there's lots of those. But the truth is, the good ones, we'd make the same moves for a single shekel as for a ten-million-dollar settlement. Because it's anger that drives us and delivers us. It's not any kind of love, either—love for the underdog or the victim, or whatever you want to call them. Some litigators like to claim that. The losers.

No, what it is, we're permanently pissed off, the winners, and practicing law is a way to be socially useful at the same time, that's all. It's like a discipline; it organizes and controls us; probably keeps us from being homicidal. A kind of Zen is what. Some people equally pissed off are able to focus their rage by becoming cops or soldiers or martial arts instructors; those who become lawyers, however, especially litigators like me, are a little too intelligent, or maybe too intellectual is all, to become cops. (I've known some pretty smart cops, but not many intellectual ones.) So instead of learning how to break bricks and two-by-fours with our hands or bust chain-snatchers in subways, we sneak off to law school and put on three-piece suits and come roaring out like banshees, all teeth and claws and fire and smoke.

Certainly we get paid well for it, which is a satisfaction, yes, but not a motivation, because the real satisfaction, the true motivation, is the carnage and the smoldering aftermath and the trophy heads that get hung up on the den wall. I love it.

That's why I spent most of six months up there in Sam Dent, practically becoming a citizen. Not my idea of a winter vacation, believe me. But anytime I hear about a case like that school bus disaster up there, I turn into a heat-seeking missile, homing in on a target that I know in my bones is going to turn out to be some bungling corrupt state agency or some multinational corporation that's cost accounted the difference between a ten-cent bolt and a million-dollar out-of-court settlement and has decided to sacrifice a few lives for the difference. They do that, work the bottom line; I've seen it play out over and over again, until you start to wonder about the human species. They're like clever monkeys, that's all. They calculate ahead of time what it will cost them to assure safety versus what they're likely to be forced to settle for damages when the missing bolt sends the bus over a cliff, and they simply choose the cheaper option. And it's up to people like me to make it cheaper to build the bus with that extra bolt, or add the extra yard of guardrail, or drain the quarry. That's the only check you've got against them. That's the only way you can ensure moral responsibility in this society. Make it cheaper.

So that winter morning when I picked up the paper and read about this terrible event in a small town upstate, with all those kids lost, I knew instantly
what the story was; I knew at once that it wasn't an "accident" at all. There are
no accidents. I don't even know what the word means, and I never trust anyone who says he does. I knew that somebody somewhere had made a decision
to cut a corner in order to save a few pennies, and now the state or the manu-
facturer of the bus or the town, somebody, was busy lining up a troop of
smoothies to negotiate with a bunch of grief-stricken bumpkins a settlement
that wouldn't displease the accountants. I packed a bag and headed north, like
I said, pissed off.

* * *

The most I could do for the Walkers was represent them in a negligence suit
that compensated them financially for the loss of their son, Sean. And that's
only part of it, the smaller part. I could also strip and hang the hide of the
sonofabitch responsible for the loss of their son—which just might save the
life of some other boy riding to school in some other small American town.

That was my intention anyhow. My mission, you might say.

Every year, though, I swear I'm not going to take any more cases involving
children. No more dead kids. No more stunned grieving parents who really
only want to be left alone to mourn in the darkness of their homes, for God's
sake, to sit on their kids' beds with the blinds drawn against the curious world
outside and weep in silence as they contemplate their permanent pain. I'm under no delusions—I know that in the end a million-dollar settlement makes
no real difference to them, that it probably only serves to sharpen their pain
by constricting it with legal language and rewarding it with money, that it
complicates the guilt they feel and forces them to question the authenticity of
their own suffering. I know all that; I've seen it a hundred times.

It hardly seems worth it, right? Thanks but no thanks, right? And I swear,
if that were the whole story, if the settlement were not a fine as well, if it were
not a punishment that, though it can never fit the crime, might at least make
the crime seem prohibitively expensive to the criminal, then, believe me, I
would not pursue these cases. They humiliate me. They make me burn inside
with shame. Win or lose, I always come out feeling diminished, like a cinder.

So I'm no Lone Ranger riding into town in my white Mercedes-Benz to
save the local sheepherders from the cattle barons in black hats; I'm clear on
that. And I don't burn myself out with these awful cases because it somehow

makes me a better person. No, I admit it, I'm on a personal vendetta; what the hell, it's obvious. And I don't need a shrink to tell me what motivates me. A shrink would probably tell me it's because I myself have lost a child and now identify with chumps like Risa and Wendell Walker and that poor sap Billy Ansel, and Wanda and Hartley Otto. The victims. Listen; identify with the victims and you become one yourself. Victims make lousy litigators.

Simply, I do it because I'm pissed off, and that's what you get when you mix conviction with rage. It's a very special kind of anger, let's say. So I'm no victim. Victims get depressed and live in the there and then. I live in the here and now.

Besides, the people of Sam Dent are not unique. We've all lost our children. It's like all the children of America are dead to us. Just look at them, for God's sake—violent on the streets, comatose in the malls, narcotized in front of the TV. In my lifetime something terrible happened that took our children away from us. I don't know if it was the Vietnam war, or the sexual colonization of kids by industry, or drugs, or TV, or divorce, or what the hell it was; I don't know which are causes and which are effects; but the children are gone, that I know. So that trying to protect them is little more than an elaborate exercise in denial. Religious fanatics and superpatriots, they try to protect their kids by turning them into schizophrenics; Episcopalians and High Church Jews gratefully abandon their kids to boarding schools and divorce one another so they can get laid with impunity; the middle class grabs what it can buy and passes it on, like poisoned candy on Halloween; and meanwhile the inner-city blacks and poor whites in the boonies sell their souls with longing for what's killing everyone else's kids and wonder why theirs are on crack.

It's too late; they're gone; we're what's left.

And the best we can do for them, and for ourselves, is rage against what took them. Even if we can't know what it'll be like when the smoke clears, we do know that rage, for better or worse, generates a future. The victims are the ones who've given up on the future. Instead, they've joined the dead. And the rest, look at them: unless they're enraged and acting on it, they're useless, unconscious; they're dead themselves and don't even know it.

* * *

Fine by me. I had my agenda too. In spite of the injuries, Nichole Burnell looked good, she talked good, and she had suffered immeasurably and would for the rest of her life. A beautiful articulate fourteen-year-old girl in a wheelchair. She was perfect. I could hardly wait to see the other side depose her.

Wendell Walker, on the other hand, when I first met him, seemed utterly defeated, gone, a dark hole in space. Useless, even to himself. I had chucked my stuff in my room and wandered back out to the motel office, to get directions to where the bus had gone over and to check out some of the local response to the event—to start work, in other words—but also to see if there was someplace in town where I could get a decent meal. It seemed unlikely, but you never know about these small towns. I once found a terrific barbecue shack in Daggle, Alabama.

The office was gloomy and dark, cold as a meat locker; behind the counter, a door leading to what I took to be the apartment where the proprietors lived was open, a crack, and a skinny band of light fell across the linoleum floor of the room. I thought I was alone, but when I walked up to the counter, looking for a bell or something to signal the woman who had checked me in, I saw a figure there, a large, heavyset man in a straight-backed chair, sitting behind the counter in the darkness as if in bright light, looking at his lap as if reading a magazine. It was a strange position, alert but frozen in place. He looked catatonic to me.

"Sorry, buddy," I said, "I didn't see you there. How's it going?"

No answer; no response whatsoever. He just went on staring down at his lap, as if he didn't hear or see me. One of those country simples, I thought. Inbreeding. Great. First local I get to talk to, and he turns out to be an alien. "The boss around?" I asked.

Nothing. Except that his tongue came out and licked dry lips. Then I recognized it: I've seen it a hundred times, but it still surprises and scares me. It's the opaque black-glass look of a man who has recently learned of the death of his child. It's the face of a person who's gone to the other side of life and is no longer even looking back at us. It always has the same history, that look: at the moment of the child's dying, the man follows his child into darkness, as if he's making a last attempt to save it; then, in panic, to be sure that he himself has not died as well, the man turns momentarily back toward us, maybe he even laughs then or says something weird, for he sees only darkness there too; and now he has returned to where his child first disappeared, fixing onto one of the bright apparitions that linger there. It's downright spooky.

"I'm sorry, bud," I said to him. "I just arrived here."

Still no response. Then he stirred slightly, turned his soft hands over, and placed them on his knees. He was wearing a Montreal Expos sweatshirt and loose khakis, a fat guy, slump-shouldered, not too bright-looking.

Suddenly, he said, "Are you a lawyer?" His voice was low but thin, flattened out, like a piece of tin. He still hadn't turned to face me, but I guess he'd taken my measure already. What the hell, I suppose I looked like a lawyer, especially up here, especially now. Something like this happens, people expect to see lawyers crawling around. Guys in suits and topcoats.

"Yes, I'm a lawyer."

"A good one?"

* * *

"So they have hired you."

"Yes."

"I see. Their child has died, and they have gone out and hired a lawyer because of it."

"Yes. Although my task is to represent them only in their anger, not their grief."

"That's how you understand your job? To represent anger?"

"Yes. You are angry, are you not? Among so many other things."

She pursed her lips thoughtfully and remained silent for a moment. The dog had started to snore. Hartley had disappeared behind a curtain, and I could hear water running into a kettle, which surprised me—I'd imagined melting chunks of ice or maybe a hand pump, not a faucet and sink. They probably had a microwave oven and a food processor back there.

"Yes," she said, expelling her breath. "Oh, yes, we are angry. Among so many other things."

"That's why I'm here, Mrs. Otto. To give your anger a voice, to be a weapon for you."

"Against whom?"

"Against whoever caused that bus to go off the road into the sandpit."

"I see. You think someone, a person, caused the accident."

"There is no such thing as an accident."

"No. No, there isn't. You are right about that. But how will you know who caused this accident that took our son from us?"

"If everyone had done his job, your son would be alive this morning and safely in school. I will simply find out who did not do his job. Then, in your name and the Walkers' and the name of whoever else decides to join you, I will sue that person and the company or agency he works for, I will sue them for negligence."

"I want that person to go to prison for the rest of his life," she declared. "I want him to die there. I don't want his money."

"It's unlikely anyone will go to prison. He or his company will have to pay in other ways. But pay they will. And we must make them pay, Mrs. Otto, not to benefit you in a material way or to compensate you for the loss of your son, Bear, which can't be done, but to protect the child you're carrying inside you now. Understand, I'm not here to speak just for your anger. I'm here to speak for the future as well. What we're talking about here is our ongoing relation to time."

"I see." And I think she did. The Walkers had seemed more muddled in their motives. The money promised by the lawsuit meant a lot to them, of course, but in a greedy, childish way, and certainly more than they were willing to admit to themselves or reveal openly to me. The Walkers were poor and in debt, and their poverty had bugged them for years, and it seemed even more unfair to them now, with their child gone, than before. But Wanda Otto, and her husband too, never struck me as having any selfish interest in the money; they cared only about its handy capacity to function as punishment and prohibition. They were too lost in their Zen Little Indians fantasy to be wholly believable, maybe, or as reliable as the Walkers were, but I admired them nonetheless.

* * *

"Well, Mr. New York Lawyer, what you've been saying makes sense," Wanda said to me. "Not much else in this world does." Then to Hartley, "We should hire this man to represent us. That way we won't have to deal with any of the others. He can advise us on how to talk to the reporters too. You'll do that?" she asked me.

"Yes. Certainly. For now, though, you should refuse all interviews. Say nothing to the press, nothing to any other lawyers. Refer everybody to me."

"Are you expensive?"

"No," I said. "If you agree to have me represent you in this suit, I will require no payment until after the suit is won, when I will require one third of the awarded amount. If there is no award made, then my services will have cost you nothing. It's a standard agreement."

"Do you have this agreement with you?"

"In my car," I said, and, not without difficulty, stood up, almost spilling my tea. I'm not used to sitting cross-legged on the floor. "I'll just be a minute. You should talk without me, anyhow, before you sign it," I added. Also, I needed a cigarette, and I hadn't noticed any ashtrays: the house was cluttered with small figurines and strange clay baskets that looked as if they were made to hold the spirits of ancestors rather than cigarette butts and ashes.

I stepped outside, coatless, still bearing my mug of tea, and the dog followed me and promptly pissed on the front tire of my car and took off down the road. I dumped the tea onto a snowbank, making my own mark. Then I got inside the car, where it was still warm, and lit a cigarette.

I felt terrific. My mind was off and running, switching options and tracking consequences like a first-class computer. Everyone has a specialty, and I guess this is mine. For twenty-five years now, and for three different firms, even after making partner, I've been the guy who handles these disaster negligence suits. I could pull away from tort cases and just handle the white-shoe stuff if I wanted—I've got the name and face for it—or I could quit the practice altogether, move permanently out to the house in East Hampton and maybe teach a course or two at Fordham; but I won't. Nothing else provides me with the rush that I get from cases like this. There is a brilliant hard-edged clarity that comes over me when I take on a suit for the Ottos and the Walkers of the world, an intensity and focus that makes me feel more alive then than at any other time.

It's almost like a drug. It's probably close to what professional soldiers feel, or bullfighters. The rest of the time, like most people, I muddle lonely through my days and nights feeling unsure, vaguely confused, conflicted, and aimless. Put me onto something like this school bus case, though, and zap! all those feelings disappear. Nothing else does it—not illicit sex, not cocaine, not driving fast late at night on the wrong lane of the highway, all of which I've tried. Nothing.

PART VII

The Law and the Loophole

Neither justice nor injustice arises out of accident. There is always legal inge-
nuity at work. The romance of law is best displayed in the lawyer's ability to
cast shadows and blow smoke, to split hairs and confound the crystal clear, to
revel in cleverness, to outwit even the most honest of witnesses. The tricks of
the lawyer's trade often require the stretching of truth. We admire such tactics
when they work to our advantage, and curse the unfairness of the system when
we become the victims of Solomonic manipulation. It is, indeed, the special
province of lawyers to coax the truth out of a "code red" and to find new
meaning in the extraction of "a pound of flesh."

Scott Turow

from PRESUMED INNOCENT

Scott Turow's bestselling 1987 legal thriller, Presumed Innocent, *addresses serious issues about the nature of law and the ethical dilemmas that attorneys face. In this excerpt, the narrator, accused of committing a murder, discusses the tactics of his defense attorney Sandy Stern, who pointedly does not ask his client whether he committed the crime.*

When I retained Sandy, within three or four hours of that bizarre meeting in Raymond's office, we spent thirty minutes together. He told me what it would cost—a $25,000 retainer, against a fee to be billed at $150 an hour for time out of court and $300 an hour in, the balance, strictly as a courtesy to me, to be returned if there was no indictment; he told me not to talk to anyone about the charges and, in particular, to make no more outraged speeches to prosecutors; he told me to avoid reporters and not to quit my job; he told me this was frightening, reminiscent of the scenes of his childhood in Latin America; he told me that he was confident that with my extraordinary background this entire matter would be favorably resolved. But Sandy Stern, with whom I have done business for better than a decade, against whom I have tried half a dozen cases, and who on matters of gravity, or of little consequence, has always known that he could accept my word—Sandy Stern has never asked me if I did it. He has inquired from time to time about details. He asked me once, quite unceremoniously, whether I'd had "a physical relationship" with Carolyn, and I told him, without flinching, yes. But Stern has remained far clear of ever putting the ultimate question. In that he is like everybody else. Even Barbara, who evinces by various proclamations a belief in my innocence, has never asked me directly. People tell you it's tough. They cling or, more often, seem visibly repulsed. But nobody has sufficient sand to come out with the only question you know they have in mind.

From Sandy this indirection seems more of his classical manner, the formal presence that lies over him like brocaded drapes. But I know it serves for more. Perhaps he does not ask because he is not certain of the verity of the answer he may get. It is a given of the criminal justice system, an axiom as certain as the laws of gravity, that defendants rarely tell the truth. Cops and prosecutors, defense lawyers and judges—everybody knows they lie. They lie solemnly; with sweaty palms and shifty eyes; or, more often, with a look of schoolboy innocence and an incensed disbelief when their credulity is assailed: They lie to protect themselves; they lie to protect their friends. They lie for the fun of it, or because that is the way they have always been. They lie about big details and small ones, about who started it, who thought of it, who did it, and who was sorry. But they lie. It is the defendant's credo. Lie to the cops. Lie to your lawyer. Lie to the jury that tries your case. If convicted, lie to your probation officer. Lie to your bunkmate in the pen. Trumpet your innocence. Leave the dirty bastards out there with a grain of doubt. Something can always change.

Thus it would be an act contrary to his professional acumen were Sandy Stern to commit himself to an unreserved faith in everything I say. Instead, he does not ask. This procedure has one further virtue. If I were to meet any new evidence by frontally contradicting what I had told Sandy in the past, legal ethics might require him to withhold me from the witness stand, where I almost certainly intend to go. Better to see everything the prosecution has, to be certain that my recollection, as the lawyers put it, has been fully "refreshed," before Sandy inquires about my version. Caught in a system where the client is inclined to lie and the lawyer who seeks his client's confidence may not help him do that, Stern works in the small open spaces which remain. Most of all, he desires to make an intelligent presentation. He does not wish to be misled, or to have his options curbed by rash declarations that prove to be untrue. As the trial approaches, he will need to know more. He may ask the question then; and I certainly will tell him the answer. For the time being, Stern has found, as usual, the most artful and indefinite means by which to probe.

O. Henry

"AFTER TWENTY YEARS"

Early-twentieth-century American short-story writer O. Henry was best known for witty turns of phrase and surprise endings. In "After Twenty Years" (1903), he portrays the long arm of the law's unwillingness to allow friendship to get in the way of justice. Yet, in a surprising twist, the law is also capable of displaying a certain level of gentleman's honor.

The policeman on the beat moved up the avenue impressively. The impressiveness was habitual and not for show, for spectators were few. The time was barely 10 o'clock at night, but chilly gusts of wind with a taste of rain in them had well nigh depeopled the streets.

Trying doors as he went, twirling his club with many intricate and artful movements, turning now and then to cast his watchful eye adown the pacific thoroughfare, the officer, with his stalwart form and slight swagger, made a fine picture of a guardian of the peace. The vicinity was one that kept early hours. Now and then you might see the lights of a cigar store or of an all-night lunch counter; but the majority of the doors belonged to business places that had long since been closed.

When about midway of a certain block the policeman suddenly slowed his walk. In the doorway of a darkened hardware store a man leaned, with an unlighted cigar in his mouth. As the policeman walked up to him the man spoke up quickly.

"It's all right, officer," he said, reassuringly. "I'm just waiting for a friend. It's an appointment made twenty years ago. Sounds a little funny to you, doesn't it? Well, I'll explain if you'd like to make certain it's all straight. About that long ago there used to be a restaurant where this store stands—'Big Joe' Brady's restaurant."

"Until five years ago," said the policeman. "It was torn down then."

The man in the doorway struck a match and lit his cigar. The light showed a pale, square-jawed face with keen eyes, and a little white scar near his right eyebrow. His scarfpin was a large diamond, oddly set.

"Twenty years ago to-night," said the man, "I dined here at 'Big Joe' Brady's with Jimmy Wells, my best chum, and the finest chap in the world. He and I were raised here in New York, just like two brothers, together. I was eighteen and Jimmy was twenty. The next morning I was to start for the West to make my fortune. You couldn't have dragged Jimmy out of New York; he thought it was the only place on earth. Well, we agreed that night that we would meet here again exactly twenty years from that date and time, no matter what our conditions might be or from what distance we might have to come. We figured that in twenty years each of us ought to have our destiny worked out and our fortunes made, whatever they were going to be."

"It sounds pretty interesting," said the policeman. "Rather a long time between meets, though, it seems to me. Haven't you heard from your friend since you left?"

"Well, yes, for a time we corresponded," said the other. "But after a year or two we lost track of each other. You see, the West is a pretty big proposition, and I kept hustling around over it pretty lively. But I know Jimmy will meet me here if he's alive, for he always was the truest, stanchest old chap in the world. He'll never forget. I came a thousand miles to stand in this door to-night, and it's worth it if my old partner turns up."

The waiting man pulled out a handsome watch, the lids of it set with small diamonds.

"Three minutes to ten," he announced. "It was exactly ten o'clock when we parted here at the restaurant door."

"Did pretty well out West, didn't you?" asked the policeman.

"You bet! I hope Jimmy has done half as well. He was a kind of plodder, though, good fellow as he was. I've had to compete with some of the sharpest wits going to get my pile. A man gets in a groove in New York. It takes the West to put a razor-edge on him."

The policeman twirled his club and took a step or two.

"I'll be on my way. Hope your friend comes around all right. Going to call time on him sharp?"

"I should say not!" said the other. "I'll give him half an hour at least. If Jimmy is alive on earth he'll be here by that time. So long, officer."

"Good-night, sir," said the policeman, passing on along his beat, trying doors as he went.

There was now a fine, cold drizzle falling, and the wind had risen from its uncertain puffs into a steady blow. The few foot passengers astir in that quarter hurried dismally and silently along with coat collars turned high and pocketed hands. And in the door of the hardware store the man who had come a thousand miles to fill an appointment, uncertain almost to absurdity, with the friend of his youth, smoked his cigar and waited.

About twenty minutes he waited, and then a tall man in a long overcoat, with collar turned up to his ears, hurried across from the opposite side of the street. He went directly to the waiting man.

"Is that you, Bob?" he asked, doubtfully.

"Is that you, Jimmy Wells?" cried the man in the door.

"Bless my heart!" exclaimed the new arrival, grasping both the other's hands with his own. "It's Bob, sure as fate. I was certain I'd find you here if you were still in existence. Well, well, well!—twenty years is a long time. The old gone, Bob; I wish it had lasted, so we could have had another dinner there. How has the West treated you, old man?"

"Bully; it has given me everything I asked it for. You've changed lots, Jimmy. I never thought you were so tall by two or three inches."

"Oh, I grew a bit after I was twenty."

"Doing well in New York, Jimmy?"

"Moderately. I have a position in one of the city departments. Come on, Bob; we'll go around to a place I know of, and have a good long talk about old times."

The two men started up the street, arm in arm. The man from the West, his egotism enlarged by success, was beginning to outline the history of his career. The other, submerged in his overcoat, listened with interest.

At the corner stood a drug store, brilliant with electric lights. When they came into this glare each of them turned simultaneously to gaze upon the other's face.

The man from the West stopped suddenly and released his arm.

"You're not Jimmy Wells," he snapped. "Twenty years is a long time, but not long enough to change a man's nose from a Roman to a pug."

"It sometimes changes a good man into a bad one," said the tall man. "You've been under arrest for ten minutes, 'Silky' Bob. Chicago thinks you may have dropped over our way and wires us she wants to have a chat with you. Going quietly, are you? That's sensible. Now, before we go on to the station here's a note I was asked to hand you. You may read it here at the window. It's from Patrolman Wells."

The man from the West unfolded the little piece of paper handed him. His hand was steady when he began to read, but it trembled a little by the time he had finished. The note was rather short.

"Bob: I was at the appointed place on time. When you struck the match to light your cigar I saw it was the face of the man wanted in Chicago. Somehow I couldn't do it myself, so I went around and got a plain clothes man to do the job. JIMMY."

W.H. Auden

"THE HIDDEN LAW"

W.H. Auden, an Anglo American poet regarded as one of the most important writers of the twentieth century, often embraced moral issues in his poetry. In his 1941 "The Hidden Law," Auden reminds his readers that there is an internal law residing in each of us—some combination of righteousness, conscience, and moral balance—that transcends both the words that appear in law books and the work of practicing lawyers.

The Hidden Law does not deny
Our laws of probability,
But takes the atom and the star
And human beings as they are,
And answers nothing when we lie.

It is the only reason why
No government can codify,
And verbal definitions mar
The Hidden Law.
Its utter patience will not try
To stop us if we want to die:
When we escape It in a car,
When we forget It in a bar,
These are the ways we're punished by
The Hidden Law

Paul Laurence Dunbar

"THE LAWYERS' WAYS"

Early-twentieth-century poet Paul Laurence Dunbar is remembered as the first African American to have gained fame among both white and black readers. A native of Ohio whose father fought in the Civil War, Dunbar was known for his use of dialect to convey the language and experience of African Americans at the turn of the century. In his 1896 "The Lawyers' Ways," Dunbar addresses the moral relativism of the adversarial system—how can we ever know what's true if competing lawyers argue their conflicting truths so persuasively?

I've been list'nin' to them lawyers
In the court house up the street,
An' I've come to the conclusion
That I'm most completely beat.
Fust one feller riz to argy,
An' he boldly waded in
As he dressed the tremblin' pris'ner
In a coat o' deep-dyed sin.

Why, he painted him all over
In a hue o' blackest crime,
An' he smeared his reputation
With the thickest kind o' grime,
Tell I found myself a-wond'rin',
In a misty way and dim,
How the Lord had come to fashion
Sich an awful man as him.

Then the other lawyer started,
An' with brimmin', tearful eyes,
Said his client was a martyr
That was brought to sacrifice.
An' he give to that same pris'ner
Every blessed human grace,
Tell I saw the light o' virtue
Fairly shinin' from his face.

Then I own 'at I was puzzled
How sich things could rightly be;
An' this aggervatin' question
Seems to keep a-puzzlin' me.
So, will some one please inform me,
An' this mystery unroll—
How an angel an' a devil
Can persess the self-same soul?

William Shakespeare

from THE MERCHANT OF VENICE

William Shakespeare's well-known selection of dialogue from Henry VI, Part II, *when Dick the Butcher says, "The first thing we do, let's kill all the lawyers," was not the first or most lasting commentary on the Bard's attitude toward members of the bar.* The Merchant of Venice, *written in 1597, offers a spectacular trial scene that is both an example of clever lawyering and an attack on the rigidity of the legal system. And yet, it also represents a traumatized cry for justice when there is nowhere else to turn. Shylock comes before the law insisting on the pound of Antonio's flesh that he contracted for earlier in the play. Portia, who is disguised as the judge, and has equally hidden conflicting interests, tries to persuade Shylock to be merciful and to instead pursue a spiritual rather than a purely legal course of action. Shylock refuses, to his peril.*

PORTIA: Is your name Shylock?
SHYLOCK: Shylock is my name.
PORTIA: Of a strange nature is the suit you follow;
Yet in such rule that the Venetian law
Cannot impugn you as you do proceed.
You stand within his danger, do you not?
ANTONIO: Ay, so he says.
PORTIA: Do you confess the bond?
ANTONIO: I do.
PORTIA: Then must the Jew be merciful.
SHYLOCK: On what compulsion must I? tell me that.
PORTIA: The quality of mercy is not strain'd,
It droppeth as the gentle rain from heaven
Upon the place beneath: it is twice blest;
It blesseth him that gives and him that takes:

'Tis mightiest in the mightiest: it becomes
The throned monarch better than his crown;
His sceptre shows the force of temporal power,
The attribute to awe and majesty,
Wherein doth sit the dread and fear of kings;
But mercy is above this sceptred sway;
It is enthroned in the hearts of kings,
It is an attribute to God himself;
And earthly power doth then show likest God's
When mercy seasons justice. Therefore, Jew,
Though justice be thy plea, consider this,
That, in the course of justice, none of us
Should see salvation: we do pray for mercy;
And that same prayer doth teach us all to render
The deeds of mercy. I have spoke thus much
To mitigate the justice of thy plea;
Which if thou follow, this strict court of Venice
Must needs give sentence 'gainst the merchant there.
SHYLOCK: My deeds upon my head! I crave the law,
The penalty and forfeit of my bond.
PORTIA: Is he not able to discharge the money?
BASSANIO: Yes, here I tender it for him in the court;
Yea, twice the sum: if that will not suffice,
I will be bound to pay it ten times o'er,
On forfeit of my hands, my head, my heart:
If this will not suffice, it must appear
That malice bears down truth. And I beseech you,
Wrest once the law to your authority:
To do a great right, do a little wrong,
And curb this cruel devil of his will.
PORTIA: It must not be; there is no power in Venice
Can alter a decree established:
'Twill be recorded for a precedent,
And many an error by the same example
Will rush into the state: it cannot be.
SHYLOCK: A Daniel come to judgment! yea, a Daniel!

O wise young judge, how I do honour thee!

PORTIA: I pray you, let me look upon the bond.

SHYLOCK: Here 'tis, most reverend doctor, here it is.

PORTIA: Shylock, there's thrice thy money offer'd thee.

SHYLOCK: An oath, an oath, I have an oath in heaven:
Shall I lay perjury upon my soul?
No, not for Venice.

PORTIA: Why, this bond is forfeit;
And lawfully by this the Jew may claim
A pound of flesh, to be by him cut off
Nearest the merchant's heart. Be merciful:
Take thrice thy money; bid me tear the bond.

SHYLOCK: When it is paid according to the tenor.
It doth appear you are a worthy judge;
You know the law, your exposition
Hath been most sound: I charge you by the law,
Whereof you are a well-deserving pillar,
Proceed to judgment: by my soul I swear
There is no power in the tongue of man
To alter me: I stay here on my bond.

ANTONIO: Most heartily I do beseech the court
To give the judgment.

PORTIA: Why then, thus it is:
You must prepare your bosom for his knife.

SHYLOCK: O noble judge! O excellent young man!

PORTIA: For the intent and purpose of the law
Hath full relation to the penalty,
Which here appeareth due upon the bond.

SHYLOCK: 'Tis very true: O wise and upright judge!
How much more elder art thou than thy looks!

PORTIA: Therefore lay bare your bosom.

SHYLOCK: Ay, his breast:
So says the bond: doth it not, noble judge?
'Nearest his heart:' those are the very words.

PORTIA: It is so. Are there balance here to weigh
The flesh?

SHYLOCK: I have them ready.

PORTIA: Have by some surgeon, Shylock, on your charge,
To stop his wounds, lest he do bleed to death.

SHYLOCK: Is it so nominated in the bond?

PORTIA: It is not so express'd: but what of that?
'Twere good you do so much for charity.

SHYLOCK: I cannot find it; 'tis not in the bond.

* * *

PORTIA: A pound of that same merchant's flesh is thine:
The court awards it, and the law doth give it.

SHYLOCK: Most rightful judge!

PORTIA: And you must cut this flesh from off his breast:
The law allows it, and the court awards it.

SHYLOCK: Most learned judge! A sentence! Come, prepare!

PORTIA: Tarry a little; there is something else.
This bond doth give thee here no jot of blood;
The words expressly are 'a pound of flesh:'
Take then thy bond, take thou thy pound of flesh;
But, in the cutting it, if thou dost shed
One drop of Christian blood, thy lands and goods
Are, by the laws of Venice, confiscate
Unto the state of Venice.

GRATIANO: O upright judge! Mark, Jew: O learned judge!

SHYLOCK: Is that the law?

PORTIA: Thyself shalt see the act:
For, as thou urgest justice, be assured
Thou shalt have justice, more than thou desirest.

GRATIANO: O learned judge! Mark, Jew: a learned judge!

SHYLOCK: I take this offer, then; pay the bond thrice
And let the Christian go.

BASSANIO: Here is the money.

PORTIA: Soft!
The Jew shall have all justice; soft! no haste:
He shall have nothing but the penalty.

GRATIANO: O Jew! an upright judge, a learned judge!

PORTIA: Therefore prepare thee to cut off the flesh.

Shed thou no blood, nor cut thou less nor more
But just a pound of flesh: if thou cut'st more
Or less than a just pound, be it but so much
As makes it light or heavy in the substance,
Or the division of the twentieth part
Of one poor scruple, nay, if the scale do turn
But in the estimation of a hair,
Thou diest and all thy goods are confiscate.
GRATIANO: A second Daniel, a Daniel, Jew!
Now, infidel, I have you on the hip.
PORTIA: Why doth the Jew pause? take thy forfeiture.
SHYLOCK: Give me my principal, and let me go.
BASSANIO: I have it ready for thee; here it is.
PORTIA: He hath refused it in the open court:
He shall have merely justice and his bond.
GRATIANO: A Daniel, still say I, a second Daniel!
I thank thee, Jew, for teaching me that word.
SHYLOCK: Shall I not have barely my principal?
PORTIA: Thou shalt have nothing but the forfeiture,
To be so taken at thy peril, Jew.
SHYLOCK: Why, then the devil give him good of it!
I'll stay no longer question.
PORTIA: Tarry, Jew:
The law hath yet another hold on you.
It is enacted in the laws of Venice,
If it be proved against an alien
That by direct or indirect attempts
He seek the life of any citizen,
The party 'gainst the which he doth contrive
Shall seize one half his goods; the other half
Comes to the privy coffer of the state;
And the offender's life lies in the mercy
Of the duke only, 'gainst all other voice.
In which predicament, I say, thou stand'st;
For it appears, by manifest proceeding,
That indirectly and directly too

Thou hast contrived against the very life
Of the defendant; and thou hast incurr'd
The danger formerly by me rehearsed.
Down therefore and beg mercy of the duke.
GRATIANO: Beg that thou mayst have leave to hang thyself:
And yet, thy wealth being forfeit to the state,
Thou hast not left the value of a cord;
Therefore thou must be hang'd at the state's charge.
DUKE: That thou shalt see the difference of our spirits,
I pardon thee thy life before thou ask it:
For half thy wealth, it is Antonio's;
The other half comes to the general state,
Which humbleness may drive unto a fine.
PORTIA: Ay, for the state, not for Antonio.
SHYLOCK: Nay, take my life and all; pardon not that:
You take my house when you do take the prop
That doth sustain my house; you take my life
When you do take the means whereby I live.
PORTIA: What mercy can you render him, Antonio?
GRATIANO: A halter gratis; nothing else, for God's sake.
ANTONIO: So please my lord the duke and all the court
To quit the fine for one half of his goods,
I am content; so he will let me have
The other half in use, to render it,
Upon his death, unto the gentleman
That lately stole his daughter:
Two things provided more, that, for this favour,
He presently become a Christian;
The other, that he do record a gift,
Here in the court, of all he dies possess'd,
Unto his son Lorenzo and his daughter.
DUKE: He shall do this, or else I do recant
The pardon that I late pronounced here.
PORTIA: Art thou contented, Jew? what dost thou say?
SHYLOCK: I am content.

Aaron Sorkin

from A FEW GOOD MEN

Aaron Sorkin, an American playwright, screenwriter, and television dramatist is known for writing clever and densely packed dialogue in works such as A Few Good Men, The American President, *and the Emmy Award–winning* West Wing. *He is also responsible for crafting one of the most exhilarating trial scenes in literature. In this scene from the film version of* A Few Good Men *(1992), naval lawyer Lieutenant Kaffee cross-examines the generally unflappable Colonel Jessep and manages to both trap and entice him to confess, in open court, that he committed a crime.*

ROSS: Colonel, do you solemnly swear that the testimony you will give in this General Court-Martial will be the truth, the whole truth, and nothing but the truth so help you God?

JESSEP: Yes I do.

ROSS: Would you state your name, rank, and current billet for the record please, sir?

JESSEP: Colonel Nathan R. Jessep, commanding officer, Marine Ground Forces, Guantánamo Bay, Cuba.

ROSS: Thank you, sir, would you have a seat, please.

KAFFEE: Yes sir. Colonel, at the time of this meeting, you gave Lieutenant Kendrick an order, is that right?

JESSEP: I told Kendrick to tell his men that Santiago wasn't to be touched.

KAFFEE: And did you give an order to Captain Markinson as well?

JESSEP: I ordered Markinson to have Santiago transferred off the base immediately.

KAFFEE: Why?

JESSEP: I felt that his life might be in danger once word of the letter got out.

KAFFEE: Grave danger?

JESSEP: Is there another kind?

Kaffee holds up a document from his table.

KAFFEE: We have the transfer order that you and Markinson co-signed, ordering that Santiago be lifted on a flight leaving Guantánamo at six the next morning. Was that the first flight off the base?

JESSEP: The six a.m. flight was the first flight off the base.

KAFFEE: Colonel, you flew up to Washington early this morning, is that right?

JESSEP: Yes.

KAFFEE: I notice you're wearing your Class A appearance in dress uniform for court today.

JESSEP: (*continuing*) As are you, Lieutenant.

KAFFEE: Did you wear that uniform on the plane?

ROSS: Please the Court, is this dialogue relevant to anything in particular?

KAFFEE: The defense didn't have an opportunity to depose this witness, your honor. I'd ask the Court for a little latitude.

RANDOLPH: A very little latitude.

KAFFEE: Colonel?

JESSEP: I wore fatigues on the plane.

KAFFEE: And you brought your dress uniform with you.

JESSEP: Yes.

KAFFEE: And a toothbrush? A shaving kit? Change of underwear?

ROSS: Your honor.

KAFFEE: (*to Ross*) Is the colonel's underwear a matter of national security?

RANDOLPH: Gentlemen. (*to Kaffee*) You better get somewhere fast with this, Lieutenant.

KAFFEE: Yes sir. Colonel?

JESSEP: I brought a change of clothes and some personal items.

KAFFEE: Thank you.

Kaffee gets a document from his table.

KAFFEE: (*continuing*) After Dawson and Downey's arrest on the night of the sixth, Santiago's barracks room was sealed off and its contents inventoried. (*reading*) Pairs of camouflage pants, six camouflage shirts, two pairs of boots, one pair of brown shoes, one pair of tennis shoes, eight khaki T-shirts, two belts, one sweater.

ROSS: Please the Court, is there a question anywhere in our future?

RANDOLPH: Lieutenant Kaffee, I have to—

KAFFEE: I'm wondering why Santiago wasn't packed.

KAFFEE: (*continuing*) I'll tell you what, we'll get back to that one in a minute.

KAFFEE: (*continuing*) This is a record of all telephone calls made from your base in the past twenty-four hours. After being subpoenaed to Washington, you made three calls.

KAFFEE: (*continuing*) I've highlighted those calls in yellow. Do you recognize those numbers?

JESSEP: I called Colonel Fitzhughes in Quantico, Virginia. I wanted to let him know I'd be in town. The second call was to set up a meeting with Congressman Raymond of the House Armed Services Committee, and the third call was to my sister Elizabeth.

KAFFEE: Why did you make that call, sir?

JESSEP: I thought she might like to have dinner tonight.

ROSS: Judge—

RANDOLPH: I'm gonna put a stop to this now.

KAFFEE: Your honor, these are the telephone records from Gitmo for August sixth. And these are fourteen letters that Santiago wrote in nine months requesting, in fact begging, for a transfer. (*to Jessep*) Upon hearing the news that he was finally getting his transfer, Santiago was so excited, that do you know how many people he called? Zero. Nobody. Not one call to his parents saying he was coming home. Not one call to a friend saying can you pick me up at the airport. He was asleep in his bed at midnight, and according to you he was getting on a plane in six hours, yet everything he owned was hanging neatly in his closet and folded neatly in his footlocker. You were leaving for one day and you packed a bag and made three phone calls. Santiago was leaving for the rest of his life, and he hadn't called a soul and he hadn't packed a thing. Can you explain that? The fact is there was no transfer order. Santiago wasn't going anywhere, isn't that right, Colonel.

ROSS: Object. Your Honor, it's obvious that Lieutenant Kaffee's intention this morning is to smear a high-ranking marine officer in the desperate hope that the mere appearance of impropriety will win him points with the jury.

ROSS: (*continuing*) It's my recommendation, sir, that Lieutenant Kaffee receive an official reprimand from the bench, and that the witness be excused with the Court's deepest apologies.

RANDOLPH: (*pause*) Overruled.

ROSS: Your honor—

RANDOLPH: The objection's noted.

KAFFEE: (*beat*) Colonel?

Jessep's smiling . . . and now he can't help but let out a short laugh.

KAFFEE: (*continuing*) Is this funny, sir?

JESSEP: No. It's not. It's tragic.

KAFFEE: Do you have an answer?

JESSEP: Absolutely. My answer is I don't have the first damn clue. Maybe he was an early morning riser and he liked to pack in the HQ. And maybe he didn't have any friends. I'm an educated man, but I'm afraid I can't speak intelligently about the travel habits of William Santiago. What I do know is that he was set to leave the base at 0600. Now are these really the questions I was called here to answer? Phone calls and footlockers? Please tell me you've got something more, Lieutenant. Please tell me there's an ace up your sleeve. These two marines are on trial for their lives. Please tell me their lawyer hasn't pinned their hopes to a phone bill. (*beat*) Do you have any other questions for me, counselor?

The courtroom is silenced.

RANDOLPH: Lieutenant Kaffee?

Kaffee says nothing. He glances over to Airmen O'Malley and Perez.

RANDOLPH: (*continuing*) Lieutenant, do you have anything further for this witness?

Kaffee doesn't respond. Jessep gets up to leave.

JESSEP: (*standing*) Thanks, Danny. I love Washington.

And Jessep starts to leave, but he's stopped by

KAFFEE: Excuse me, I didn't dismiss you.

Jessep turns around.

JESSEP: I beg your pardon.

KAFFEE: I'm not through with my examination. Sit down.

JESSEP: Colonel.

KAFFEE: What's that?

JESSEP: (*to Randolph*) I'd appreciate it if he addressed me as "Colonal" or "Sir." I believe I've earned it.

RANDOLPH: Defense counsel will address the witness as "Colonel" or "Sir."

JESSEP: (*to Randolph*) I don't know what the hell kind of an outfit you're running here.

RANDOLPH: And the witness will address this Court as "Judge" or "Your Honor." I'm quite certain I've earned it. Take your seat, Colonel. . . .

JESSEP: *(continuing)* What would you like to discuss now! My favorite color?

KAFFEE: Colonel, the six a.m. flight was the first one off the base?

JESSEP: Yes.

KAFFEE: There wasn't a flight that left seven hours earlier and landed at Andrews Air Force Base at two a.m.?

RANDOLPH: Lieutenant, I think we've covered this, haven't we?

KAFFEE: Your Honor, these are the Tower Chief's Logs for both Guantánamo Bay and Andrews Air Force Base. The Guantánamo log lists no flight that left at eleven p.m., and the Andrews log lists no flight that landed at two a.m. I'd like to admit them as Defense Exhibits "A" and "B."

RANDOLPH: I don't understand. You're admitting evidence of a flight that never existed?

KAFFEE: We believe it did, sir. *(glancing at the paper, then motioning to the airmen)* Defense'll be calling Airman Cecil O'Malley and Airman Anthony Perez. They were working the ground crew at Andrews at two a.m. on the seventh.

ROSS: Your Honor, these men weren't on the list. Rebuttal witnesses, Your Honor, called specifically to refute testimony offered under direct examination.

RANDOLPH: I'll allow the witnesses.

JESSEP: This is ridiculous.

KAFFEE: Colonel, a moment ago—

JESSEP: Check the Tower Logs, for Christ's sake.

KAFFEE: We'll get to the airmen in just a minute, sir. A moment ago you said that you ordered Kendrick to order his men not to touch Santiago.

JESSEP: That's right.

KAFFEE: And Kendrick was clear on what you wanted?

JESSEP: Crystal.

KAFFEE: Any chance Kendrick ignored the order?

JESSEP: Ignored the order?

KAFFEE: Any chance he just forgot about it?

JESSEP: No.

KAFFEE: Any chance Kendrick left your office and said, "The old man's wrong"?

JESSEP: No.

KAFFEE: When Kendrick spoke to the platoon and ordered them not to touch Santiago, any chance they ignored him?

JESSEP: Have you ever spent time in an infantry unit, son?

KAFFEE: No sir.

JESSEP: Ever served in a forward area?

KAFFEE: No sir.

JESSEP: Ever put your life in another man's hands, ask him to put his life in yours?

KAFFEE: No sir.

JESSEP: We follow orders, son. We follow orders or people die. It's that simple. Are we clear?

KAFFEE: Yes sir.

JESSEP: Are we clear?

KAFFEE: Crystal.

KAFFEE: (*continuing; beat*) Colonel, I have just one more question before I call Airman O'Malley and Airman Perez: If you gave an order that Santiago wasn't to be touched, and your orders are always followed, then why would he be in danger, why would it be necessary to transfer him off the base?

And Jessep has no answer. He sits there, and for the first time, seems to be lost.

JESSEP: Private Santiago was a substandard marine. He was being transferred off the base because—

KAFFEE: But that's not what you said. You said he was being transferred because he was in grave danger.

JESSEP: (*pause*) Yes. That's correct, but—

KAFFEE: You said, "He was in danger." I said, "Grave danger." You said—

JESSEP: Yes, I recall what—

KAFFEE: I can have the Court Reporter read back your—

JESSEP: I know what I said. I don't need it read back to me like I'm a damn—

KAFFEE: Then why the two orders? (*beat*) Colonel? (*beat*) Why did you—

JESSEP: Sometimes men take matters into their own hands.

KAFFEE: No sir. You made it clear just a moment ago that your men never take matters into their own hands. Your men follow orders or people die. So Santiago shouldn't have been in any danger at all, should he have, Colonel?

JESSEP: You little bastard.

ROSS: Your Honor, I have to ask for a recess to—

KAFFEE: I'd like an answer to the question, Judge.

RANDOLPH: The Court'll wait for an answer.

KAFFEE: If Kendrick told his men that Santiago wasn't to be touched, then why did he have to be transferred?

KAFFEE: (*continuing*) Colonel?

KAFFEE: (*continuing*) Kendrick ordered the code red, didn't he? Because that's what you told Kendrick to do.

ROSS: Object!

RANDOLPH: Counsel.

KAFFEE: And when it went bad, you cut these guys loose.

ROSS: Your Honor—

RANDOLPH: That'll be all, counsel.

KAFFEE: You had Markinson sign a phony transfer order—

ROSS: Judge—

KAFFEE: You doctored the log books.

ROSS: Damn it Kaffee!

KAFFEE: I'll ask for the fourth time. You ordered—

JESSEP: You want answers?

KAFFEE: I think I'm entitled to them.

JESSEP: You want answers?!

KAFFEE: I want the truth.

JESSEP: You can't handle the truth!

JESSEP: (*continuing*) Son, we live in a world that has walls. And those walls have to be guarded by men with guns. Who's gonna do it? You? You, Lieutenant Weinberg? I have a greater responsibility than you can possibly fathom. You weep for Santiago and you curse the marines. You have that luxury. You have the luxury of not knowing what I know: that Santiago's death, while tragic, probably saved lives. And my existence, while grotesque and incomprehensible to you, saves lives. (*beat*) You don't want the truth. Because deep down, in places you don't talk about at parties, you want me on that wall. You need me there. (*boasting*) We use words like honor, code, loyalty . . . we use these words as the backbone to a life spent defending something. You use 'em as a punch line. (*beat*) I have neither the time nor the inclination to explain myself to a man who rises and sleeps under the blanket of the very freedom I provide, then questions the manner in which I provide it. I'd prefer you just said thank you and went on your way. Otherwise, I suggest you pick up a weapon and stand a post. Either way, I don't give a damn what you think you're entitled to.

KAFFEE: (*quietly*) Did you order the code red?

JESSEP: (*beat*) I did the job you sent me to do.

KAFFEE: Did you order the code red?

JESSEP: (*pause*) You're goddamn right I did.

Silence. From everyone. Randolph, Ross, the MPs, they're all frozen. Jo and Sam are likewise. Jessep seems strangely, quietly relieved. Kaffee simply takes control of the room now.

KAFFEE: Please the court, I suggest the jury be dismissed so that we can move to an immediate Article 39A Session. The witness has rights.

Silence. Randolph looks to Ross.

RANDOLPH: Lieutenant Ross?

KAFFEE: (*as a friend*) Jack.

Ross looks at Kaffee, then Jessep, then nods his head "yes" to Randolph.

RANDOLPH: The Sergeant at Arms will take the jury to an anteroom where you'll wait until further instruction.

JESSEP: What the hell's going on?

JESSEP: (*continuing; to Captain*) Captain, what the hell's going on? I did my job. I'd do it again. Now I'm getting on a plane and going back to my base.

RANDOLPH: MPs, guard the prisoner.

ROSS: Guard the prisoner.

JESSEP: What the hell—

ROSS: Colonel Jessep, you have the right to remain silent. Any statement you do make can be used against you in a trial by court-martial or other judicial or administrative proceeding. You have the right . . .

Ross continues reading Jessep his rights, over

JESSEP: I'm being charged with a crime? I'm—that's what this is (*to Ross*) Marine! (*Ross keeps going*) Marine! (*Ross is doing his job*) I'm being charged with a crime? I'm—that's what's happening? This—I'm—this is funny, you know that, this is—

And Jessep lunges at Kaffee, and Kaffee would be dead but for the three MPs who leap in to restrain Jessep. Sam and Jo have come to their feet and stand behind Kaffee.

JESSEP: (*continuing; to Kaffee*) I'm gonna tear your eyes right outta your head and piss in your dead skull. You fucked with the wrong marine.

ROSS: Colonel Jessep, do you understand those rights as I have just read them to you?

JESSEP: I saved lives. That boy was there was weak link. I saved lives, you hear me?

JESSEP: (*continuing*) You fuckin' people. (*beat*) You have no idea how to defend a nation.

JESSEP: (*continuing; to Kaffee*) All you did was weaken a country today, Kaffee. That's all you did. You put people in danger. Sweet dreams, son.

KAFFEE: Don't call me son. (*beat*) I'm a lawyer, and an officer of the United States Navy. And you're under arrest you son of a bitch.

PART VIII

Layman's Law

Justice can sometimes be achieved without judges and lawyers. It can take place completely outside the presence of juries. In such circumstances, court-houses are far off in the background. Sometimes all it takes is the simple wisdom of ordinary citizens—those without law degrees, black robes, and silver tongues—who have a better sense of how to make things right than a stadium full of Supreme Court justices. The law would benefit greatly from a women's perspective, whether in examining a crime scene, or in teaching a child not to snatch a purse. Clients understand what their lawyers do not: that the true value of a case is measured not just in money but also in human dignity. And sometimes all the legal wisdom in the world will not resolve conflict without the common courtesy of a simple apology.

Susan Glaspell

from "A JURY OF HER PEERS"

American dramatist, novelist, and short-story writer Susan Glaspell's most lasting work is "A Jury of Her Peers," published in 1929. Like Ibsen's A Doll's House, *Glaspell's short story offers a feminist perspective and critique of the legal system. In the story, a male sheriff and county attorney investigate a crime scene and mockingly dismiss the women who are there waiting for them to finish. Meanwhile, the male "professionals" miss all the important clues, while the women see right through the crime, comprehend certain sensitivities, and, in the process, thwart the law and do the right thing.*

"I'm glad you came with me," Mrs. Peters said nervously, as the two women were about to follow the men in through the kitchen door.

Even after she had her foot on the door-step, her hand on the knob, Martha Hale had a moment of feeling she could not cross that threshold. And the reason it seemed she couldn't cross it now was simply because she hadn't crossed it before. Time and time again it had been in her mind, "I ought to go over and see Minnie Foster"—she still thought of her as Minnie Foster, though for twenty years she had been Mrs. Wright. And then there was always something to do and Minnie Foster would go from her mind. But *now* she could come.

The men went over to the stove. The women stood close together by the door. Young Henderson, the county attorney, turned around and said, "Come up to the fire, ladies."

Mrs. Peters took a step forward, then stopped. "I'm not—cold," she said.

And so the two women stood by the door, at first not even so much as looking around the kitchen.

The men talked for a minute about what a good thing it was the sheriff had sent his deputy out that morning to make a fire for them, and then Sheriff Peters stepped back from the stove, unbuttoned his outer coat, and leaned his

hands on the kitchen table in a way that seemed to mark the beginning of official business. "Now, Mr. Hale," he said in a sort of semi-official voice, "before we move things about, you tell Mr. Henderson just what it was you saw
when you came here yesterday morning."

The county attorney was looking around the kitchen.

"By the way," he said, "has anything been moved?" He turned to the sheriff. "Are things just as you left them yesterday?"

Peters looked from cupboard to sink; from that to a small worn rocker a little to one side of the kitchen table.

"It's just the same."

"Somebody should have been left here yesterday," said the county attorney.

"Oh—yesterday," returned the sheriff, with a little gesture as of yesterday
having been more than he could bear to think of. "When I had to send Frank
to Morris Center for that man who went crazy—let me tell you. I had my
hands full yesterday. I knew you could get back from Omaha by today,
George, and as long as I went over everything here myself—"

"Well, Mr. Hale," said the county attorney, in a way of letting what was
past and gone go, "tell just what happened when you came here yesterday
morning."

Mrs. Hale, still leaning against the door, had that sinking feeling of the
mother whose child is about to speak a piece. Lewis often wandered along and
got things mixed up in a story. She hoped he would tell this straight and plain,
and not say unnecessary things that would just make things harder for Minnie
Foster. He didn't begin at once, and she noticed that he looked queer—as if
standing in that kitchen and having to tell what he had seen there yesterday
morning made him almost sick.

* * *

"I didn't see or hear anything. I knocked at the door. And still it was all
quiet inside. I knew they must be up—it was past eight o'clock. So I knocked
again, louder, and I thought I heard somebody say, 'Come in.' I wasn't sure—
I'm not sure yet. But I opened the door—this door," jerking a hand toward the
door by which the two women stood, "and there, in that rocker"—pointing to
it—"sat Mrs. Wright."

Everyone in the kitchen looked at the rocker. It came into Mrs. Hale's mind
that that rocker didn't look in the least like Minnie Foster—the Minnie Foster

of twenty years before. It was a dingy red, with wooden rungs up the back, and the middle rung was gone, and the chair sagged to one side.

"How did she—look?" the county attorney was inquiring.

"Well," said Hale, "she looked—queer."

"How do you mean—queer?"

As he asked it he took out a note-book and pencil. Mrs. Hale did not like the sight of that pencil. She kept her eye fixed on her husband, as if to keep him from saying unnecessary things that would go into that note-book and make trouble.

Hale did speak guardedly, as if the pencil had affected him too.

"Well, as if she didn't know what she was going to do next. And kind of—done up."

"How did she seem to feel about your coming?"

"Why, I don't think she minded—one way or other. She didn't pay much attention. I said, 'Ho' do, Mrs. Wright? It's cold, ain't it?' And she said. 'Is it?'—and went on pleatin' at her apron.

"Well, I was surprised. She didn't ask me to come up to the stove, or to sit down, but just set there, not even lookin' at me. And so I said: 'I want to see John.'

"And then she—laughed. I guess you would call it a laugh.

"I thought of Harry and the team outside, so I said, a little sharp, 'Can I see John?' 'No,' says she—kind of dull like. 'Ain't he home?' says I. Then she looked at me. 'Yes,' says she, 'he's home.' 'Then why can't I see him?' I asked her, out of patience with her now. 'Cause he's dead,' says she, just as quiet and dull—and fell to pleatin' her apron. 'Dead?' says I, like you do when you can't take in what you've heard.

"She just nodded her head, not getting a bit excited, but rockin' back and forth.

"'Why—where is he?' says I, not knowing *what* to say.

"She just pointed upstairs—like this"—pointing to the room above.

"I got up, with the idea of going up there myself. By this time I—didn't know what to do. I walked from there to here; then I says: 'Why, what did he die of?'

"'He died of a rope around his neck,' says she; and just went on pleatin' at her apron."

Hale stopped speaking, and stood staring at the rocker, as if he were still seeing the woman who had sat there the morning before. Nobody spoke; it was as if every one were seeing the woman who had sat there the morning before.

"And what did you do then?" the county attorney at last broke the silence.

"I went out and called Harry. I thought I might—need help. I got Harry in, and we went upstairs." His voice fell almost to a whisper. "There he was— lying over the—"

"I think I'd rather have you go into that upstairs," the county attorney interrupted, "where you can point it all out. Just go on now with the rest of the story."

"Well, my first thought was to get that rope off. It looked—"

He stopped, his face twitching.

"But Harry, he went up to him, and he said, 'No, he's dead all right, and we'd better not touch anything.' So we went downstairs.

"She was still sitting that same way. 'Has anybody been notified?' I asked. 'No,' says she, unconcerned.

"'Who did this, Mrs. Wright?' said Harry. He said it businesslike, and she stopped pleatin' at her apron. 'I don't know,' she says. 'You don't *know*?' says Harry. 'Weren't you sleepin' in the bed with him?' 'Yes,' says she, 'but I was on the inside.' 'Somebody slipped a rope round his neck and strangled him, and you didn't wake up?' says Harry. 'I didn't wake up,' she said after him.

"We may have looked as if we didn't see how that could be, for after a minute she said, 'I sleep sound.'"

* * *

"You're convinced there was nothing important here?" he asked the sheriff. "Nothing that would—point to any motive?"

The sheriff too looked all around, as if to re-convince himself.

"Nothing here but kitchen things," he said, with a little laugh for the insignificance of kitchen things.

The county attorney was looking at the cupboard—a peculiar, ungainly structure, half closet and half cupboard, the upper part of it being built in the wall, and the lower part just the old-fashioned kitchen cupboard. As if its queerness attracted him, he got a chair and opened the upper part and looked in. After a moment he drew his hand away sticky.

"Here's a nice mess," he said resentfully.

The two women had drawn nearer, and now the sheriff's wife spoke.

"Oh—her fruit," she said, looking to Mrs. Hale for sympathetic understanding.

She turned back to the county attorney and explained: "She worried about that when it turned so cold last night. She said the fire would go out and her jars might burst."

Mrs. Peters' husband broke into a laugh.

"Well, can you beat the women! Held for murder, and worrying about her preserves!"

The young attorney set his lips.

"I guess before we're through with her she may have something more serious than preserves to worry about."

"Oh, well," said Mrs. Hale's husband, with good-natured superiority, "women are used to worrying over trifles."

The two women moved a little closer together. Neither of them spoke. The county attorney seemed suddenly to remember his manners—and think of his future.

"And yet," said he, with the gallantry of a young politician, "for all their worries, what would we do without the ladies?"

The women did not speak, did not unbend. He went to the sink and began washing his hands. He turned to wipe them on the roller towel—whirled it for a cleaner place.

"Dirty towels! Not much of a housekeeper, would you say, ladies?"

He kicked his foot against some dirty pans under the sink.

"There's a great deal of work to be done on a farm," said Mrs. Hale stiffly.

"To be sure. And yet"—with a little bow to her—"I know there are some Dickson County farm-houses that do not have such roller towels." He gave it a pull to expose its full length again.

"Those towels get dirty awful quick. Men's hands aren't always as clean as they might be."

"Ah, loyal to your sex, I see," he laughed. He stopped and gave her a keen look. "But you and Mrs. Wright were neighbors. I suppose you were friends, too."

Martha Hale shook her head.

"I've seen little enough of her of late years. I've not been in this house—it's more than a year."

"And why was that? You didn't like her?"

"I liked her well enough," she replied with spirit. "Farmers' wives have their hands full, Mr. Henderson. And then—" She looked around the kitchen.

"Yes?" he encouraged.

"It never seemed a very cheerful place," said she, more to herself than to him.

"No," he agreed; "I don't think anyone would call it cheerful. I shouldn't say she had the home-making instinct."

"Well, I don't know as Wright had, either," she muttered.

"You mean they didn't get on very well?" he was quick to ask.

"No; I don't mean anything," she answered, with decision. As she turned a little away from him, she added: "But I don't think a place would be any the cheerfuller for John Wright's bein' in it."

* * *

"Yes—Mrs. Peters," he said, his glance resting on the woman who was not Mrs. Peters, the big farmer woman who stood behind the sheriff's wife. "Of course Mrs. Peters is one of us," he said, in a manner of entrusting responsibility. "And keep your eye out, Mrs. Peters, for anything that might be of use. No telling; you women might come upon a clue to the motive—and that's the thing we need."

Mr. Hale rubbed his face after the fashion of a showman getting ready for a pleasantry.

"But would the women know a clue if they did come upon it?" he said; and, having delivered himself of this, he followed the others through the stair door.

The women stood motionless and silent, listening to the footsteps, first upon the stairs, then in the room above them.

* * *

"Do you think she—did it?'

A frightened look blurred the other thing in Mrs. Peters' eyes.

"Oh, I don't know," she said, in a voice that seemed to shrink away from the subject.

"Well, I don't think she did," affirmed Mrs. Hale stoutly. "Asking for an apron, and her little shawl. Worryin' about her fruit."

"Mr. Peters says—." Footsteps were heard in the room above; she stopped, looked up, then went on in a lowered voice: "Mr. Peters says—it looks bad for her. Mr. Henderson is awful sarcastic in a speech, and he's going to make fun of her saying she didn't—wake up."

For a moment Mrs. Hale had no answer. Then, "Well, I guess John Wright didn't wake up—when they was slippin' that rope under his neck," she muttered.

"No, it's *strange*," breathed Mrs. Peters. "They think it was such a—funny way to kill a man."

She began to laugh; at sound of the laugh, abruptly stopped.

"That's just what Mr. Hale said," said Mrs. Hale, in a resolutely natural voice. "There was a gun in the house. He says that's what he can't understand."

"Mr. Henderson said, coming out, that what was needed for the case was a motive. Something to show anger—or sudden feeling."

'Well, I don't see any signs of anger around here," said Mrs. Hale, "I don't—" She stopped. It was as if her mind tripped on something. Her eye was caught by a dish-towel in the middle of the kitchen table. Slowly she moved toward the table. One half of it was wiped clean, the other half messy. Her eyes made a slow, almost unwilling turn to the bucket of sugar and the half empty bag beside it. Things begun—and not finished.

After a moment she stepped back, and said, in that manner of releasing herself:

"Wonder how they're finding things upstairs? I hope she had it a little more red up there. You know,"—she paused, and feeling gathered—"it seems kind of *sneaking:* locking her up in town and coming out here to get her own house to turn against her!"

"But, Mrs. Hale," said the sheriff's wife, "the law is the law."

"I s'pose 'tis," answered Mrs. Hale shortly.

She turned to the stove, saying something about that fire not being much to brag of. She worked with it a minute, and when she straightened up she said aggressively:

"The law is the law—and a bad stove is a bad stove. How'd you like to cook on this?"—pointing with the poker to the broken lining. She opened the oven door and started to express her opinion of the oven; but she was swept into her own thoughts, thinking of what it would mean, year after year, to have that stove to wrestle with. The thought of Minnie Foster trying to bake in that oven—and the thought of her never going over to see Minnie Foster—.

She was startled by hearing Mrs. Peters say: "A person gets discouraged—and loses heart."

The sheriff's wife had looked from the stove to the sink—to the pail of water which had been carried in from outside. The two women stood there silent, above them the footsteps of the men who were looking for evidence against the woman who had worked in that kitchen. That look of seeing into things, of seeing through a thing to something else, was in the eyes of the sheriff's wife now. . . .

* * *

They returned to an inspection of the block for the quilt. Mrs. Hale was looking at the fine, even sewing, and preoccupied with thoughts of the woman who had done that sewing, when she heard the sheriff's wife say, in a queer tone:

"Why, look at this one."

She turned to take the block held out to her.

"The sewing," said Mrs. Peters, in a troubled way. "All the rest of them have been so nice and even—but—this one. Why, it looks as if she didn't know what she was about!"

Their eyes met—something flashed to life, passed between them; then, as if with an effort, they seemed to pull away from each other. A moment Mrs. Hale sat there, her hands folded over that sewing which was so unlike all the rest of the sewing. Then she had pulled a knot and drawn the threads.

"Oh, what are you doing, Mrs. Hale?" asked the sheriff's wife, startled.

"Just pulling out a stitch or two that's not sewed very good," said Mrs. Hale mildly.

"I don't think we ought to touch things," Mrs. Peters said, a little helplessly.

"I'll just finish up this end," answered Mrs. Hale, still in that mild, matter-of-fact fashion.

She threaded a needle and started to replace bad sewing with good. For a little while she sewed in silence. Then, in that thin, timid voice, she heard:

"Mrs. Hale!"

"Yes, Mrs. Peters?"

"What do you suppose she was so—nervous about?"

* * *

One piece of the crazy sewing remained unripped. Mrs. Peter's back turned, Martha Hale now scrutinized that piece, compared it with the dainty, accurate sewing of the other blocks. The difference was startling. Holding this block made her feel queer, as if the distracted thoughts of the woman who had perhaps turned to it to try and quiet herself were communicating themselves to her.

Mrs. Peters' voice roused her.

"Here's a bird-cage," she said. "Did she have a bird, Mrs. Hale?"

"Why, I don't know whether she did or not." She turned to look at the cage Mrs. Peters was holding up. "I've not been here in so long." She sighed. "There was a man round last year selling canaries cheap—but I don't know as she took one. Maybe she did. She used to sing real pretty herself."

Mrs. Peters looked around the kitchen.

"Seems kind of funny to think of a bird here." She half laughed—an attempt to put up a barrier. "But she must have had one—or why would she have a cage? I wonder what happened to it."

"I suppose maybe the cat got it," suggested Mrs. Hale, resuming her sewing.

"No; she didn't have a cat. She's got that feeling some people have about cats—being afraid of them. When they brought her to our house yesterday, my cat got in the room, and she was real upset and asked me to take it out."

"My sister Bessie was like that," laughed Mrs. Hale.

The sheriff's wife did not reply. The silence made Mrs. Hale turn round. Mrs. Peters was examining the bird-cage.

"Look at this door," she said slowly. "It's broke. One hinge has been pulled apart."

Mrs. Hale came nearer.

"Looks as if someone must have been—rough with it."

Again their eyes met—startled, questioning, apprehensive. For a moment neither spoke nor stirred. Then Mrs. Hale, turning away, said brusquely:

"If they're going to find any evidence, I wish they'd be about it. I don't like this place."

* * *

"Not having children makes less work," mused Mrs. Hale, after a silence, "but it makes a quiet house—and Wright out to work all day—and no company when he did come in. Did you know John Wright, Mrs. Peters?"

"Not to know him. I've seen him in town. They say he was a good man."

"Yes—good," conceded John Wright's neighbor grimly. "He didn't drink, and kept his word as well as most, I guess, and paid his debts. But he was a hard man, Mrs. Peters. Just to pass the time of day with him—." She stopped, shivered a little. "Like a raw wind that gets to the bone." Her eye fell upon the cage on the table before her, and she added, almost bitterly: "I should think she would've wanted a bird!"

Suddenly she leaned forward, looking intently at the cage. "But what do you s'pose went wrong with it?"

"I don't know," returned Mrs. Peters; "unless it got sick and died."

But after she said it she reached over and swung the broken door. Both women watched it as if somehow held by it.

* * *

They turned to the sewing basket.

"Here's some red," said Mrs. Hale, bringing out a roll of cloth. Underneath that was a box. "Here, maybe her scissors are in here—and her things." She held it up. "What a pretty box! I'll warrant that was something she had a long time ago—when she was a girl."

She held it in her hand a moment; then, with a little sigh, opened it.

Instantly her hand went to her nose.

"Why—!"

Mrs. Peters drew nearer—then turned away.

"There's something wrapped up in this piece of silk," faltered Mrs. Hale.

"This isn't her scissors," said Mrs. Peters, in a shrinking voice.

Her hand not steady, Mrs. Hale raised the piece of silk. "Oh, Mrs. Peters!" she cried. "It's—"

Mrs. Peters bent closer.

"It's the bird," she whispered.

"But, Mrs. Peters!" cried Mrs. Hale. "*Look* at it! Its *neck*—look at its neck! It's all—other side *to*."

She held the box away from her.

The sheriff's wife again bent closer.

"Somebody wrung its neck," said she, in a voice that was slow and deep.

And then again the eyes of the two women met—this time clung together in a look of dawning comprehension, of growing horror. Mrs. Peters looked from the dead bird to the broken door of the cage. Again their eyes met. And just then there was a sound at the outside door. Mrs. Hale slipped the box under the quilt pieces in the basket, and sank into the chair before it. Mrs. Peters stood holding to the table. The county attorney and the sheriff came in from outside.

"Well, ladies," said the county attorney, as one turning from serious things to little pleasantries, "have you decided whether she was going to quilt it or knot it?"

"We think," began the sheriff's wife in a flurried voice, "that she was going to—knot it."

He was too preoccupied to notice the change that came in her voice on that last.

"Well, that's very interesting, I'm sure," he said tolerantly. He caught sight of the bird-cage.

"Has the bird flown?"

"We think the cat got it," said Mrs. Hale in a voice curiously even.

He was walking up and down, as if thinking something out.

"Is there a cat?" he asked absently.

Mrs. Hale shot a look up at the sheriff's wife.

"Well, not *now*," said Mrs. Peters. "They're superstitious, you know; they leave."

She sank into her chair.

The county attorney did not heed her. "No sign at all of anyone having come in from the outside," he said to Peters, in the manner of continuing an interrupted conversation. "Their own rope. Now let's go upstairs again and go over it, piece by piece. It would have to have been someone who knew just the—"

The stair door closed behind them and their voices were lost.

The two women sat motionless, not looking at each other, but as if peering into something and at the same time holding back. When they spoke now it was as if they were afraid of what they were saying, but as if they could not help saying it.

"She liked the bird," said Martha Hale, low and slowly. "She was going to bury it in that pretty box."

"When I was a girl," said Mrs. Peters, under her breath, "my kitten—there was a boy took a hatchet, and before my eyes—before I could get there—" She covered her face an instant. "If they hadn't held me back I would have"— she caught herself, looked upstairs where footsteps were heard, and finished weakly—"hurt him."

Then they sat without speaking or moving.

"I wonder how it would seem," Mrs. Hale at last began, as if feeling her way over strange ground—"never to have had any children around?" Her eyes made a slow sweep of the kitchen, as if seeing what that kitchen had meant through all the years. "No, Wright wouldn't like the bird," she said after that—"a thing that sang. She used to sing. He killed that too." Her voice tightened.

Mrs. Peters moved uneasily.

"Of course we don't know who killed the bird."

"I knew John Wright," was Mrs. Hale's answer.

"It was an awful thing was done in this house that night, Mrs. Hale," said the sheriff's wife. "Killing a man while he slept—slipping a thing round his neck that choked the life out of him."

Mrs. Hale's hand went out to the bird-cage.

"We don't *know* who killed him," whispered Mrs. Peters wildly. "We don't *know.*"

Mrs. Hale had not moved. "If there had been years and years of—nothing, then a bird to sing to you, it would be awful—still—after the bird was still."

It was as if something within her not herself had spoken, and it found in Mrs. Peters something she did not know as herself.

"I know what stillness is," she said, in a queer, monotonous voice. "When we homesteaded in Dakota, and my first baby died—after he was two years old—and me with no other then—"

Mrs. Hale stirred.

"How soon do you suppose they'll be through looking for the evidence?"

"I know what stillness is," repeated Mrs. Peters, in just that same way. Then she too pulled back. "The law has got to punish crime, Mrs. Hale," she said in her tight little way.

"I wish you'd seen Minnie Foster," was the answer, "when she wore a white dress with blue ribbons, and stood up there in the choir and sang."

The picture of that girl, the fact that she had lived neighbor to that girl for twenty years, and had let her die for lack of life, was suddenly more than she could bear.

* * *

"No, Peters," said the county attorney incisively; "it's all perfectly clear, except the reason for doing it. But you know juries when it comes to women. If there was some definite thing—something to show. Something to make a story about. A thing that would connect up with this clumsy way of doing it."

In a covert way Mrs. Hale looked at Mrs. Peters. Mrs. Peters was looking at her. Quickly they looked away from each other. The outer door opened and Mr. Hale came in.

"I've got the team round now," he said. "Pretty cold out there."

"I'm going to stay here awhile by myself," the county attorney suddenly announced. "You can send Frank out for me, can't you?" he asked the sheriff. "I want to go over everything. I'm not satisfied we can't do better."

Again, for one brief moment, the two women's eyes found one another.

The sheriff came up to the table.

"Did you want to see what Mrs. Peters was going to take in?"

The county attorney picked up the apron. He laughed.

"Oh, I guess they're not very dangerous things the ladies have picked out."

Mrs. Hale's hand was on the sewing basket in which the box was concealed. She felt that she ought to take her hand off the basket. She did not seem able to. He picked up one of the quilt blocks which she had piled on to cover the box. Her eyes felt like fire. She had a feeling that if he took up the basket she would snatch it from him.

But he did not take it up. With another little laugh, he turned away, saying:

"No; Mrs. Peters doesn't need supervising. For that matter, a sheriff's wife is married to the law. Ever think of it that way, Mrs. Peters?"

Mrs. Peters was standing beside the table. Mrs. Hale shot a look up at her; but she could not see her face. Mrs. Peters had turned away. When she spoke, her voice was muffled.

"Not—just that way," she said.

"Married to the law!" chuckled Mrs. Peters' husband.

* * *

Hale went to look after the horses. The sheriff followed the county attorney into the other room. Again—for one final moment—the two women were alone in that kitchen.

Martha Hale sprang up, her hands tight together, looking at that other woman, with whom it rested. At first she could not see her eyes, for the sheriff's wife had not turned back since she turned away at that suggestion of being married to the law. But now Mrs. Hale made her turn back. Her eyes made her turn back. Slowly, unwillingly, Mrs. Peters turned her head until her eyes met the eyes of the other woman. There was a moment when they held each other in a steady, burning look in which there was no evasion or flinching. Then Martha Hale's eyes pointed the way to the basket in which was hidden the thing that would make certain the conviction of the other woman—that woman who was not there and yet who had been there with them all through that hour.

For a moment Mrs. Peters did not move. And then she did it. With a rush forward, she threw back the quilt pieces, got the box, tried to put it in her handbag. It was too big. Desperately she opened it, started to take the bird out. But there she broke—she could not touch the bird. She stood there helpless, foolish.

There was the sound of a knob turning in the inner door. Martha Hale snatched the box from the sheriff's wife, and got it in the pocket of her big coat just as the sheriff and the county attorney came back into the kitchen.

"Well, Henry," said the county attorney facetiously, "at least we found out that she was not going to quilt it. She was going to—what is it you call it, ladies?"

Mrs. Hale's hand was against the pocket of her coat.

"We call it—knot it, Mr. Henderson."

Langston Hughes

from "THANK YOU, M'AM"

One of the leaders and best-known writers of the Harlem Renaissance movement, Langston Hughes was an American poet, playwright, novelist, and short-story writer. In this excerpt from his short story "Thank You, M'am," Hughes offers an alternative to strict legal justice. When an adolescent attempts to snatch a black woman's purse, the boy learns a lesson about dignity and kindness that could never have been duplicated in juvenile detention.

She was a large woman with a large purse that had everything in it but a hammer and nails. It had a long strap, and she carried it slung across her shoulder. It was about eleven o'clock at night, dark, and she was walking alone, when a boy ran up behind her and tried to snatch her purse. The strap broke with the sudden single tug the boy gave it from behind. But the boy's weight and the weight of the purse combined caused him to lose his balance. Instead of taking off full blast as he had hoped, the boy fell on his back on the sidewalk and his legs flew up. The large woman simply turned around and kicked him right square in his blue-jeaned sitter. Then she reached down, picked the boy up by his shirtfront, and shook him until his teeth rattled.

After that the woman said, "Pick up my pocketbook, boy, and give it here."

She still held him tightly. But she bent down enough to permit him to stoop and pick up her purse. Then she said, "Now ain't you ashamed of yourself?"

Firmly gripped by his shirtfront, the boy said, "Yes'm."

The woman said, "What did you want to do it for?"

The boy said, "I didn't aim to."

She said, "You a lie!"

By that time two or three people passed, stopped, turned to look, and some stood watching.

"If I turn you loose, will you run?" asked the woman.

"Yes'm," said the boy.

"Then I won't turn you loose," said the woman. She did not release him.

"Lady, I'm sorry," whispered the boy.

"Um-hum! Your face is dirty. I got a great mind to wash your face for you. Ain't you got nobody home to tell you to wash your face?"

"No'm," said the boy.

"Then it will get washed this evening," said the large woman, starting up the street, dragging the frightened boy behind her.

He looked as if he were fourteen or fifteen, frail and willow-wild, in tennis shoes and blue jeans.

The woman said, "You ought to be my son. I would teach you right from wrong. Least I can do right now is to wash your face. Are you hungry?"

"No'm," said the being-dragged boy. "I just want you to turn me loose."

"Was I bothering *you* when I turned that corner?" asked the woman.

"No'm."

"But you put yourself in contact with *me*," said the woman. "If you think that that contact is not going to last awhile, you got another thought coming. When I get through with you, sir, you are going to remember Mrs. Luella Bates Washington Jones."

Sweat popped out on the boy's face and he began to struggle. Mrs. Jones stopped, jerked him around in front of her, put a half nelson about his neck, and continued to drag him up the street. When she got to her door, she dragged the boy inside, down a hall, and into a large kitchenette-furnished room at the rear of the house. She switched on the light and left the door open. The boy could hear other roomers laughing and talking in the large house. Some of their doors were open, too, so he knew he and the woman were not alone. The woman still had him by the neck in the middle of her room.

* * *

"You gonna take me to jail?" asked the boy, bending over the sink.

"Not with that face, I would not take you nowhere," said the woman. "Here I am trying to get home to cook me a bite to eat and you snatch my pocketbook! Maybe you ain't been to your supper either, late as it be. Have you?"

"There's nobody home at my house," said the boy.

"Then we'll eat," said the woman. "I believe you're hungry—or been hungry—to try to snatch my pocketbook!"

"I want a pair of blue suede shoes," said the boy.

"Well, you didn't have to snatch *my* pocketbook to get some suede shoes," said Mrs. Luella Bates Washington Jones. "You could've asked me."

"M'am?"

The water dripping from his face, the boy looked at her. There was a long pause. A very long pause. After he had dried his face and not knowing what else to do, dried it again, the boy turned around, wondering what next. The door was open. He could make a dash for it down the hall. He could run, run, run, *run*!

The woman was sitting on the daybed. After a while she said, "I were young once and I wanted things I could not get."

There was another long pause. The boy's mouth opened. Then he frowned, not knowing he frowned.

The woman said, "Um-hum! You thought I was going to say *but*, didn't you? You thought I was going to say, *but I didn't snatch people's pocketbooks*. Well, I wasn't going to say that." Pause. Silence. "I have done things, too, which I would not tell you, son—neither tell God, if He didn't already know. Everybody's got something in common. So you set down while I fix us something to eat. You might run that comb through your hair so you will look presentable."

In another corner of the room behind a screen was a gas plate and an icebox. Mrs. Jones got up and went behind the screen. The woman did not watch the boy to see if he was going to run now, nor did she watch her purse, which she left behind her on the day-bed. But the boy took care to sit on the far side of the room, away from the purse, where he thought she could easily see him out of the corner of her eye if she wanted to. He did not trust the woman *not* to trust him. And he did not want to be mistrusted now.

* * *

"Eat some more, son," she said.

When they were finished eating, she got up and said, "Now here, take this ten dollars and buy yourself some blue suede shoes. And next time, do not make the mistake of latching onto *my* pocketbook *nor nobody else's*—because shoes got by devilish ways will burn your feet. I got to get my rest now. But from here on in, son, I hope you will behave yourself."

She led him down the hall to the front door and opened it. "Good night! Behave yourself, boy!" she said, looking out into the street as he went down the steps.

The boy wanted to say something other than, "Thank you, m'am," to Mrs. Luella Bates Washington Jones, but although his lips moved, he couldn't even say that as he turned at the foot of the barren stoop and looked up at the large woman in the door. Then she shut the door.

Jonathan Harr

from A CIVIL ACTION

In Jonathan Harr's 1995 bestselling nonfiction book, A Civil Action *(later adapted into a feature film starring John Travolta), a law firm is headed for financial ruin when its senior partner takes a case on behalf of a community where families have been exposed to contaminated water. Originally, the lawyer, Jan Schlichtmann, was interested only in the money. Later, he is motivated by both money and principle. In this excerpt, he meets with his clients to discuss a proposed settlement and discovers, once again, that money is not the only compensation that injured parties need and require.*

Schlichtmann had asked the families to come into his office for a meeting the next morning, a Saturday. He had to inform them about Eustis's offer and the status of the trial.

Kathy Boyer arrived early that morning and began clearing piles of documents from the conference room table. She washed the dishes and coffee cups in the kitchen sink, made two pots of fresh coffee, and when she finished those tasks, she went out to buy a box of breakfast pastries. By then, Donna Robbins, Kathryn Gamache, and Kevin and Patricia Kane had arrived. Donna went back to the kitchen and offered to help Kathy. The Aufieros, the Toomeys, Anne Anderson, and the Zonas gathered in the conference room, sipping coffee and chatting with Conway.

None of the families had seen the office since last February, on the eve of trial. Only a year ago it had seemed to sparkle with luxury and order. Now some of Schlichtmann's clients noticed that it looked shabby. The potted plants had died and their bare stems gave the place a forlorn look. Behind the conference room door was a gaping hole in the plaster wall where Schlichtmann had flung the door open with such force that the knob had punched a ragged circle in the wall. In the kitchen alcove, a fluorescent light had dimmed and was blinking fitfully on and off. The vacuum cleaner had broken and the carpets, unvacuumed for weeks now, were stained by ground-in dirt.

In the conference room Schlichtmann stood before his clients, who had taken seats around the table. He was dressed in a short-sleeved shirt and chinos and looked gaunt, his hair almost completely gray.

"The lawyer's perspective this morning is not very good," he told the families. He talked about the risk of facing a divided jury in the next phase of the trial. It might be possible to win, he said, if the jury gave him the benefit of the doubt. But at every step along the way, the Grace defense would try to put doubt in the jury's mind. "The most difficult thing we face is this jury asking themselves, How do I make a decision when there are doctors and scientists out there who can't agree? They might decide to take the easy way out and not decide."

Then he told the families that he had gone to New York to discuss settlement with a Grace executive. "He put some money on the table," Schlichtmann said. "I'm going to tell you the figure, but I don't want it to go out outside this room." Schlichtmann looked around at his clients. Some of them nodded, others sat impassively.

"He offered six point six million dollars. He's decided to stop negotiating until the judge rules on the motions. He's hoping the judge will dismiss all— or at least some—of the claims."

Everyone in the room knew which claims had been put in jeopardy by the jury's date.

"When we start talking about money," continued Schlichtmann, "people get emotionally involved. That's a reality of life. In this case, that reality is backed up by a very personal claim. You'll all have to agree that you will act as one unit. There'll be no talk about this is for Toomey and not for Robbins or Zona, no talk about whose claim is more viable than someone else's claim." Schlichtmann paused to gauge his clients' reaction. They looked expectantly at him. No one said anything.

"If the eight families can't do that," Schlichtmann said, "then we're in real trouble. If there's a problem between families, then I won't know who I am representing. If there's a problem, it means that each family will have to get its own attorney."

Thirty seconds of silence ensued. Schlichtmann waited for a response. People looked cautiously at each other, wondering who would speak first.

Richard Toomey, whose dead son, Patrick, had the strongest of the remaining claims, sat directly across the table from where Schlichtmann stood. Toomey's eyes were half closed, his hands folded across his large barrel chest. He was the first to break the silence, in a voice clear and strong. "We're all in this together," he said. "That's how we started, and that's how we'll stay."

Anne Anderson smiled in sudden relief, and everyone began to say, as if in chorus, "We're unanimous, we're together."

At ease now, and with a sense of common purpose, they began to talk freely among themselves about the prospects of settling or going ahead with the trial. Again it was Toomey who spoke most forcefully.

"A settlement is one thing," he said, "but I'm not willing to throw out the verdict in order to settle. They're guilty of polluting. My child died from their stupidity. I didn't get into this for the money. I got into this because I want to find them guilty for what they did. I want the world to know that."

Most seemed to agree with this. Pasquale Zona said, "A settlement without disclosure is no settlement at all."

But Anne saw it differently. "I think you have to accept that Grace never, ever said they did anything. The world will come crashing down before they do that."

Pasquale Zona's son, Ron, who was twenty-five years old now, a strapping, husky youth, seemed affronted by this. "Saying they're not guilty of any illness or death," Ron Zona said with disgust. "That's why we're in this thing to begin with."

Anne glanced at him. "Look at how many experts say that smoking causes lung cancer, but the tobacco companies still deny it. I don't know about you people," she continued, "but I don't think I'm any match for their lawyers. I don't feel strong. I find myself crying a lot. They'll tear us apart, make mincemeat of us."

"They put their socks on the same way you do," said Ron Zona. "If we don't go to the second phase, what was the sense of this trial? That's what we got into this for, to prove that it causes illness."

Some voiced their fear that if they went ahead with the trial, they risked losing everything. Others maintained that was the chance they'd taken when they began this odyssey. Donna Robbins was of two minds, about whether they could prevail in the second phase. "But six point six million," she said, "I don't think that hurts them enough."

Schlichtmann listened to his clients for a while—and then he intervened. He asked for a show of hands—how many people thought they could win in the second phase? The Toomeys, the Zonas, Kevin Kane, and Donna Robbins raised their hands. How many thought they'd lose? Seven people, among them Patricia Kane and Anne, raised their hands. "Anybody who's studied this will realize the second phase is weaker than the first," said Anne.

The group was divided, but with the exception of young Ron Zona, no one hewed adamantly to their position. Donna Robbins asked Schlichtmann what would happen if he advised them to accept a settlement and they said no.

"I'll keep going," replied Schlichtmann. "I'm representing you, not controlling you."

It was Patricia Kane who, near the end, seemed to speak for everyone. "I think we'd all love to settle as long as we don't have to compromise the verdict," she said. "I don't think it's a matter of money. But we all want the jury's verdict to stand against Grace."

The families, in a somber mood, left the office shortly before one o'clock. Schlichtmann said good-bye to them in the conference room and he remained there after they had gone, deep in thought, his long legs up on the table.

Conway came in and sat across from him. "Well, what do you think?"

Schlichtmann cocked his head and gave Conway a wry look. "I think I'd have trouble winning this case in front of my own clients."

"They're a reflection of you," said Conway.

"They're good people. If you have to die, they're good people to die for." Schlichtmann paused. "Goddamn it, I wish it had turned out differently."

Bernard Malamud

from "AN APOLOGY"

American novelist and short-story writer Bernard Malamud wrote movingly about broken-down immigrants, mostly Jewish, accented and dispossessed, sometimes wretched, often poignant. In "An Apology," from 1957, a peddler teaches a police officer that the most valuable form of relief in the aftermath of loss and injury might just be a common courtesy.

Early one morning, during a wearying hot spell in the city, a police car that happened to be cruising along Canal Street drew over to the curb and one of the two policemen in the car leaned out of the window and fingered a come-here to an old man wearing a black derby hat, who carried a large carton on his back, held by clothesline rope to his shoulder, and dragged a smaller carton with his other hand.

"Hey, Mac."

But the peddler, either not hearing or paying no attention, went on. At that, the policeman, the younger of the two, pushed open the door and sprang out. He strode over to the peddler and, shoving the large carton on his back, swung him around as if he were straw. The peddler stared at him in frightened astonishment. He was a gaunt, shriveled man with very large eyes which at the moment gave the effect of turning lights, so that the policeman was a little surprised, though not for long.

"Are you deaf?" he said.

The peddler's lips moved in a way that suggested he might be, but at last he cried out, "Why do you push me?" and again surprised the policeman with the amount of wail that rang in his voice.

"Why didn't you stop when I called you?"

"So who knows you called me? Did you say my name?"

"What is your name?"

The peddler clamped his sparse yellow teeth rigidly together.

"And where's your license?"

"What license?—who license?"

"None of your wisecracks—your license to peddle. We saw you peddle."

The peddler did not deny it.

"What's in the big box?"

"Hundred watt."

"Hundred what?"

"Lights."

"What's in the other?"

"Sixty watt."

"Don't you know it's against the law to peddle without a license?"

Without answering, the peddler looked around, but there was no one in sight except the other policeman in the car and his eyes were shut as if he was catching a little lost sleep.

The policeman on the sidewalk opened his black summons book.

"Spill it, Pop, where do you live?"

The peddler stared down at the cracked sidewalk.

"Hurry up, Lou," called the policeman from the car. He was an older man, though not so old as the peddler.

"Just a second, Walter, this old guy here is balky."

With his pencil he prodded the peddler, who was still staring at the sidewalk but who then spoke, saying he had no money to buy a license.

"But you have the money to buy bulbs. Don't you know you're cheating the city when you don't pay the legitimate fees?"

"   "
" . . ."

"Talk, will you?"

"Come on, Lou."

"Come on yourself, this nanny goat won't talk."

The other policeman slowly got out of the car, a heavy man with gray hair and a red face shiny with perspiration.

"You better give him the information he wants, mister."

The peddler, holding himself stiff, stared between them. By this time some people had gathered and were looking on, but Lou scattered them with a wave of his arm.

"All right, Walter, give me a hand. This bird goes to the station house."

Walter looked at him with some doubt, but Lou said, "Resisting an officer in the performance of his duty."

He took the peddler's arm and urged him forward. The carton of bulbs slipped off his shoulder, pulling him to his knees.

"Veh is mir."

Walter helped him up and they lifted him into the car. The young cop hauled the large carton to the rear of the car, opened the trunk, and shoved it in sideways. As they drove off, a man in front of one of the stores held up a box and shouted, "Hey, you forgot this one," but neither of them turned to look back, and the peddler didn't seem to be listening.

On their way to the station house they passed the Brooklyn Bridge. "Just a second, Lou," said Walter. "Could you drive across the bridge now and stop at my house? My feet are perspiring and I'd like to change my shirt."

"After we get this character booked."

But Walter querulously insisted it would take too long, and though Lou didn't want to drive him home he finally gave in. Neither of them spoke on the way to Walter's house, which was not far from the bridge, on a nice quiet street of three-story brownstone houses with young trees in front of them, newly planted not far from the curb.

When Walter got out, he said to the peddler, "If you were in Germany they would have killed you. All we were trying to do was give you a summons that would maybe cost you a buck fine." Then he went up the stone steps.

After a while Lou became impatient waiting for him and honked the horn. A window shade on the second floor slid up and Walter in his underwear called down, "Just five minutes, Lou—I'm just drying my feet."

He came down all spry and they drove back several blocks and onto the bridge. Midway across, they had to slow down in a long traffic line, and to their astonishment the peddler pushed open the door and reeled out upon the bridge, miraculously ducking out of the way of the trailers and trucks coming from the other direction. He scooted across the pedestrians' walk and clambered with ferocious strength up on the railing of the bridge.

But Lou, who was very quick, immediately pursued him and managed to get his hand on the peddler's coattails as he stood poised on the railing for the jump.

With a yank Lou pulled him to the ground. The back of his head struck against the sidewalk and his derby hat bounced up, twirled, and landed at his feet. However, he did not lose consciousness. He lay on the ground moaning and tearing with clawlike fingers at his chest and arms.

Both the policemen stood there looking down at him, not sure what to do since there was absolutely no bleeding. As they were talking it over, a fat woman with moist eyes who, despite the heat, was wearing a white shawl over her head and carrying, with the handle over her pudgy arm, a large basket of salted five-cent pretzels passed by and stopped out of curiosity to see what had happened.

Seeing the man on the ground she called out, "Bloostein!" but he did not look at her and continued tearing at his arms.

"Do you know him?" Lou asked her.

"It's Bloostein. I know him from the neighborhood."

"Where does he live?"

She thought for a minute but didn't know. "My father said he used to own a store on Second Avenue but he lost it. Then his missus died and also his daughter was killed in a fire. Now he's got the seven years' itch and they can't cure it in the clinic. They say he peddles with light bulbs."

"Don't you know his address?"

"Not me. What did he do?"

"It doesn't matter what he tried to do," said Walter.

"Goodbye, Bloostein, I have to go to the schoolyard," the fat lady apologized. She picked up the basket and went with her pretzels down the bridge.

By now Bloostein had stopped his frantic scratching and lay quietly on the sidewalk. The sun shone straight into his eyes but he did nothing to shield them.

Lou, who was quite pale, looked at Walter and Walter said, "Let him go."

They got him up on his feet, dusted his coat, and placed his dented hat on his head. Lou said he would get the bulbs out of the car, but Walter said, "Not here, down at the foot of the bridge."

They helped Bloostein back to the car and in a few minutes let him go with his carton of bulbs at the foot of the bridge, not far from the place where they had first chanced to see him.

But that night, after their tour of duty, when Lou drove him home, Walter got out of the car and saw, after a moment of disbelief, that Bloostein himself was waiting for him in front of his house.

"Hey, Lou," he called, but Lou had already driven off so he had to face the peddler alone. Bloostein looked, with his carton of bulbs, much as he had that morning, except for the smudge where the dent on his derby hat had been, and his eyes were fleshy with fatigue.

"What do you want here?" Walter said to him.

The peddler parted his lips, then pointed to his carton. "My little box lights."

"What about it?"

"What did you do with them?"

Walter thought a few seconds and remembered the other box of bulbs.

"You sure you haven't gone back and hid them somewhere?" he asked sternly.

Bloostein wouldn't look at him.

The policeman felt very hot. "All right, we'll try and locate them, but first I have to have my supper. I'm hungry."

* * *

They then rode to the address he had been given but no one knew where the one who had the bulbs was. Finally a bald-headed, stocky man in an undershirt came down from the top floor and said he was the man's uncle and what did Walter want.

Walter convinced him it wasn't serious. "It's just that he happens to know where these bulbs are that we left behind by mistake after an arrest."

The uncle said if it wasn't really serious he would give him the address of the social club where he could find his nephew. The address was a lot farther uptown and on the East Side.

"This is foolish," Walter said to himself as he came out of the house. He thought maybe he could take his time and Bloostein might go away, so he stopped at another beer parlor and had several more as he watched a ten-round fight on television.

He came out sweaty from the beers. But Bloostein was there.

* * *

Bloostein was perched like a skinny owl on the back seat gazing at him.

Walter capped the bottle but did not start the car. He sat for a long time at the wheel, moodily meditating. At the point where he was beginning to feel down in the dumps, he got a sudden idea. The idea was so simple and good he quickly started the motor and drove downtown straight to Canal, where there was a hardware store that stayed open to midnight. He almost ran into the place and in ten minutes came out with a wrapped carton containing five dozen 60-watt bulbs.

"The joyride's finished, my friend."

The peddler got out and Walter unloaded the large carton and left it standing on the sidewalk near the smaller one.

He drove off quickly.

Going over the bridge he felt relieved, yet at the same time a little anxious to get to sleep because he had to be up at six. He garaged the car and then walked home and upstairs, taking care to move about softly in the bathroom so as not to waken his son, a light sleeper, or his wife, who slept heavily but couldn't get back to sleep once she had been waked up. Undressing, he got into bed with her, but though the night was hot he felt like a cake of ice covered with a sheet. After a while he got up, raised the shade, and stood by the window.

The quiet street was drenched in moonlight, and warm dark shadows fell from the tender trees. But in the tree shadow in front of the house were two strange oblongs and a gnarled, grotesque-hatted silhouette that stretched a tormented distance down the block. Walter's heart pounded heavily, for he knew it was Bloostein.

He put on his robe and straw slippers and ran down the stairs. "What's wrong?"

Bloostein stared at the moonlit sidewalk.

"What do you want?"

" . . . "

"You better go, Bloostein. This is too late for monkey business. You got your bulbs. Now you better just go home and leave me alone. I hate to have to call the police. Just go home."

Then he lumbered up the stone steps and the flight of carpeted stairs. Inside the bedroom he could hear his son moan in his sleep. Walter lay down and slept, but was awakened by the sound of soft rain. Getting up, he stared out. There was the peddler in the rain, with his white upraised face looking at the window, so near he might be standing on stilts.

Hastening into the hall, Walter rummaged in a closet for an umbrella but couldn't find one. Then his wife woke and called in a loud whisper, "Who's there?" He stood motionless and she listened a minute and evidently went back to sleep. Then because he couldn't find the umbrella he got out a light summer blanket, brought it into the little storage room next to the bedroom, and, taking the screen out of the window, threw the blanket out to Bloostein so he wouldn't get too wet. The white blanket seemed to float down.

He returned to bed, by an effort of the will keeping himself there for hours. Then he noticed that the rain had stopped and he got up to make sure. The blanket lay heaped where it had fallen on the sidewalk. Bloostein was standing away from it, under the tree.

Walter's straw slippers squeaked as he walked down the stairs. The heat had broken and now a breeze came through the street, shivering the leaves in summer cold.

In the doorway he thought, What's my hurry? I can wait him out till six, then just let the mummy try to follow me into the station house.

"Bloostein," he said, going down the steps, but as the old man looked up, he felt a sickening emptiness.

Staring down at the sidewalk he thought about everything. At last he raised his head and slowly said, "Bloostein, I owe you an apology. I'm really sorry the whole thing happened. I haven't been able to sleep. From my heart I'm truly sorry."

Bloostein gazed at him with enormous eyes reflecting the moon. He answered nothing, but it seemed he had shrunk and so had his shadow.

Walter said good night. He went up and lay down under the sheet. "What's the matter?" said his wife.

"Nothing."

She turned over on her side. "Don't wake Sonny."

"No."

He rose and went to the window. Raising the shade, he stared out. Yes, gone. He, his boxes of lights and soft summer blanket. He looked again, but the long, moon-whitened street had never been so empty.

PART IX

The Law and Longing

There is a curious gravitational pull that summons citizens to answer the call of the courthouse bell. We find the law irresistible, for so many reasons. We begin by clamoring for justice and are drawn to morally crusading attorneys who fight for fairness and equality. Sometimes we are forced to look elsewhere for satisfaction. But we are all united by the moral imperative to know the truth.

Thomas Wolfe

from THE HILLS BEYOND

Thomas Wolfe, acclaimed novelist of the American South and author of Look
Homeward, Angel, *died before completing the manuscript that was later edited
to become the collection of stories entitled* The Hills Beyond, *published posthu-
mously in 1941. It tells the story of the Joyner family of North Carolina and contains Wolfe's characteristically romantic prose, lush portraiture, and nostalgia for
the past. In this excerpt, he describes a courthouse in a small southern town and the
majestic hold that it has on the citizens who are called before it.*

Later, it seemed to Edward Joyner that his whole childhood had been haunted
by the ringing of the courthouse bell. It got into almost every memory he had
of early youth. It beat wildly, with advancing and receding waves of sound
through stormy autumn days. In the sharp, sweet loveliness of spring, the
bloom of April and the green of May, the courthouse bell was also there: it
gave a brazen pulse to haunting solitudes of June, getting into the rustling of
a leaf, speaking to morning with its wake-o'-day of "Come to court," and jar-
ring the drowsy torpor of the afternoon with "Court again."

It was a rapid and full-throated cry, a fast stroke beating on the heels of
sound. Its brazen tongue, its hard and quickening beat, were always just the
same, yet never seemed the same. The constant rhythm of its strokes beat
through his heart and brain and soul with all the passionate and mad excite-
ments of man's fate and error, and he read into the sound his own imagined
meanings.

He never heard it as a boy without a faster beating of the pulse, a sharp, dry
tightening of the throat, a numb aerial buoyancy of deep excitement. At
morning, shining morning in the spring, it would seem to speak to him of
work-a-day, to tell him that the world was up and doing, advancing to the rattling traffics of full noon. In afternoon it spoke with still another tongue,

breaking the dull-eyed hush of somnolent repose with its demand for action. It spoke to bodies drowsing in the midday warmth, and told them they must rudely break their languorous siesta. It spoke to stomachs drugged with heavy food, crammed full of turnip greens and corn, string beans and pork, hot biscuits and hot apple pie, and it told them it was time to gird their swollen loins for labor, that man's will and character must rise above his belly, that work was doing, and that night was not yet come.

Again, in morning, it would speak of civil actions, of men at law and the contentions of a suit. Its tone was full of writs and summonses, of appearances and pleadings. Sometimes it's hard, fast tongue would now cry out: "Appear!"

"Appear, appear, appear, appear, appear, appear, appear!"

Again:

"Your property is mine—is mine—is mine—is mine—is mine!"

Or, yet again, harsh, peremptory, unyielding, unexplained:

"You come to court—to court—to court—to court—to court—to court!"

Or, more brusque and more commanding still, just:

"Court—court—court—court—court—court—court!"

In afternoon, the courthouse bell would speak of much more fatal punishment—of murder on trial, of death through the heated air, of a dull, slow-witted mountain wretch who sat there in the box, with a hundred pairs of greedy eyes upon him, and, still half unaware of what he did, let out the killer's sudden sob, itself like blood and choking in the throat, and instantly the sun went blood-smeared in the eyes, with the feel and taste of blood throughout, upon the sultry air, upon the tongue and in the mouth, and across the very visage of the sun itself, with all the brightness of the day gone out. Then, as the clanging stroke continued, a cloud-shape passed upon the massed green of a mountain flank, and the gold-bright sun of day returned, and suddenly there were bird-thrumming wood notes everywhere, swift and secret, bullet-wise within the wilderness, and the drowsy stitch and drone of three o'clock through coarse, sweet grasses of the daisied fields, and there beneath his feet the boy beheld the life-blood of a murdered man soaking quietly down before him into an unsuspected hand's breadth of familiar earth—all as sudden, swift, and casual as this, all softly done as the soft thrummings in the wood. And as the brazen strokes went on, he saw again the prisoner in the box, all unknowing still of the reason why he did it, a stunned animal caught in the steel traps of law, and now, with those hundred pairs of greedy eyes upon him, the courthouse bell was pounding on the torpor of hot afternoon the stark imperative of its inflexible command:

"To kill—to kill—to kill—to kill—to kill—to kill!"

And then, dying out upon the heated air, just:

"Kill—kill—kill kill kill kill killkillkill . . . !"

It is doubtful if people of a younger and more urban generation can realize the way the county courthouse shaped human life and destiny through all America some sixty years ago. In Libya Hill the courthouse was the center of the community, for Libya Hill had been the county courthouse before it was a town. The town grew up around the courthouse, made a Square, and straggled out along the roads that led away to the four quarters of the earth.

And for the country people round about, the courthouse was even more the center of life and interest than it was for the townsfolk. The countrymen came into town to trade and barter, to buy and sell; but when their work was over, it was always to the courthouse that they turned. When court was being held, one could always find them here. Here, in the Square outside, were their mules, their horses, their ox-teams, and their covered wagons. Here, inside the building, were their social converse and their criminal life. Here were their trials, suits, and punishments, their relatives accused, their friends and enemies acquitted or convicted, their drawling talk of rape and lust and murder—the whole shape and pattern of their life, their look, their feel, their taste, their smell.

Here was, in sum, the whole framework of America—the abysmal gap between its preachment and performance, its grain of righteousness and its hill of wrong. Not only in the voices and the persons of these country people, these mountaineers who sat and spat and drawled and loitered on the courthouse steps, but in the very design and structure of the courthouse building itself did the shape and substance of their life appear. Here in the pseudo-Greek façade with the false front of its swelling columns, as well as in the high, square dimensions of the trial courtroom, the judge's bench, the prisoner's box, the witness stand, the lawyers' table, the railed-off area for participants, the benches for spectators behind, the crossed flags of the state and of the nation, the steel engraving of George Washington—in all these furnishings of office there was some effort to maintain the pomp of high authority, the outward symbols of a dignified, impartial execution of the law. But, alas, the execution of the law was, like the design and structure of the courthouse itself, not free from error, and not always sound. The imposing Doric and Corinthian columns were often found, upon inspection, to be just lath and brick and plaster trying to be stone. No matter what pretensions to a classic austerity the courtroom itself might try to make, the tall and gloomy-looking windows were generally unwashed. No matter what effect of Attic graces the fake façade might have upon the slow mind of the countryman, the wide, dark corridors were full of drafts and unexpected ventilations, darkness, creaking boards, squeaking stairways, and the ominous dripping of an unseen tap.

And the courthouse smell was like the smell of terror, crime, and justice in America—a certain essence of our life, a certain sweat out of ourselves, a certain substance that is ours alone, and unmistakable. What was this smell of courthouse justice in America? What were the smells of terror, law, and crime in this great land? It was a single and yet most high, subtle, and composite stink: made up of many things, yet, like the great union that produced it, one smell and one alone—one and indivisible!

It was—to get down to its basic chemistries—a smell of sweat, tobacco juice, and urine; a smell of sour flesh, feet, clogged urinals, and broken-down latrines. It was, mixed in and subtly interposed with these, a smell of tarry disinfectant, a kind of lime and alum, a strong ammoniac smell. It was a smell of old dark halls and old used floorways, a cool, dark, dank, and musty cellar-smell. It was a smell of old used chairs with creaking bottoms, a smell of sweated woods and grimy surfaces; a smell of rubbed-off arm rests, bench rests, chair rests, of counters, desks, and tables; a smell as if every inch of woodwork in the building had been oiled, stewed, sweated, grimed, and polished by man's flesh.

In addition to all these, it was a smell of rump-worn leathers, a smell of thumb-worn calfskin, yellowed papers, and black ink. It was a smell of brogans, shirt-sleeves, overalls, and sweat and hay and butter. It was a kind of dry, exciting smell of chalk, of starched cuffs that rattled—a smell that went with the incessant rattling of dry papers, the crackling of dry knuckles and parched fingers, the rubbing of dry, chalky hands—a country lawyer smell of starch and broadcloth.

And oh, much more than these—and *all* of these—it was a smell of fascination and of terror, a smell of throbbing pulse and beating heart and the tight and dry constriction of the throat. It was a smell made up of all the hate, the horror, the fear, the chicanery, and the loathing that the world could know; a smell made up of the intolerable anguish of man's nerve and heart and sinew, the sweat and madness of man's perjured soul enmeshed in trickery—a whole huge smell of violence and crime and murder, of shyster villainies and broken faith. And to this high and mountainous stench of error, passion, guilt, graft, and wrong, there was added one small smell of justice, fairness, truth, and hope.

The county courthouse was, in short, America—the wilderness America, the sprawling, huge, chaotic, criminal America. It was murderous America soaked with murdered blood, tortured and purposeless America, savage, blind, and mad America, exploding through its puny laws, its pitiful pretense. It was America with all its almost hopeless hopes, its almost faithless faiths— America with the huge blight on her of her own error, the broken promise of her lost dream and her unachieved desire; and it was America as well with her unspoken prophecies, her unfound language, her unuttered song. And just for all these reasons it was for us all our own America—with all her horror, beauty, tenderness, and terror—with all we know of her that never has been proved, that has never yet been uttered—the only one we know, the only one there is.

E.L. DOCTOROW

from THE BOOK OF DANIEL

American novelist E.L. Doctorow's third novel, The Book of Daniel, *fictionalized the prosecution of Julius and Ethel Rosenberg, who were accused of spying for the Russians during the cold war. While this novel is a virtual tutorial on the tyrannical politics of the Red Scare, it also is a commentary on the way in which the legal system often capitulates to the politics of an era. Here we see a description of Jacob Ascher, the lawyer representing the Isaacsons (i.e., the Rosenbergs)—a moral attorney forced to defend his clients within a legal system that has abandoned its commitment to civil liberties.*

So Ascher came into our lives, the first Surrogate. Ascher was not a left-wing lawyer. He had spent his professional life practicing in the Bronx, primarily in civil law. He was what my Aunt Frieda called a Jewish gentleman. Ascher was the kind of lawyer who quietly handles all the legal affairs of his Synagogue for years without compensation. He was in his sixties when I first saw him, the large features of his face showing the signs of his emphysema. His mouth was stretched wide, his eyes deep-set and slightly bulging. I felt the weight of my grief when Ascher was around because, like a doctor, he would not have been there unless something was wrong. But I didn't dislike him. He had enormous hands, and a gruff condescension to children that I did not find inappropriate or offensive.

Ascher was a pillar of the Bronx bar. He was not brilliant, but his law was sound, and his honor as a man, as a religious man, was unquestionable. He was an honest lawyer, and was dogged for his clients. I picture him on Yom Kippur standing in the pew with his homburg on his head, and a tallis around his shoulders. Ascher could wear a homburg and a tallis at the same time.

He was not my parents' first choice. My parents were not accustomed to dealing with lawyers, or accountants, or bank tellers. I think now my father must have called a half-dozen lawyers on the recommendations of his friends, before he found Ascher. Lawyers were not anxious to handle any case involving the FBI, even left-wing lawyers. When my father was trying to find a lawyer while fending off the FBI visits, the case was open-ended, as any sharp lawyer understood. Maybe Ascher understood this too. He certainly understood that this was a bad time in history for anyone whom the law turned its eye on who was a Red, or a "progressive" as Communists had come to characterize themselves. Since 1946, indecent things had happened in the country. He lectured Rochelle as if she might not know. The Democrats under Harry Truman competed with the Republicans in Congress to see who could be rougher on the Left. People were losing their jobs and their careers for things they said or appeals they had supported fifteen years before. People were accused, investigated and fired from their jobs without knowing what the charges were, or who made them. People were blacklisted in their professions. Public confessions of error had become a national rite, just as in Russia. Witnesses naming friends and acquaintances seen at meetings twenty years before were praised by Congressmen. Informing was the new ethic. Ex-Communists who would testify about Party methods, and who would write confessionals, made lots of money. The measure of their success was the magnitude of their sin. It was the time of the Red Menace. The fear of Communists taking over the PTA and Community Chest affected the lives of ordinary people in ordinary towns. Anyone who knew anyone who was a Communist felt tainted. Everything that could be connected to the Communists took on taint. People who defended their civil liberties on principle. The First, Fifth and Fourteenth Amendments to the Constitution. Pablo Picasso, because he had attended the Communists' World Peace Congress in Paris and painted doves for peace. Doves. Peace. There was a new immigration control bill and alien deportation bill, and a control of American citizens abroad bill. And there was an internal security bill providing for concentration camps for anyone who might be expected to commit espionage. And there were now people who couldn't get passports, and there were now people who couldn't find jobs, and there were now people jailed for contempt, and there were now people who couldn't find Mark Twain in the library because the Russians liked him and he was a best seller over there.

* * *

This was hardly the kind of talk my mother could find comforting. Ascher was not a tactful man. He lacked a bedside manner. You accepted the way he

was because of his obvious integrity, and because you had no choice. Ascher
was not a political man, you could imagine him voting for anyone he found
morally recognizable, no matter what the party. If anything, he was conser-
vative. He perceived in the law a codification of the religious sense of life.
He was said to have worked for years on a still unfinished book demonstrating
the contributions of the Old Testament to American law. For Ascher witch-
hunting was paganism. Irrationality was a sin. He came to our cold house and
sat without taking off his coat, and with his homburg shoved back on his
head, he asked a few questions and answered a few questions, and nodded and
sighed, and shook his head. For Ascher, my parents' communism was easily
condoned because it was pathetic and gutsy at the same time. One of the
people who wrote about Paul and Rochelle, a Jewish literary critic, said that
they were so crass and hypocritical that they even called on their Jewish faith
to sustain sympathy for themselves in their last months. This writer could not
have understood Ascher. Or the large arms of ethical sanctity he could wrap
around an atheistic Communist when in the person of a misfit Jew as ignorant
as my father of the real practical world of men and power. Ascher understood
how someone could forswear his Jewish heritage and take for his own the per-
fectionist dream of heaven on earth, and in spite of that, or perhaps because of
it, still consider himself a Jew.

Fyodor Dostoevsky

from THE BROTHERS KARAMAZOV

The master of moral inquiries within the setting of psychological crime novels, Fyodor Dostoevsky authored both Crime and Punishment *and* The Brothers Karamazov, *two of the most important novels in the genre of law and literature. The latter, written in 1880 and excerpted here, contains a lengthy, suspenseful, and morally complex murder trial in which a son is accused of killing his father.*

The day after the events just described, at ten o'clock in the morning, our district court opened its session and the trial of Dmitri Karamazov began.

I will say beforehand, and say emphatically, that I am far from considering myself capable of recounting all that took place in court, not only with the proper fullness, but even in the proper order. I keep thinking that if one were to recall everything and explain everything as one ought, it would fill a whole book, even quite a large one. Therefore let no one grumble if I tell only that which struck me personally and which I have especially remembered. I may have taken secondary things for the most important, and even overlooked the most prominent and necessary features . . . But anyway I see that it is better not to apologize. I shall do what I can, and my readers will see for themselves that I have done all I could.

And, first of all, before we enter the courtroom, I will mention something that especially surprised me that day. By the way, as it turned out later, it surprised not only me but everyone else as well. That is: everyone knew that this case interested a great many people, that everyone was burning with impatience for the trial to begin, that for the whole two months past there had been a great deal of discussion, supposition, exclamation, anticipation among our local society. Everyone also knew that the case had been publicized all over Russia, but even so they never imagined that it had shaken all and sundry to such a burning, such an intense degree, not only among us but everywhere, as became clear at the trial that day. By that day visitors had come to us not only from the provincial capital but from several other Russian cities, and lastly from Moscow and Petersburg. Lawyers came, several noble persons even came, and ladies as well. All the tickets were snapped up. For the most respected and noble of the men visitors, certain quite unusual seats were even reserved behind the table at which the judges sat: a whole row of chairs appeared there, occupied by various dignitaries—a thing never permitted before. There turned out to be an especially large number of ladies—our own and visitors—I would say even not less than half the entire public. The lawyers alone, who arrived from all over, turned out to be so numerous that no one knew where to put them, since the tickets had all been given out, begged, besought long ago. I myself saw a partition being temporarily and hastily set up at the end of the courtroom, behind the podium, where all these arriving lawyers were admitted, and they even considered themselves lucky to be able at least to stand there, because in order to make room, the chairs were removed from behind this partition, and the whole accumulated crowd stood through the whole "case" in a closely packed lump, shoulder to shoulder. Some of the ladies, especially among the visitors, appeared in the gallery of the courtroom extremely dressed up, but the majority of the ladies were not even thinking about dresses. Hysterical, greedy, almost morbid curiosity could be read on their faces. One of the most characteristic peculiarities of this whole society gathered in the courtroom, which must be pointed out, was that, as was later established by many observations, almost all the ladies, at least the great majority of them, favored Mitya and his acquittal. Mainly, perhaps, because an idea had been formed of him as a conqueror of women's hearts. . . . I know positively that in our town itself several serious family quarrels even took place on account of Mitya. Many ladies quarreled hotly with their husbands owing to a difference of opinion about this whole terrible affair, and naturally, after that, all the husbands of these ladies arrived in court feeling not only ill disposed towards the defendant but even resentful of him. And generally it can be stated positively that the entire male contingent, as opposed to the ladies, was aroused against the defendant. One saw stern, scowling faces, some even quite angry, and not a few of them. It was also true that Mitya had managed to insult many of them personally during his stay in our town. Of course, some of the visitors were even almost merry and quite indifferent to Mitya's fate in itself, although, again, not to the case under consideration; everyone was concerned with its outcome, and the majority of the men decidedly wished to see the criminal punished, except perhaps for the lawyers, who cared not about the moral aspect of the case, but only, so to speak, about its contemporary legal aspect. Everyone was excited by the coming of the famous Fetyukovich. His talent was known everywhere, and this was not the first time he had come to the provinces to defend a celebrated criminal case. And after his defense such cases always became famous all over Russia and were remembered for a long time. There were several anecdotes going around concerning both our prosecutor and the presiding judge. It was said that our prosecutor trembled at the thought of meeting Fetyukovich, that they were old enemies from way back in Petersburg, from the beginning of their careers, that our vain Ippolit Kirillovich, who ever since Petersburg had always thought himself injured by someone, because his talents were not properly appreciated, had been resurrected in spirit by the Karamazov case and even dreamed of resurrecting his flagging career through it, and that his only fear was Fetyukovich. But the opinions concerning his trembling before Fetyukovich were not altogether just. Our prosecutor was not one of those characters who lose heart in the face of danger; he was, on the contrary, of the sort whose vanity grows and takes wing precisely in pace with the growing danger. And generally it must be noted that our prosecutor was too ardent and morbidly susceptible. He would put his whole soul into some case and conduct it as if his whole fate and his whole fortune depended on the outcome. In the legal world this gave rise to some laughter, for our prosecutor even achieved a certain renown precisely by this quality, if not everywhere, at least more widely than one might have supposed in view of his modest position in our court. The laughter was aimed especially at his passion for psychology. In my opinion they were all mistaken: as a man and as a character, our prosecutor seems to me to have been much more serious than many people supposed. But from his very first steps this ailing man was simply unable to show himself to advantage, either at the beginning of his career or afterwards for the rest of his life.

As for our presiding judge, one can simply say of him that he was an educated and humane man, with a practical knowledge of his task, and with the most modern ideas. He was rather vain, but not overly concerned with his career. His chief goal in life was to be a progressive man. He had a fortune and connections besides. He took, as it turned out later, a rather passionate view of the Karamazov case, but only in a general sense. He was concerned with the phenomenon, its classification, seeing it as a product of our social principles, as characteristic of the Russian element, and so on and so forth. But his attitude towards the personal character of the case, its tragedy, as well as towards the persons of the participants, beginning with the defendant, was rather indifferent and abstract, as, by the way, it perhaps ought to have been.

Long before the appearance of the judges, the courtroom was already packed. Our courtroom is the best hall in town, vast, lofty, resonant. To the right of the judges, who were placed on a sort of raised platform, a table and two rows of chairs were prepared for the jury. To the left was the place for the defendant and his attorney. In the center of the hall, close to the judges, stood a table with the "material evidence." . . . At a certain distance farther back in the hall began the seats for the public, but in front of the balustrade stood several chairs for those witnesses who would remain in the courtroom after giving their evidence. At ten o'clock the members of the court appeared, consisting of the presiding judge, a second judge, and an honorary justice of the peace. Of course, the prosecutor also appeared at once. The presiding judge was a stocky, thick-set man, of less than average height, with a hemorrhoidal face, about fifty years old, his gray-streaked hair cut short, wearing a red ribbon—I do not remember of what order. To me, and not only to me but to everyone, the prosecutor looked somehow too pale, with an almost green face, which for some reason seemed suddenly to have grown very thin, perhaps overnight, since I had seen him just two days before looking quite himself. The presiding judge began by asking the marshal if all the jurors were present . . . I see, however, that I can no longer go on in this way, if only because there were many things I did not catch, others that I neglected to go into, still others that I forgot to remember, and, moreover, as I have said above, if I were to recall everything that was said and done, I literally would not have time or space. I know only that neither side—that is, neither the defense attorney nor the prosecutor—objected to very many of the jurors. But I do remember who the twelve jurors consisted of: four of our officials, two merchants, and six local peasants and tradesmen. In our society, I remember, long before the trial, the question was asked with some surprise, especially by the ladies: "Can it be that the fatal decision in such a subtle, complex, and psychological case is to be turned over to a bunch of officials, and even to peasants?" and "What will some ordinary official make of it, not to mention a peasant?" Indeed, all four of the officials who got on the jury were minor persons of low rank, gray-haired old men—only one of them was a little younger—scarcely known in our society, vegetating on meager salaries, with old wives, no doubt, whom they could not present anywhere, and each with a heap of children, perhaps even going barefoot; who at most found diversion in a little game of cards somewhere in their off hours, and who most assuredly had never read a single book. . . . "What can such people possibly grasp of such a case?" Nevertheless their faces made a certain strangely imposing and almost threatening impression; they were stern and frowning.

Finally the presiding judge announced the hearing of the case of the murder of the retired titular councillor Fyodor Pavlovich Karamazov—I do not quite remember how he put it then. The marshal was told to bring in the defendant, and so Mitya appeared. A hush came over the courtroom, one could have heard a fly buzz. I do not know about the others, but on me Mitya's looks made a most unpleasant impression. Above all, he appeared a terrible dandy, in a fresh new frock coat. I learned later that he had specially ordered himself a frock coat for that day from Moscow, from his former tailor, who had his measurements. He was wearing new black kid gloves and an elegant shirt. He walked in with his yard-long strides, looking straight and almost stiffly ahead of him, and took his seat with a most intrepid air. Right away, at once, the defense attorney, the famous Fetyukovich, also appeared, and a sort of subdued hum, as it were, swept through the courtroom. He was a tall, dry man, with long, thin legs, extremely long, pale, thin fingers, a clean-shaven face, modestly combed, rather short hair, and thin lips twisted now and then into something halfway between mockery and a smile. He looked about forty. His face would even have been pleasant had it not been for his eyes, which, in themselves small and inexpressive, were set so unusually close together that they were separated only by the thin bone of his thin, long-drawn nose. In short, his physiognomy had something sharply birdlike about it, which was striking. He was dressed in a frock coat and a white tie. I remember the presiding judge's first questions to Mitya—that is, about his name, social position, and so forth. Mitya answered sharply, but somehow in an unexpectedly loud voice, so that the judge even shook his head and looked at him almost in surprise. Then the list of persons called for questioning in court—that is, of witnesses and experts—was read.

* * *

All became hushed as the first words of the famous orator resounded. The whole room fixed their eyes on him. He began with extreme directness, simplicity, and conviction, but without the slightest presumption. Not the slightest attempt at eloquence, at notes of pathos, at words ringing with emotion. This was a man speaking within an intimate circle of sympathizers. His voice was beautiful, loud, and attractive, and even in this voice itself one seemed to hear something genuine and guileless. But everyone realized at once that the orator could suddenly rise to true pathos—and "strike the heart with an unutterable power." He spoke perhaps less correctly than Ippolit Kirillovich, but without long phrases, and even more precisely. There was one thing the ladies did not quite like: he somehow kept bending forward, especially at the beginning of his speech, not really bowing, but as if he were rushing or flying at his listeners, and this he did by bending precisely, as it were, with half of his long back, as if a hinge were located midway down that long and narrow back that enabled it to bend almost at a right angle. He spoke somehow scatteredly at the beginning, as if without any system, snatching up facts at random, but in the end it all fell together. His speech could be divided into two halves: the first half was a critique, a refutation of the charges, at times malicious and sarcastic. But in the second half of the speech he seemed to change his tone and even his method, and all at once rose into pathos, and the courtroom seemed to be waiting for it and all began trembling with rapture. He went straight to work, and began by saying that although his practice was in Petersburg, this was not the first time he had visited the towns of Russia to defend a case, though he did so only when he was convinced of the defendant's innocence or anticipated it beforehand. "The same thing happened to me in the present case," he explained. "Even in the initial newspaper reports alone, I caught a glimpse of something that struck me greatly in favor of the defendant. In a word, I was interested first of all in a certain juridical fact, which appears often enough in legal practice, though never, it seems to me, so fully or with such characteristic peculiarities as in the present case. This fact I ought to formulate only in the finale of my speech, when I have finished my statement; however, I shall express my thought at the very beginning as well, for I have a weakness for going straight to the point, not storing up effects or sparing impressions. This may be improvident on my part, yet it is sincere. This thought of mine—my formula—is as follows: the overwhelming totality of the facts is against the defendant, and at the same time there is not one fact that will stand up to criticism, if it is considered separately, on its own! Following along through rumors and the newspapers, I was becoming more and more firmly set in my thought, when suddenly I received an invitation from the defendant's relatives to come and defend him. I hastened here at once, and here became finally convinced. It was in order to demolish this terrible totality of facts and show how undemonstrable and fantastic each separate accusing fact is, that I undertook the defense of this case."

Thus the defense attorney began, and suddenly he raised his voice:

"Gentlemen of the jury, I am a newcomer here. All impressions fell upon me without preconceived ideas. The defendant, a man of stormy and unbridled character, had not offended me to begin with, as he had perhaps a hundred persons in this town, which is why many are prejudiced against him beforehand. Of course, I also admit that the moral sense of local society has been justly aroused: the defendant is stormy and unbridled. Nonetheless he was received in local society; even in the family of the highly talented prosecutor he was warmly welcomed." (*Nota bene*: At these words two or three chuckles came from the public, quickly suppressed, but noticed by all. We all knew that the prosecutor had admitted Mitya to his house against his will, solely because for some reason he interested the prosecutor's wife—a highly virtuous and respectable, but fantastic and self-willed, lady, who in certain cases, for the most part trifling, loved to oppose her husband. Mitya, by the way, had visited their home rather infrequently.) "Nevertheless, I make so bold as to assume," the defense attorney went on, "that even in such an independent mind and just character as my opponent's, a somewhat erroneous prejudice against my unfortunate client might have formed. Oh, it's quite natural: the unfortunate man deserved all too well to be treated with prejudice. And an offended moral and, even more so, aesthetic sense is sometimes implacable. Of course, in the highly talented speech for the prosecution, we have all heard a strict analysis of the defendant's character and actions, a strictly critical attitude towards the case; and, above all, such psychological depths were demonstrated to explain the essence of the matter, that a penetration to those depths could by no means have taken place were there even the slightest amount of deliberate and malicious prejudice with regard to the person of the defendant. But there are things that are even worse, even more ruinous in such cases than the most malicious and preconceived attitude towards the matter. Namely, if we are, for example, possessed by a certain, so to speak, artistic game, by the need for artistic production, so to speak, the creation of a novel, especially seeing the wealth of psychological gifts with which God has endowed our abilities. While still in

Petersburg, still only preparing to come here, I was warned—and I myself knew without any warning—that I would meet here as my opponent a profound and most subtle psychologist, who has long deserved special renown for this quality in our still young legal world. But psychology, gentlemen, though a profound thing, is like a stick with two ends." (A chuckle from the public.) "Oh, you will of course forgive the triviality of my comparison; I am not a master of eloquent speaking."

Sophocles

from OEDIPUS, THE KING

Perhaps the very first work of dramatic literature to involve a trial—with a Greek chorus as a jury and a plot conceit focused on the search for the truth—Sophocles's ancient Greek tragedy Oedipus Rex, *written in 427 B.C., is a meditation on the moral imperatives of discovering the truth. The failure to prosecute an unpunished crime leads to the moral decay of a civilization. Here we see Oedipus, the king of Thebes, forced to investigate a murder that the gods have fated to be the source of his own undoing.*

OEDIPUS: Well, be it mine to track them to their source.
Right well hath Phoebus, and right well hast thou,
Shown for the dead your care, and ye shall find,
As is most meet, in me a helper true,
Aiding at once my country and the God.
Not for the sake of friends, or near or far,
But for mine own, will I dispel this curse;
For he that slew him, whosoe'er he be,
Will wish, perchance, with such a blow to smite
Me also. Helping him, I help myself.
And now, my children, rise with utmost speed
From off these steps, and raise your suppliant boughs;
And let another call my people here,
The race of Cadmus, and make known that I
Will do my taskwork to the uttermost:
So, as God wills, we prosper, or we fail.

* * *

OEDIPUS: Thou prayest, and for thy prayers, if thou wilt hear
My words, and treat the dire disease with skill,

Thou shalt find help and respite from thy pain,—
My words, which I, a stranger to report,
A stranger to the deed, will now declare:
For I myself should fail to track it far,
Unless some footprints guided me aright.
But now, since here I stand, the latest come,
A citizen to citizens, I speak
To all the sons of Cadmus. Lives there one
Who knows of Laitus, son of Labdacus,
The hand that slew him; him I bid to tell
His tale to me; and should it chance he shrinks,
Fearing the charge against himself to bring,
Still let him speak; no heavier doom is his
Than to depart uninjured from the land;
Or, if there be that knows an alien arm
As guilty, let him hold his peace no more;
I will secure his gain and thanks beside.
But if ye hold your peace, if one through fear
Shall stifle words his bosom friend may drop,
What then I purpose let him hear from me:
That man I banish, whosoe'er he be,
From out the land whose power and throne are mine;
And none may give him shelter, none speak to him,
Nor join with him in prayer and sacrifice,
Nor pour for him the stream that cleanses guilt;
But all shall thrust him from their homes, abhorred,
Our curse and our pollution, as the word
Prophetic of the Pythian God has shown:
Such as I am, I stand before you here,
A helper to the God and to the dead.
And for the man who did the guilty deed,
Whether alone he lurks, or leagued with more,
I pray that he may waste his life away,
For vile deeds vilely dying; and for me,
If in my house, I knowing it, he dwells,
May every curse I speak on my head fall.

And this I charge you do, for mine own sake,
And for the God's, and for the land that pines,
Barren and god-deserted. Wrong 'twould be,
E'en if no voice from heaven had urged us on,
That ye should leave the stain of guilt uncleansed,
Your noblest chief, your king himself, being slain.
Yea, rather, seek and find. And since I reign,
Wielding the might his hand did wield before,
Filling his couch, and calling his wife mine,
Yea, and our children too, but for the fate
That fell on his, had grown up owned by both;
But so it is. On his head fell the doom;
And therefore will I strive my best for him,
As for my father, and will go all lengths
To seek and find the murderer, him who slew
The son of Labdacus, and Polydore,
And earlier Cadmus, and Agenor old;
And for all those who hearken not, I pray
The Gods to give then neither fruit of earth,
Nor seed of woman, but consume their lives
With this dire plague, or evil worse than this.
And you, the rest, the men from Cadmus sprung,
To whom these words approve themselves as good,
May righteousness befriend you, and the Gods,
In full accord, dwell with you evermore.

Jerome Lawrence and Robert Edwin Lee

from INHERIT THE WIND

The 1955 Broadway play and 1960 feature film Inherit the Wind *fictionalized the 1925 Scopes Monkey trial in Tennessee, in which a schoolteacher was sent to prison for teaching Charles Darwin in a state whose laws mandated the teaching of the Bible as the final word on creation. In this excerpt, and in a bizarre although dramatic twist, Henry Drummond, the attorney representing the schoolteacher, cross-examines the prosecuting attorney, Mathew Harrison Brady, who is being called as an expert witness on the Bible.*

DRUMMOND: The individual human mind. In a child's power to master the multiplication table there is more sanctity than in all your shouted "Amens!", "Holy, Holies!" and "Hosannahs!" An idea is a greater monument than a cathedral. And the advance of man's knowledge is more of a miracle than any sticks turned to snakes, or the parting of waters! But are we now to halt the march of progress because Mr. Brady frightens us with a fable? (*Turning to the jury, reasonably*) Gentlemen, progress has never been a bargain. You've got to pay for it. Sometimes I think there's a man behind a counter who says, "All right, you can have a telephone; but you'll have to give up privacy, the charm of distance. Madam, you may vote; but at a price; you lose the right to retreat behind a powder-puff or a petticoat. Mister, you may conquer the air; but the birds will lose their wonder, and the clouds will smell of gasoline!" (*Thoughtfully, seeming to look beyond the courtroom*) Darwin moved us forward to a hilltop, where we could look back and see the way from which we came. But for this view, this insight, this knowledge, we must abandon our faith in the pleasant poetry of Genesis.

BRADY: We must *not* abandon faith! Faith is the important thing!

DRUMMOND: Then why did God plague us with the power to think? Mr. Brady, why do you deny the *one* faculty which lifts man above all other creatures on the earth: the power of his brain to reason. What other merit have we? The elephant *is* larger, the horse *is* stronger and swifter, the butterfly more beautiful, the mosquito more prolific, even the simple sponge *is* more durable! Or does a *sponge* think?

BRADY: I don't know. I'm a man, not a sponge.

(*There are a few snickers at this; the crowd seems* to *be slipping away from* BRADY *and aligning itself more and more with* DRUMMOND.)

DRUMMOND: Do you think a sponge thinks?

BRADY: If the Lord wishes a sponge to think, it thinks.

DRUMMOND: Does a man have the same privileges that a sponge does?

BRADY: Of course.

DRUMMOND: (*Roaring, for the first time: stretching his arm toward* CATES) This man wishes to be accorded the same privilege as a sponge! *He wishes to think!*

BRADY: But your client is wrong! He *is* deluded! He has lost his way!

DRUMMOND: It's sad that we aren't all gifted with your positive knowledge of Right and Wrong, Mr. Brady. (DRUMMOND *strides to one of the uncalled witnesses seated behind him and takes from him a rock, about the size of a tennis ball.* DRUMMOND *weighs the rock in his hand as he saunters back toward* BRADY) How old do you think this rock is?

BRADY: (*Intoning*) I am more interested in the Rock of Ages, than I am in the Age of Rocks.

DRUMMOND: Dr. Page of Oberlin College tells me that this rock is at least ten million years old.

BRADY: (*Sarcastically*) Well, well, Colonel Drummond! You managed to sneak in some of that scientific testimony after all. (DRUMMOND *opens up the rock, which splits into two halves. He shows it to* BRADY.)

DRUMMOND: Look, Mr. Brady. These are the fossil remains of a pre-historic marine creature, which was found in this very county and which lived here millions of years ago, when these very mountain ranges were submerged in water.

BRADY: I know. The Bible gives a fine account of the flood. But your professor is a little mixed up on his dates. That rock is not more than six thousand years old.

DRUMMOND: How do you know?

BRADY: A fine Biblical scholar, Bishop Usher, has determined for us the exact date and hour of the Creation. It occurred in the year 4004 B.C.

DRUMMOND: That's Bishop Usher's opinion.

BRADY: It is not an opinion. It is literal fact, which the good Bishop arrived at through careful computation of the ages of the prophets as set down in the Old Testament. In fact, he determined that the Lord began the Creation on the 23rd of October in the Year 4004 B.C. at—uh, at 9 A.M.!

DRUMMOND: That Eastern Standard Time? (*Laughter*) Or Rocky Mountain Time? (*More laughter*) It wasn't daylight-saving time, was it? Because the Lord didn't make the sun until the fourth day!

BRADY: (*Fidgeting*) That is correct.

DRUMMOND: (*Sharply*) The first day. Was it a twenty-four-hour day?

BRADY: The Bible says it was a day.

DRUMMOND: There wasn't any sun. How do you know how long it was?

BRADY: (*Determined*) The Bible says it was a day.

DRUMMOND: A normal day, a literal day, a twenty-four-hour day? (*Pause.* BRADY *is unsure.*)

BRADY: I do not know.

DRUMMOND: What do you think?

BRADY: (*Floundering*) I do not think about things that . . . I do not think about!

DRUMMOND: Do you ever think about things that you do think about? Isn't it possible that first day was *twenty-five* hours long? There was no way to measure it, no way to tell! *Could* it have been twenty-five hours?

BRADY: (*Hesitates—then*) It is . . . *possible* . . .

DRUMMOND: Oh. You interpret that the first day recorded in the Book of Genesis could be of indeterminate length.

BRADY: (*Wriggling*) I mean to state that the day referred to is not necessarily a twenty-four-hour day.

DRUMMOND: It could have been thirty hours! Or a month! Or a year! Or a hundred years! (*He brandishes the rock underneath* BRADY's *nose*) *Or* ten million years!

DAVENPORT: I protest! This is not only irrelevant, immaterial—it is *illegal!* (*There is excited reaction in the courtroom. The* JUDGE *pounds for order, but the emotional tension will* not *subside.*) I demand to know the purpose of Mr. Drummond's examination! What is he trying to do?

BRADY: I'll tell you what he's trying to do! He wants to destroy everybody's belief in the Bible, and in God!

DRUMMOND: You know that's not true. I'm trying to stop you bigots and ignoramuses from controlling the education of the United States! And you know it!

JUDGE: (*Shouting*) I shall ask the bailiff to clear the court, unless there is order here.

BRADY: How dare you attack the Bible?

DRUMMOND: The Bible is a book. A good book. But it's not the *only* book.

BRADY: It is the revealed word of the Almighty. God spake to the men who wrote the Bible.

DRUMMOND: And how do you know that God didn't "spake" to Charles Darwin?

BRADY: I know, because God tells me to oppose the evil teachings of that man.

DRUMMOND: Oh. God speaks to you.

BRADY: Yes.

DRUMMOND: He tells you exactly what's right and what's wrong?

BRADY: (*Doggedly*) Yes.

DRUMMOND: And you act accordingly?

BRADY: Yes.

DRUMMOND: So you, Matthew Harrison Brady, through oratory, legislation, or whatever, pass along God's orders to the rest of the world! (*Laughter begins*) Gentlemen, meet the "Prophet From Nebraska!"

(BRADY's *oratory is unassailable; but his vanity—exposed by* DRUMMOND's *prodding—is only funny. The laughter is painful to* BRADY.)

BRADY: (*Almost inarticulate*) I—Please—!

DRUMMOND: (*With increasing tempo, closing in*) Is that the way of things? God tells Brady what is good! To be against Brady is to be against God!

(*More laughter.*)

BRADY: (*Confused*) No, no! Each man is a free agent—

DRUMMOND: Then what is Bertram Cates doing in the Hillsboro jail? (*Some applause*) Suppose Mr. Cates had enough influence and lung power to railroad through the State Legislature a law that only *Darwin* should be taught in the schools!

BRADY: Ridiculous, ridiculous! There is only one great Truth in the world—

DRUMMOND: The Gospel according to Brady! God speaks to Brady, and Brady tells the world! Brady, Brady, Brady, Almighty!

(DRUMMOND *bows grandly. The crowd laughs.*)

BRADY: The Lord is my strength—

DRUMMOND: What if a lesser human being—a Cates, or a Darwin—has the audacity to think that God might whisper to *him*? That an un-Brady thought might still be holy? Must men go to prison because they are at odds with the self-appointed prophet? (BRADY *is now trembling so that it is impossible for him to speak. He rises, towering above his tormentor—rather like a clumsy, lumbering bear that is baited by an agile dog*) Extend the Testaments! Let us have a Book of Brady! We shall hex the Pentateuch, and slip you in neatly between Numbers and Deuteronomy! (*At this, there is another burst of laughter.* BRADY *is almost in a frenzy.*)

BRADY: (*Reaching for a sympathetic ear, trying to find the loyal audience which has slipped away from him*) My friends—Your Honor—My Followers—Ladies and Gentlemen—

DRUMMOND: The witness is excused.

ACKNOWLEDGMENTS

This anthology brings together, in one handsome collection, some of the finest writers who have ever written about the law. This acknowledgments section is an equally august gathering of some very fine friends, supporters, and colleagues—many of whom are quite handsome and attractive, too.

Thank you to Paul and Judy Berkman, Sandee Brawarsky, Marjory Dobbin, Sam Dubbin, Keni Fine, Eva Fogelman, Sol Haber, Tom Hameline, Angela Himsel, Tracey Hughes, Annette Insdorf, Andrea and Bill Kirsh, Myrna Kirkpatrick, Andy Kovler, Alex Mauskop, Marcus Retter, Paula Rackoff, Carol and Seymour Sarnoff, David Stern, Ivan Strausz, Robert Weil, and Susan Wolfson. I've probably forgotten someone here, so, if I have, let me preemptively apologize in print.

There are various children in my life who deserve their own sentence: Elska and Zofii, Maya, Solènne, and Basia Tess.

Danny Goldhagen could easily have had many of my earlier books dedicated to him, and, if there are future books, one will find his name on it, but for now, let this serve as a global and retroactive dedication.

As always, I must thank my agent, Ellen Levine, a loyal friend and partner, who has guided my career. And my editor, Diane Wachtell, who conceived this idea of *Law Lit* and who recruited me to anthologize all those who make no apologies for the law. At The New Press I would like to thank Sarah Fan for the various movements of the manuscript. Finally, I am always grateful to Don Walker of the Harry Walker Agency, the Trident Media Group, and Susan Schulman of the Susan Schulman Literary Agency for their continued promotional activities on my behalf.

This book could not have been composed by a novelist alone. One would have to possess a legal job as well, and for that I must thank Dean William Treanor at Fordham Law School, my friend and patron, for creating a platform for me to teach, write, and direct the Forum on Law, Culture & Society. I must thank Helen Herman, who is the Executive Producer of the Forum and a loyal friend, and Mathew Diller, the law school's associate dean, for his friendship. I would also like to extend my gratitude to the faculty secretarial staff at Fordham Law School for their assistance in preparing the manuscript, especially Larry Bridgett and Emma L. Mercer, and also to Pat Erts, Kim Holder, Gabriel Peguero, Debra Rivera, and Kathleen Ruggiero, and, of course, Dan Auld for overseeing everyone's efforts.

David Margolick, lawyer, writer, and friend, led me to one of the most notable and special selections in this book, and along the way we shared a nice writer's moment.

I would like to acknowledge the law and literature faculty around the country. I very much hope that *Law Lit* will do honor to the books we teach and love.

Finally, I had three outstanding, dedicated, and brilliant law students who assisted me in all phases of *Law Lit*. This book truly could not have been published without them. They are Jessica Lichtenstein, Adam Ostreicher, and Lea Speiss, who spent countless thankless hours and to whom I now humbly offer my thanks.

PERMISSIONS AND SOURCES

Excerpt from "After Twenty Years" from *The Four Million* by O. Henry, copyright © 1912 by Doubleday, Page and Co.

"The Hidden Law" from *Collected Poems* by W.H. Auden, copyright © 1941 by W.H. Auden. Used by permission of Random House, Inc.

Excerpt from "The Lawyers' Ways" from *The Complete Poems of Paul Laurence Dunbar* by Paul Laurence Dunbar, copyright © 1913 by Dodd, Mead, and Co.

Excerpt from *The Merchant of Venice* by William Shakespeare from *The Complete Works of William Shakespeare*, http:shakespeare.mit.edu/.

Excerpt from *A Few Good Men* by Aaron Sorkin, copyright © 1991. Permission granted courtesy of Warner Bros. Entertainment Inc.

Excerpt from "A Jury of Her Peers" by Susan Glaspell, from *The Best Short Stories of 1917*, ed. Edward J. O'Brien (Small, Maynard & Company, 1917).

Excerpt from "Thank You, M'am" from *Short Stories* by Langston Hughes, copyright © 1996 by Ramona Bass and Arnold Rampersad. Reprinted by permission of Hill and Wang, a division of Farrar, Straus and Giroux, LLC. Also reprinted by permission of Harold Ober Associates Incorporated.

Excerpt from *A Civil Action* by Jonathan Harr, copyright © 1995 by Jonathan Harr. Used by permission of Random House, Inc.

Excerpt from "An Apology" from *The People and Uncollected Stories* by Bernard Malamud, copyright © 1989 by Ann Malamud. Reprinted by permission of Farrar, Straus and Giroux, LLC.

Excerpt from *The Hills Beyond* by Thomas Wolfe, copyright © 1935, 1936, 1937, 1939, 1941 by Maxwell Perkins as Executor of the Estate of Thomas Wolfe. Copyright renewed © 1969 by Paul Gitlin, Administrator, C.T.A of the Estate of Thomas Wolfe. Reprinted with permission of McIntosh & Otis, Inc.